Seven keys to imagination

Seven keys to imagination

creating the future by imagining the unthinkable – and delivering it

Piero Morosini

Marshall Cavendish
Editions

Copyright © 2010 Piero Morosini

First published in 2010 by Marshall Cavendish Editions
An imprint of Marshall Cavendish International

PO Box 65829
London EC1P 1NY
United Kingdom
info@marshallcavendish.co.uk

and

1 New Industrial Road
Singapore 536196
genrefsales@sg.marshallcavendish.com
www.marshallcavendish.com/genref

Marshall Cavendish is a trademark of Times Publishing Limited

Other Marshall Cavendish offices: Marshall Cavendish International (Asia)
Private Limited, 1 New Industrial Road, Singapore 536196 • Marshall Cavendish
Corporation. 99 White Plains Road, Tarrytown NY 10591-9001, USA • Marshall
Cavendish International (Thailand) Co Ltd. 253 Asoke, 12th Floor, Sukhumvit 21
Road, Klongtoey Nua, Wattana, Bangkok 10110, Thailand • Marshall Cavendish
(Malaysia) Sdn Bhd, Times Subang, Lot 46, Subang Hi-Tech Industrial Park, Batu
Tiga, 40000 Shah Alam, Selangor Darul Ehsan, Malaysia

A CIP record for this book is available from the British Library

978-9-814-27689-4

Printed and bound in Great Britain by
TJ International Ltd, Padstow, Cornwall

To Siwar, Munay Quinti, Rumiñawi and the Otorongo

contents

....

About the author

PIERO MOROSINI is an internationally recognized author and keynote speaker who helps individuals and organizations apply imagination in order to create new and successful futures.

Piero has been selected as one of the world's next-generation thought leaders in management (*Next Generation Business Handbook*, Wiley, 2004), and was a worldwide award winner for thought leadership at Accenture. His work has been published in books (*The Common Glue*, Elsevier, 2005; *Managing Complex Mergers*, Financial Times/Prentice Hall, 2004; *Managing Cultural Differences*, Pergamon Press, 1998), video cases, case studies and articles in the international media, and in leading academic journals.

Piero is a Peruvian and Italian national, and holds a PhD in management as well as an MA and an MBA at the Wharton School, Philadelphia. He lives in Lima, Peru, where he carries out social work in support of the Andean communities' ancestral art and culture. He is married, with a son and a daughter.

Contact: sevenkeystoimagination@gmail.com

figures and tables

 **prelude**

It always seems impossible until it's done.

Nelson Mandela (1918–)

IDYLICALLY LOCATED ON A HILL overlooking Rimini – the dazzling summer resort along the Italian coastline of the Adriatic– the San Patrignano community could be mistaken for one of the holiday seaside villages that are so common in the Mediterranean region. Andrea Muccioli, the community's head, describes with contained pride the achievements of his "ragazzi" (kids):

 In 1989 we set ourselves the difficult – and for an outsider a bit foolish – commitment of rebuilding the Italian breeding of world-class showjumping horses in Italy. And after just five years our horses won gold medals in both the individual and team competitions at the 1994 World Championship at The Hague. Nobody had ever done this before and I believe no one will again. Our annual San Patrignano horse jumping event has ever since been one of the world's best […]. Since we started producing wine professionally in 1994, we have also won every major prize for best wines in Italy, and we can show similar levels of excellence in each of the 57 business activities we run now [in 2009].

San Patrignano was also, in 2009, a community managed by 2,000 hardened drug users in rehabilitation, the largest such community in the world. Founded in 1978 by Vincenzo Muccioli, a Rimini-based insurance broker, San Patrignano defines itself as a family community for the inclusion of the outcast, boasting a 72 per cent drug rehabilitation rate – the world's highest. Members of the community – referred to as 'guests' – must complete an educational training that lasts three years on average, using neither therapists nor drug replacements such as methadone. The whole educational programme, which costs the community an annual €10,000 per guest, is offered entirely free. (In comparison, the annual costs of methadone-based therapies or incarceration typically amount to over €20,000 per person, an amount that is usually paid either by the patient or by the state, or a combination of both, with success rates of up to 50 per cent in the best institutions.) San Patrignano's guests learn a profession inside the community by choosing from 57 different activities, ranging from wine production and gourmet cuisine to fine handicrafts, artistic photography and prize horse breeding. In all these activities, San Patrignano demands world-class standards of excellence from its guests, and achieves them. In fact, from the outset, the community has applied a self-support policy, depending on the sale of its own products and services and private fundraising activities to sustain its entire financial needs.

Vincenzo Muccioli died unexpectedly in September 1995, leaving his 31-year-old son Andrea, a trained lawyer, to succeed him. Andrea describes his father:

> He was a man with a great humanity, a great capacity to project himself in others. He was, in my opinion, a man of the Renaissance, a man out of his time, but in another sense a man very much in our own time. Because a person that anticipates his own times is someone who really belongs to them. You need a great sensitivity and a great intuition to do this. This is what we call a capacity for vision. He was that kind of man.

Just before his untimely death, Vincenzo Muccioli gave an insight into how his unlikely transformation from successful insurance broker to head of a most remarkable family-style community had started inadvertently, sparked off by his regular evening walk home from work through Rimini's central piazza:

> When I look back to the beginning of this whole story and I

look around, it seems light-years away from me; while instead the memories, the images, are so much alive and stuck in my mind, it seems yesterday. My spirit of observation led me to notice what was happening around me. I'm not able to walk around and miss the trees, the flowers or the grass… there is Life! And so, by walking around my city, I couldn't miss people feeling bad, suffering from serious problems, living a drama… there it was, all this youth, disconnected and switched off. There had to be a reason for this situation. But it seemed to me that other people did not want to realize what was going on. Unlike them, I wanted to get closer to these young people.

While back in the mid 1970s Vincenzo Muccioli was pondering with an open mind why so many youngsters in Rimini were falling prey to drug addiction, in Arteixo, A Coruña, a humble city in Galicia, northwestern Spain, Amancio Ortega, an unassuming local tailor, was preparing the opening of his first Zara store of fashion apparel. Ortega had started out in the textile sector at a very young age as a clerk in two clothing retailers. But in 1963, at the age of 27, he created his own garment manufacturing company. Already set to make his mark, during the years following the opening of the first Zara store in 1975, Ortega had begun formulating in his mind a new model for his business, which could bring to market what he called "instant fashion". During the early 1980s, Ortega determinedly sought a means that would allow him to design, produce and deliver new items every week, something previously unimaginable within the fashion industry, where until then the launching of a new collection only happened, as a general rule, once every season.

Ortega's dream remained unfulfilled until he met José Maria Castellano, a computer expert, who joined him in 1984. Together, they set to work developing a revolutionary distribution model for fashion retailing. Just one year later, Ortega integrated Zara into a new holding company, Industria de Diseño Textil, or Inditex SA. By the end of that decade, the company had a network of 85 Zara stores in Spain and one in Portugal, all of them profiting from the lean and mean "design to dressing room" model the two men had developed. Throughout the 1990s, Inditex set out to pursue an impressive international expansion programme, adding other retail chains to its network through acquisitions as well as internal developments.

The key to Zara's success was its ability to consistently deliver new cheap-chic and fair quality fashion items to its stores all over the world twice a week, and do this so economically that, in the process, the company could generate far bigger profits than its rivals. Before Zara, the clothing industry followed design, production and distribution processes that took up to nine months. Ortega proved the industry wrong time and again and achieved the impossible. On a mission to take long lead times out of the equation, Zara began responding quickly and inexpensively to shifts in consumer tastes and to newly emerging trends. First throughout Spain and then in the main shopping streets of New York, Milan, Paris and London, Ortega's bet paid off – and left the industry giants scrambling to catch up.

In May 2001, Inditex sold 26 per cent of its shares on the Spanish Stock Exchange in a bold move that sent waves rippling through the Spanish market. This turned Amancio Ortega – who had retained 61 per cent ownership of the company – into Spain's richest person and one of the world's wealthiest individuals, with an estimated worth of more than €6 billion at the time. But Ortega continued to shun all media attention, never giving interviews and making it clear to all that what he enjoyed most was being amongst his team of designers at the company headquarters in remote Arteixo. Indeed, he would routinely be spotted having lunch with other employees in the company cafeteria rather than out partying with supermodels.

In 2005, Inditex had reached only half the sales of the US company Gap – then the world's largest apparel retailer – and ranked third behind Sweden's H&M. However, Zara's spectacular international growth was far quicker than its rivals. It continued its pace even during the first quarter of 2009, in defiance of a global recessionary economy that damaged every other big name in the fashion industry. Mostly as a result of Zara's performance, in June 2009 its parent company Inditex became the number one apparel retailer in the world, with sales nearing €10 billion across 4,300 stores all over the world (from a total of

€5.67 billion in revenues and 2,244 stores just five years earlier, in 2004), dethroning former reigning leader Gap, whose growth had peaked at 3,100 stores.

Contrary to how it might appear, Zara's successful move to overtake the world's largest fashion retailers had not happened overnight; the company had shown remarkable and sustained growth for more than a decade. Revenues had tripled between 1996 and 2000. From there, sales skyrocketed even further, from €4 billion in 2001 to €9.4 billion in 2007. This exceptional success was not accidental, but was instead the result of a process that had begun thirty years earlier with Amancio Ortega's original vision, carefully executed by him in conjunction with the company's leadership group.

These amazing real stories reveal a golden thread of seven essential elements that are common to both. These seven elements explain the astonishing success not only of the examples we have looked at so far, but of many other extraordinary leaders and organizations that I have examined over the past decade. I call these elements the "seven keys to imagination", because they can be recognized, developed and applied by all individuals, teams and organizations who have the courage and determination to unlock their power to imagine and create successful futures for themselves (see Figure 1 on the following page). The first two keys – *trade-on mindset* and *customer obsession* – let you imagine radically new, unimaginable futures by correctly observing in your surroundings important things that most people keep missing. The last four keys – *Wiraqocha leaders, tinkunacuy, gentlemen's promises* and *common glue* – allow imaginative individuals and teams to deliver in the real world the challenging mental images about a new future that were conceived in the first place. And the third key – *purposeful mission* – connects the mental worlds of imagined futures to actual reality by unlocking a transformation that turns a free flow of imaginary thoughts into a more deliberate and results-oriented creative process.

In fact, in both the story of San Patrignano and the case of Zara, their founders started out with an open mind and a positive disposition by putting themselves in other people's shoes: the

FIGURE 1 : Seven keys to imagination

youngsters who had become addicted to drugs, in the case of Vincenzo Muccioli; women of all ages who aspired to always wear something new and fashionable but could not always afford to buy it, in the case of Amancio Ortega. Their mental operation – which I call "customer obsession" – stemmed from both opportunity and chance to a certain extent, but it was neither easy nor short-lived. Andrea Muccioli described his father Vincenzo as someone with "a great capacity to project himself in others". At first, however, he was constantly rejected by the young drug addicts of Rimini, but he kept approaching them until he eventually gained their trust. Likewise, Ortega's profound understanding of the desire of women of modest income to dress fashionably developed into a long-lasting obsession, leading him to defy the most established norms of the international fashion industry over the ensuing decades.

The key to the first sentence in the previous paragraph is "open mind and a positive disposition" rather than "putting themselves in other people's shoes" *per se*. Here, the art is not in the concept: I found that it is the particularly open mindset of individuals such as Muccioli and Ortega, and the ease with which these men acted out their personal qualities, developed over their previous life-experiences, which allowed their imaginations to eventually fly in unsuspected directions. By putting themselves in other people's shoes with such mindset and disposition, they could observe things that others kept missing. They found something new. And, in their minds, they started to add new, hypothetical images to those they observed in the real world. Thus, by engaging with them with an open mind, Muccioli found that drug addicts actually were neither sick people nor intrinsically losers, but just marginalized individuals who lacked a family, and this discovery led him to imagine San Patrignano not as a hospital or a clinic but as a large, loving and supporting family where these youngsters could get – like any other youngster – their fair chance at becoming real winners. And Ortega's mental images of Zara as a veritable fashion bazaar, where all sorts of "instant fashions" could be purchased by women of all ages and incomes at impossibly low prices that nevertheless gave the company superior profitability, stemmed from his realization that fashion – by then an exclusive reserve of the elite – was a universal aspiration of all women. Zara's revolution turned "affordable fashion" or "democratic fashion" – an oxymoron before the company existed – into new labels for the freshest and fastest growing areas of the global fashion market.

From the outset, an "open mind and a positive disposition" were also showcased by Muccioli's and Ortega's bold aspirations to do much more with a lot less than their peers. I call the fundamentally win–win mentality underpinning these kinds of ambitions "trade-on mindset" or "trade-on thinking". Individuals with a trade-off instead of a trade-on mindset typically conceive any given pair of important elements in an issue as mutually exclusive factors. As a result, these people typically set trade-off goals that favour the achievement of one factor at the expense of the other. For instance, most conventional drug rehabilitation institutions offering considerably better results than their peers do so by accruing higher than average cost. These additional costs are then transferred to either the drug abuser or the country's social security system (or a combination of both). Similarly, the fashion industry was historically built on the premise of high quality and exclusivity that came at a high cost (and to the privileged few who could afford it, this meant high prices). Both San Patrignano and Zara dramatically challenged the conventional trade-off thinking and the prevailing status quo of their own contexts by making radical trade-on promises and actually delivering on them. In the process, they created unprecedented customer experiences that, at the time, were simply inconceivable for most people.

Some people's ability to adopt the perspectives of others and imagine the unimaginable as a result – vividly illustrated by men such as Muccioli and Ortega – can be found throughout history and in all areas of human activity. However, the psychological literature warns us that the ability to recognize and accept these universal faculties of the human mind is not the same as the skill to use them. Most people, in fact, have to face a series of mental impediments that consciously or unconsciously inhibit their trade-on mindset and perspective-taking abilities, and filter quite selectively the images they allow themselves to form in their minds. In order to unlock their imagination fully, these people have to train their minds in a similar way to when engaging in physical training: regularly, wisely and patiently. People who are well trained in the art of unlocking their imagination keep surprising us more because of their sheer ability to imagine the unimaginable and act on it than because of the intrinsic mental images they are able to evoke. After all, there are today thousands of drug abusers who get regularly rehabilitated in San Patrignano-like communities that have sprung up all over the world under the inspiration of Vincenzo Muccioli. And for women the world over, shopping in Zara has become a routine they now expect – and get – from an increasing number of fashion retailers. In both of these cases – as well as many similar ones – it is the unusual insight of the initial image of the future that surprised us. After the initial image became a new reality, most people would accept and even engage in it, making it a routine part of their worlds.

The ease with which people like Ortega or Muccioli step naturally into the future, just by holistically applying in new ways and in unsuspected places certain essential subjective learnings stemming from their previous life-experience events, is inspiring. This contrasts greatly with other people's approaches that favour the design of future scenarios as logical step-wise projections of a status quo "objectively" defined and shared by experts. Neither San Patrignano nor Zara could have been conceived back in the mid 1970s as logical step-wise projections of, on the one hand, the current medical approach to drug rehabilitation or, on the other, the existing state of the global fashion industry. In fact, the founders of San Patrignano and Zara did not engage in any such logical projections when imagining their future creations. Vincenzo Muccioli was simply a man of "great sensitivity and great intuition" who had developed a Renaissance-style humanistic ability to observe his surroundings with curiosity and an open mind. His wife described him also as a compassionate man, the type who would show up at home for dinner accompanied by a beggar or a homeless person he had just met in the street and offered shelter to. One evening, Muccioli stumbled across some young drug addicts, and the rest, as they say, is history. Likewise, Ortega was a hard-working man from Galicia, a region famous in history for the generations of industrious migrants who left for South America, looking for a better future away from the perennial poverty of their birthplace. Growing up as a tailor and as an apparel salesman in such an environment, he came to conceive of fashion as something that every woman should be able to afford instantly and constantly, and turned such life insights into a mission.

For imaginative individuals and organizations, a *purposeful mission* to serve others transforms an effortless flow of new imaginary thoughts into a more deliberate and results-oriented creative process that ought to deliver in the real world the challenging mental images of the future that were evoked in the first place. However, once more, in this area the art is not in the concept. Consider San Patrignano's arresting mission, "we train marginalized people and bring them to achieve extraordinary things"; or Zara's mantra, "to bring fashion to the masses". As we have seen, these kinds of purposeful missions radically break with the prevailing status quo and originally stemmed from observing an issue with an open mind and from somebody else's perspective – be it a suffering drug abuser or a disappointed female customer.

Moreover, these purposeful missions emerge quite naturally from, and fit strongly with, the initial observer's emotional core – in other words, with what truly makes his or her eyes sparkle, with what resonates loudly with the moving experiences and deep lessons he or she has absorbed over a lifetime. That's how Vincenzo Muccioli and Amancio Ortega could turn radically new mental images, born of insightful observations, into purposeful, lifetime missions focused on real people.

The next step in the creative process sees the transformation of imaginative men or women armed with a purposeful mission into recruiters. They look for capable people who can be different – and often are extremely different – from them, but who share their deeply emotional and passionate connection with a radically new purposeful mission. I was also amazed to find that, beyond the vast differences in their fields of activities, cultural backgrounds and so on, successful imaginative leaders deliberately look for five specific qualities in the people they recruit. These are wholeness (a person's ability to transcend dilemmas or seemingly conflicting views), tolerance (the ability to observe and selectively discard one's own mental models about others in order to empathize with them), walk-the-talk (the quality of demonstrating coherence between thoughts, values, words and actions in one's own behaviour), generosity (the willingness to give one's own time to face-to-face mentoring, coaching and supporting others, irrespective of their position), and patience (the perseverance and endurance a person shows in the process of building a common language with other people who speak different technical and/or native languages). In this book, I call those people who passionately share a purposeful mission and display these five qualities *Wiraqocha leaders*, in allusion to the Hamawtha Wiraqocha, the legendary Andean wise man who many thousands of years ago recognized these traits and taught the ancient Peruvian people how to nurture them in order to positively unleash the full power of individuals and communities. In Renaissance Europe or in ancient Persia, they would have called Hamawtha Wiraqocha a magus, or a wizard, because of his ability to build things that could scarcely be imagined and to teach such knowledge to others. In a way, Wiraqocha leadership is what created Macchu Picchu and other incredibly imaginative works of art and engineering that the ancient Peruvians built throughout their vast Andean realms, and the remains of which can still be admired today.

It often takes time and perseverance for the imaginative leader to recruit his or her Wiraqocha leadership group. Vincenzo Muccioli had to start San Patrignano with the help of his own family, together with a few drug abusers determined to recover their own lifes. Andrea Muccioli observes that this has remained the main entrance criteria for selecting new "guests":

 The only criterion we use – and we don't have any other important criteria for selection – is personal determination. We assess the will of the individual to make a very difficult and very tiring journey of growth. This is the only thing that counts.

Over the ensuing years, as new drug abusers joined the community, they would be given a "guardian angel", another guest who was in his or her second year there, and who would provide the newly arrived person with total and continuous support and affection, teaching him or her to observe the few but non-negotiable rules of the community. It was in this organic and gradual way that San Patrignano's world-class approach to drug rehabilitation developed. Likewise, it took years for Amancio Ortega to find José Maria Castellano, the right computer expert who enthusiastically embraced this mission of providing fashion for the masses instead of fussing about the supposed impracticality of such a dream. José Maria Castellano went on recruiting the Wiraqocha leadership group that created Zara as the first fashion retailer with an integrated logistical and manufacturing operation that could deliver new fashion items twice a week, reliably and inexpensively, to thousands of retail stores around the world. This required people with a common mindset that favoured rapid change, quick responses and informal face-to-face coaching on the job within the extremely fast-paced Zara environment. A Zara executive remarks that attracting people with these traits is key across all the culturally diverse locations where the company operates:

 As things move so fast, there's no one to teach you in a formal way. You need to be proactive and make yourself useful, keep a young mindset, and be open to change.

Once a Wiraqocha leadership group is formed, their imaginative members set a very special creative process in motion. Its strong social initiation and experimentation components are reminiscent of *tinkunacuy*, a Qheshwa word denoting the ancient pre-marriage practice of living together in Peru's Andean civilizations. Within certain Andean communities, whenever a young couple contemplate future marriage, they move in together for a number of months. If the experience of living together is satisfactory, they go on to marry. If it is not, the couple give up their marriage hopes and return to being single individuals, ready for tinkunacuy with another partner in the community. Similarly, the creative process that both San Patrignano and Zara engaged in at the start of their journeys bears little resemblance to the rigorous goal-setting approaches that are traditionally in place in the strategic planning function of many large multinational organizations. Rather, Wiraqocha leaders tend to craft their commitments as the final step of a loosely organized team-based social process of imaginative discovery, creative exchanges and experiential learning, closely knit with the customer and other key actors.

This tinkunacuy-like social experimentation process, usually lasting about six months, allows them to imagine and experience at first hand new scenarios and ways to fulfil their purposeful missions to their end-customers without preconceptions, objectives or expectations of any kind. As the social experimentation process unfolds over time, the free flow of dialogues and mental images, serendipitous events, continuous feedback and open experimentation starts to get a visual structure in the form of a new prototype that has the capability of fulfilling the organization's purposeful mission. The prototype gets increasingly tested and enhanced through the imaginative incorporation of "multi-complementors". These are players whose products, services or technologies perform the seemingly magical function of reducing the costs of building the new prototype while simultaneously increasing its attractiveness to customers. It is at this point that a strategic direction and specific commitments are formally set in place that promise the delivery of the new prototype to the customer within tight deadlines.

The ability to identify new multicomplementors is a hallmark of imaginative trade-on thinking. When built into a new and exciting customer experience, these multicomplementors help imaginative organizations both to fulfil their purposeful missions in unprecedented ways and to achieve superior financial performance. Thus, San Patrignano's use of community work carried out with standards of excellence turned key players in areas such as high-quality wine production, the breeding of fine horses or the manufacturing of design furniture into multicomplementors of drug rehabilitation. Some of these players were crucial to San Patrignano's success. For example, from the outset the community attracted people with the required professional know-how: a range of old, retired *maestri* (master artisans) who – in another example of trade-on thinking – were happy to teach their unique skills to San Patrignano's guests for nothing. By engaging in these professional activities with standards of excellence, San Patrignano's guests could at the same time work effectively towards their own rehabilitation and help self-finance the community through the sale of their products and services to outside customers. Likewise, one of the main drivers of Zara's superior profitability is its use of global integrated logistics as a central component of the fashion industry, which gives the company its systematic just-in-time capability to swiftly deliver new designs to their customers anywhere in the world, while at the same time removing inventory cost. In the mid 1980s, this radical industrial approach, which turned logistics players such as DHL or just-in-time manufacturers like Toyota into natural multicomplementors of Zara, was unimaginable to any other player in the fashion industry. However, when Ortega went about developing Zara's unique just-in-time logistics capabilities in 1984, he and computer expert Castellano looked to both DHL and Toyota for inspiration.

The output of the *tinkunacuy* creative process is a radical prototype giving concrete form and function to the team's original ideas of the future. A second valuable end result of this process is a strategic sense of direction, and the making of what I call *gentlemen's promises* that will turn the new prototype into a larger scale reality. A gentleman's promise is a serious pledge that commits a team or an entire organization to create a vastly superior customer experience in ways that were previously considered unthinkable. This step marks the initiation of a collective process that will turn mental imagination and creativity into actual innovations and real experiences for people like you and me. It is precisely because they aim at achieving – usually within very tight, explicit deadlines – what most people consider to be unimaginable or even impossible things that these promises have an intense effect upon those on both the giving and the receiving end. Although their aims can be projected over months or even years, gentlemen's promises immediately set people in motion, capturing everyone's imagination and emotions in the process.

The closer that people get to an organization's gentleman's promises – as customers, work-members or simply spectators – the stronger the upheaval in their minds and hearts. Over the 1980s, it was a shock to the Italian medical establishment to learn about San Patrignano's ability to rehabilitate 72 per cent of drug abusers with neither therapists nor methadone and at an annual cost of just €10,000 per person. When it became obvious over the ensuing decade that San Patrignano's extraordinary "treatment" for drug abusers consisted simply of making them live and work within a supporting family community that created and brought out world-class products and services, the initial disbelief turned into the overwhelming mix of awe, emotion and humility that we normally experience in the presence of the miraculous. Yet, right from the outset, back in the 1970s, San Patrignano has continued to achieve, year after year, its "72:10,000" gentleman's promise, and to demand and achieve its breathtaking standards of excellence in everything it does. Likewise, when pundits and competitors alike realized Zara could provide all women with desirable, inexpensive and brand-new fashion items twice a week – and in a way that generated superior company profits – they found it hard to understand how this was done, even on close examination. In fact, turning against the common wisdom of the fashion world, where secrecy is the norm prior to releasing new collections, Zara would habitually allow its competitors to review its operations without concern. Following one such visit, Amancio Ortega commented:

We had a team of 22 people here from The Limited [the group
behind a number of successful retail chains, including Victoria's
Secret, Limited Express, Bath & Body Works and Henri Bendel]
trying to work out how we do things, and even after several
days they could not get it.

Inside the company's headquarters, visitors found a striking
minimalist complex, designed in-house, with little fixed furniture; large open spaces decorated all in white and with intense,
natural illumination. Here, Zara's initial gentleman's promise of
inexpensively delivering fair-quality new fashion items twice a
week in thousands of stores all over the world is renewed, monitored and achieved again and again, week after week, with the
precision of a high-quality Swiss timepiece. In a few years during
the early 1980s, Zara changed the industry life-cycle from about
four seasonal collections per year to around 104 (yes, that figure
is correct: 104!). Something so impossible to imagine, even for
certain fashion professionals, that they would find it difficult to
understand even when actually seeing it at work.

All gentlemen's promises share three remarkable characteristics. First of all, in a very obvious way, they enable the imaginative organization to achieve its purposeful mission. When the
imaginative organization achieves its gentleman's promises, you
know that its purposeful mission has been met and that a radically new imagined future has become a reality. That's it. Thus,
San Patrignano's "72:10,000" gentleman's promise and its associated pursuit of world-class excellence in all they do within a
supporting family community very obviously attain their mission
of "training marginalized people and bringing them to achieve
extraordinary things". Likewise, Zara's gentleman's promises
of inexpensively delivering all kinds of new, low-priced fashion
items twice a week to thousands of very large stores located in
the most prestigious central streets of scores of cities – ranging
from Milan and Los Angeles to Shanghai and São Paulo – very
closely enact its mission of "bringing fashion to the masses". Purposeful missions and gentlemen's promises are, in the minds and
hearts of imaginative Wiraqocha leaders, two sides of the same
coin.

Secondly, gentlemen's promises evidently reflect a trade-on mindset by combining aims that seem contradictory to most, especially to those people permeated by conventional trade-off thinking. Take San Patrignano's "72:10,000" gentleman's promise, for example. That is the world's highest drug rehabilitation rate – far superior to the average 40 to 50 per cent rate achieved in state-of-the-art institutions in Europe or in the US – achieved at nearly half the cost per individual compared with those same institutions. Or take Zara's double-digit margins and superior profitability, together with significantly lower prices for its ever-changing fashion items, which nevertheless maintain a fair quality and striking new design features that keep its faithful customers coming back every week. In both of these cases, there is a clear promise to deliver vastly superior customer value at a significantly lower cost to the organization. Thus, thanks to their skill in making gentlemen's promises with a trade-on mindset, imaginative Wiraqocha leaders are able to set new standards that spectacularly transcend the bounds of conventional trade-off thinking. The former leads to radical, rather than slight, shifts in the status quo: think of San Patrignano's standards of excellence achieved at low cost and with the outcasts of society, or Zara's ability to inexpensively change its collections in thousands of stores around the world 104 instead of four times per year.

The third crucial characteristic of gentlemen's promises is that, in a strictly etymological sense of the word, they constitute serious and honourable commitments by those making them, and this characteristic is more extraordinary than it may seem at first. By setting gentlemen's promises, Wiraqocha leaders commit an entire organization to create, within ambitious deadlines, new imagined futures that radically break with the past and bear little resemblance to the status quo. As these leaders put their personal dignity and reputation at stake when they make their commitments, they also assume the full consequences of success or failure. This is in profound contrast with the goal-setting processes of most large organizations I know. There, strategic objectives are set as explicit, logical step-wise projections of past results into the future, making the imagined future merely a modified version of past occurrences of pre-defined factors. Because strategic objectives usually are associated with specific macro-economic as well as market forecasts, responsibility for attaining a specific set of results is often made dependent upon the actual materialization of such predictions. Instead, gentlemen's promises are radical personal commitments stemming from a mental future imagined by open-minded observers *independently* from past results, but in tune with the observer's insightful observations stemming from his or her subjective life experiences – in other words, inner experiences, not necessarily professional ones. Vincenzo Muccioli was neither a physician nor an expert in drug rehabilitation when he imagined a radical new way of recuperating drug abusers, and committed his family and a few outcasts to the promise of building San Patrignano. And, although Amancio Ortega did have a life experience in the clothing sector when he came to imagine the democratization of fashion, the radical promises involved in Zara's new approach required such a broad range of new and sophisticated skills (from advanced computer systems to just-in-time industrial automation and integrated large-scale logistics) that it was way beyond what anyone in the clothing industry back in the 1980s could imagine being applicable to fashion – let alone have brought into reality.

The discovery of multicomplementors and the setting of gentlemen's promises shift the focus of imaginative Wiraqocha leaders towards building the organizational capabilities that will creatively deliver their imagined futures within a rigorous set of deadlines. In order to do this successfully, they invariably build a strong *common glue* within their organizations. This common glue represents the special kind of cooperative relationships that Wiraqocha leaders nurture amongst themselves and within their organizations in order to build mutual trust and operate as a cohesive, imaginative and creative team that fulfils its gentleman's promises to its customers. In addition to Wiraqocha leaders and a set of gentleman's promises, an imaginative organization needs to draw upon three other mutually reinforcing social capabilities in order to build strong common glue.

First, it needs to develop a common language, not only in a strictly linguistic sense, but also in the sense of implanting a set of shared values and a common career development approach for the leadership group, as well as a common set of performance measures for the organization as a whole. Common language constitutes a group's platform for mutual understanding that turns the diversity of a team into a collective capability for imaginative and creative leadership.

Secondly, the organization needs to develop cross-boundary networks; in other words the capability to put in place and lead interfunctional and multicultural teams, dialogues, processes, projects and virtual communities in order to achieve the gentleman's promises of the organization. Especially within large multinational organizations such as Zara, the development of cross-boundary networks is greatly fostered by the enactment of knowledge-sharing processes, as well as by the use of personnel policies for expatriate, repatriate, educational and reward programmes that facilitate the smooth and continual rotation of key members across organizational and geographic divides.

No less important than these is the capability to create and carry out communication rituals: a set of frank, moving, regular and organization-wide symbolic actions that continuously renovate the organization's strong emotional commitment to both its purposeful mission and its customers. I still remember the feeling of excitement as I was driving up to Rimini for the first time to join the San Patrignano family for lunch. It was April 1999, and I approached the community unaware that what I was about to see would profoundly change the images that, in my mind, had come to be associated with the words "drug abusers". I was received at a large dining room with huge windows overlooking a breathtaking Italian valley that stretches majestically all the way down to the Mediterranean. There, all two thousand guests eat together every day, neatly organized by professional group at tables that seat about a dozen people each. The buzz reverberated under a vast ceiling towering above us, filling the entire space with its cheerful echoes until we heard the ringing sound of a spoon against a glass. Complete silence followed. I could hear the subdued murmur of tree branches creaking outside. After a minute of stillness, all of a sudden the noise resumed.

Andrea Muccioli pointed at an empty chair in front of us and explained the ritual silence: "It is for my father, Vincenzo, who died four years ago." The excellent lunch was cooked and served by the community's guests, and eaten in exactly one hour. After lunch, people from all professional groups mixed freely and informally over coffee. As I toured the immaculately clean community during the afternoon, I felt two thousand pairs of eyes watching me with warm, welcoming glances. I visited several working areas (or "working cells" as San Patrignano's guests call them): the winery, the printshop, the horse stables, the photography lab, the blacksmith's facilities, the carpentry shop... In all of them, I saw the same happy camaraderie, the same dedication to quality work of the highest standards, the same determination to stay clean of drugs, the same tearful eyes when evoking Vincenzo.

Zara's common glue is so strong that it materializes in the instantly recognizable shop designs of its thousands of stores, which in 2009 could be found in more than seventy countries. Inside each store, the commercial personnel – 80 per cent of whom are women – act both as salespeople and as antennae capturing emerging customer trends, to be fed back in real time to headquarters, which in turn delivers in a couple of weeks and on a global scale new fashion items to match the newly spotted trends. In a flexible, fast-paced environment, Zara created a strong culture and a common process of informal communication and in-store decision-making through constant practice and levels of investment in education and in-job training that were unprecedented in the fashion industry. The latter included programmes at the world's top business schools, combined with a six-month rotation training across all company departments (though mainly in the stores); visits to the main fashion capitals of the world; massive training programmes for all of its retail staff; personalized training plans for every employee in the corporate areas; and a year-long personnel training plan for store managers. As a whole, the company invested hundreds of millions of euros in educational programmes for its personnel every year, leading the American magazine *Fortune* to rate Inditex third in Europe and eleventh in the world in its 2007 survey on Top Companies for

Leaders – the only company in the fashion industry to achieve this level of recognition.

A strength of purpose similar to what I sensed in San Patrignano and Zara can also be found in other organizations that are able to beat the seemingly insurmountable odds of geographic distance, cultural differences and organizational divides to build strong common glue around fairly different missions, but all aimed at the same end result of bringing new futures to life that others can scarcely imagine. Over the years, I would eventually bring to light the intangible elements at the core of this common glue, in a book that quantitatively analysed a large statistical sample of thousands of people across scores of highly diverse organizations all over the world.[1] But it is the images of these extraordinary leaders and their organizations, rather than the statistical figures involved, that remain fixed in my memory.

Which brings us back to imagination and the initial themes of our story. What makes some people imagine radically different futures? How do individuals like Vincenzo Muccioli and Amancio Ortega manage to turn those extreme mental futures into reality? We have already sketched out some responses to these questions in the previous pages. In addition to this, I found that taking a different – I am almost tempted to use the word "imaginative" – look at what the notion of imagination has historically entailed provides us with powerful new insights that lead us to further answers.

part one

preparing the way

the magic of imagination

The power of Thought, the magic of the Mind.

Lord Byron (1788–1824), English poet

THE OLD AND WEALTHY PATRIARCH Cosimo de'
Medici had probably had a premonition of his own death when
he ordered a copy of an old Greek manuscript to be translated at
once. One of the agents he had commissioned to collect rare books
for his admirable library had just found the ancient document in
Macedonia and secretly brought it to him. The year was 1463, and
Cosimo had been for most of the previous three decades the real
power behind the scenes at the influential Republic of Florence,
which, partly due to him, was at the time widely regarded as one
of the cradles of the Italian and European Renaissance. Cosimo
told Marsilio Ficino – head of the modern Platonic Academy that
Cosimo had established 24 years before to translate into Latin
and study the complete works of Plato – to immediately halt all
other work and concentrate solely on translating the mysterious
manuscript.

It contained a copy of fourteen of the fifteen treatises of the
Corpus Hermeticus, a secret synthesis of all knowledge attributed
to Hermes Trismegistus, a legendary Egyptian magus, high priest
and king of remote antiquity whose teachings were supposed to
have inspired Aristotle and Plato. Ficino managed to make the
translation in a few months and presented it to his patron just

before old Cosimo died in 1464. We will never know for certain whether Cosimo found what he was looking for in the manuscript. However, the impact of the *Corpus Hermeticus* on fifteenth century European thinkers was nothing short of revolutionary, unleashing a powerfully creative intellectual and artistic movement that was to stamp its decisive imprint on the ensuing centuries. Indeed, well over five hundred years later, on the eve of the 21st century, I still found its unmistakable mindset at work in the imagination of such leaders as Vincenzo Muccioli, creator of the San Patrignano drug rehabilitation community, and Amancio Ortega, whose Zara chain of fashion stores turned the idea of "fashion for the masses" from a seeming oxymoron into the largest, fastest growing and most profitable area of the global clothing industry.

✳ *it's a kind of magic*

One of the first representatives of the new Renaissance mindset was Ficino himself. Deeply influenced by the *Corpus Hermeticus*, he created a practical method for conditioning the imagination to receive archetypal images that facilitated the acquisition of universal knowledge. This method was inspired directly by the use of talismanic images in the *Corpus Hermeticus*, where geometric and anthropomorphic figures organized in 36 decans (or segments of 10 degrees, into which the 360 degrees of the circle of the zodiac are divided) were given specific practical applications. Ficino, a trained physician, would advise his patients to focus on certain talismanic images as part of their treatment in order to attract the benign influence of life-giving planets, such as Jupiter and Venus, and dispel the detrimental effects of Saturn or Mars. However, it was on the artistic realms that Ficino's approach for the conditioning of the imagination, expanded by thinkers such as Pico della Mirandola to include Cabalistic and mystical practices, found some of its most arresting applications. In fact, there is now considerable evidence that not only did some of the leading Renaissance artists, such as Botticelli, Raphael, Pinturicchio and Leonardo, use the kinds of talismanic approaches suggested by Ficino to conceive sublimely beautiful figures in their imagination, but often the talismans themselves were the real subjects in some of their most enigmatic masterpieces, such as Botticelli's *Primavera*, Leonardo's two versions of the *Virgin of the Rocks* or Pinturicchio's allegorical paintings at the Appartamenti Borgia in the Vatican.[1]

Ficino's method was called natural magic (*magia naturalis*) by his contemporaries, and the label explains much of the secretive approach of its practitioners, the renaissance magi, who had to come to terms with the Catholic Church's declared opposition to all sorts of medieval necromancers, conjurors, magicians, tricksters and jugglers. In 1486, however, and at the age of 24, Pico della Mirandola, an Italian nobleman of prodigious memory, wrote 900 theses to synthesize all human knowledge, dedicating 26 of them to *magia naturalis* as a legitimate practice, not forbidden by law, and allied to both science and religion. Pico moreover sharply distinguished between it and all the other kinds of magic, which, according to him, were bad, demonic and groundless practices rightly condemned by the Catholic Church. Instead, Ficino and Pico described natural magic as a great natural philosophy operating through subjective concentration on magical images that attracted into the personality of the Renaissance magus an inner understanding and the ability to harness the power of natural forces at will. Pico advised that such conditioning of the imagination was greatly facilitated through a sensible way of life and certain musical and verbal rituals conducive to heightening a person's inward emotional and psychological perception:

 In natural magic nothing is more efficacious than the Hymns of Orpheous, if there be applied to them a suitable music, and disposition of soul, and the other circumstances known to the wise.[2]

Underlying Ficino's and Pico's natural magic, there is a theory and a practical method that regard imagination as the prime cognitive power for reaching truth. Not only did these notions stem from the *Corpus Hermeticus*'s pointed use of archetypal images within a cosmic framework, but they were also in full accordance with Aristotle's perspective that "to think is to speculate with images", as well as with Renaissance Neoplatonist views about images – especially ancient ones –actually possessing within themselves the essential (or "divine") reflection of an Idea. In her classic 1964 work about the European Hermetic tradition of the Renaissance, Frances A. Yates explains the singular fifteenth-century mode of thought about images:

> An ancient image of Justice was not just a picture, but actually contained within it some echo, taste, substance, of the divine Idea of Justice. This helps us to understand the way in which Ficino thinks of those star images descending from "the more ancient Platonists", though, in the case of such images, the relation to the Idea is even closer, through the cosmology of *mens, anima mundi, corpus mundi* in which the images have a definite place.[3]

Parallel to the creation of wonderful artistic works, the Renaissance magi's cognitive method of conditioning the imagination through archetypal images was applied to the creation of the first modern systems of artificial memory. This was the work of Giordano Bruno (1548–1600) and his followers, who, in a series of classical volumes, devised a mathematical hierarchy of correspondences between a set of concepts and a vast array of both simple and complex geometric images that were reminiscent of the *Corpus Hermeticus* talismans. Bruno's geometric correspondences could move and rotate within imaginary circular fields, allowing a person to mentally store, retrieve, organize and even investigate new relationships between any given set of concepts. In a 1679 letter to the Dutch mathematician and astronomer Huyghens, Gottfried Leibniz, the great German mathematician and inventor of the binary system used in virtually all of today's computer architectures, speculated that his "geometrical characteristic" – a generalized Euclidean system of symbolic techniques highly reminiscent of Bruno's conceptual and geometric correspondences – could allow for the description of plants and animals and the invention of machines to take place entirely in the imagination, without the aid of any concrete figures or models.[4] However, Bruno's dynamic use of imaginary geometrical fields as memory systems was so far ahead of its time that its first true offspring emerged only with the nineteenth-century development of topology and existential graphs as new mathematical theories, and subsequently with the twentieth-century scientific application of semantic fields to disciplines such as neural networks theory, computer science, artificial intelligence and topological "life space" psychology.

In creating his imaginary memory fields, Bruno, a Renaissance magus who was condemned and burned at the stake by the Catholic Church's Holy Inquisition, was building upon a medieval mnemonic tradition expounded by philosophers such as Ramón Llull (1232–1314), whose roots went back to the classical Graeco-Roman world. This ancient "art of memory" consisted not of the simple retention or regurgitation of large amounts of material, but rather equated memory with the capability to imagine images that allows its practitioners to mentally store, organize and manipulate these materials in order to generate new ideas or deconstruct old ones. A favourite mnemonic exercise at the Renaissance schools was to imagine a beautiful palace where the student would mentally move from room to room. In each space the student would "find" some key words, data or conceptual categories. He would then tour and explore at will the lovely palace in his imagination, making new relationships arise between the concepts stored within its rooms. The art of memory was widely practised in the educated circles of both ancient and medieval Europe, and was central to the equipment of Roman orators such as Cicero, who is sometimes credited as the anonymous author of the *Ad Herennium*, a classical work that explained the method at length.[5]

Neither the Renaissance magi nor the ancient philosophers thought of "visual memory" as different from "auditory memory" or "tactile memory" in the way that we often do today. Instead, they followed Aristotle's view that the activities of mental retention, retrieval and use of sense perceptions were best carried out through a single mental process that transformed these perceptions into phantasms (mind-pictures made of light; equivalent to *imago* in Latin), or *eikon* (mental copies) that were imprinted in the brain and could be scanned by the "eye of the mind". In her *Book of Memory,* Mary Carruthers's fascinating study of memory in medieval culture, she observes that the modern experimental work of cognitive psychologists offers startling corroboration of the ancient idea that any kind of sense perception that enters the mind in a "seeable" form attains a higher degree of stability, permanence and usability in our memories.[6] In fact, the American psychologist Allan Paivio demonstrated in the 1970s that mental images facilitate memory performance far more effectively than memories that are only represented in verbal or in abstract form. For example, Paivio's subjects remembered concrete substantives such as "glass" more easily than abstract nouns like "value" because of the greater information carried by mental images than by words. Later experimental psychologists such as Stephen Kosslyn showed that mental imagery can even be used both to access implicit memory – that is, memories that are involuntarily called to mind to guide our behaviour, such as when driving a car or when eating correctly at a table – and to alter such implicit information (which, in turn, will affect our behaviour).[7]

From the outset, the Renaissance magus's focus on imagination as the prime cognitive faculty to harness the power of natural forces was applied to the design of clever mechanical machines. The endless array of creative mechanisms ranged from optical lenses, magnetic attractors and astronomical clocks, to hearing and medical devices, rapidly revolving wheels producing distorted figures, speaking bronze heads, hydrostatic weighing machines, perpetual motion mechanisms, musical machines, galleys that move without sails or oars, mechanical eagles to communicate with besieged towns, and so on. The emphasis on designing ingenious mechanistic devices within natural magic – called artificial magic by some of its chief representatives, such as the German Athanasius Kircher (c. 1601–80) and his disciple Kaspar Schott (1608–66) – was recognized as a forerunner of experimental science and technology by the award-winning American historian Lynn Thorndike (1882–1965). In fact, by browsing through the pages of some of artificial magic's most representative books, such as Schott's *Universal Magic of Nature and Art*, one can identify at least 26 sub-divisions of artificial magic that read more like speculative mechanical applications.[8] Thus magic with mirrors is a study on the projection of optical illusions; thaumaturgic magic is concerned with machinery such as gears, horseless chariots, cyclometers and astronomical spheres; and hydrostatic magic studies why ice floats on water. Here, the intellectual aspiration clearly is both mechanistic and operative, and such emphasis is quite deliberate. Indeed, in the opening pages of his *Universal Magic*, Schott introduces the "later magic" as being either natural, artificial or prohibited; he then vows to remove superstition from natural magic and warns against prohibited magic, which involves an explicit or implicit pact with a demon.

Yet it would be hasty to see in Schott's artificial magic the methods of later experimental science. Conditioned imagination is still very obviously at work as the prime cognitive method underlying the fantastic mechanisms and naturalistic speculations of his work, for these are mostly mere pictorial machines and mental conjectures that are well ahead of the technology of their time. Thus, when Schott in the "static magic" section of *Universal Magic* contemplates methods for measuring weight without instruments, he does not quite indicate why or how these new approaches work. In another section, he presents wondrous weight-lifting mechanisms but admits his inability to solve the problems of weight resistance that prevent their actual construction. Can we regard Schott's beautifully illustrated *Universal Magic* treatises – originally printed in four volumes between 1657 and 1659 – as precursors of Leibniz's geometric methods for "describing machines entirely in the imagination"? Although this remains a speculation, the amazing mechanical designs stemming from Schott's vivid imagination led Lynn Thorndike, an outstanding twentieth-century historian of medieval science, to hesitantly ask: "Are the marvels which they work through magicians real or only seeming?" [9]

Kaspar Schott's teacher, Athanasius Kirchner, has been regarded by some as the last Renaissance man. When he died, at the close of the seventeenth century, the curtain was falling on the bright Renaissance period, ushering in a new era when the mechanistic and operative impulse of natural magic – itself so different from the religious contemplation that dominated medieval intellectual life – was rapidly giving way to the new principles of experimental science. The latter was not so much an offspring of natural magic as a new cognitive paradigm developed under the same will to operate the natural forces that motivated the Renaissance magi. Yet there were many points of contact between Renaissance natural magic and the emerging scientific method. Not only did some of natural magic's central insights – such as its artificial memory systems and the systematic development of ingenious machines – also find a place in the new emerging science, but some of its first representatives were also practitioners of natural magic. The Englishman John Dee (1527–c. 1609), an accomplished mathematician and scientist who also inhabited the world of natural magic, is a typical example. But it is the promethean figure of Leonardo da Vinci (1452–1519) who provides the real archetype of a Renaissance magus, designing fabulous machines, pioneering experimental science and creating supremely beautiful works of art with equal ease.

It is perhaps within the overarching and holistic framework of natural magic, with its concept of the boundless power of the imagination and of a living and interconnected cosmos, that the universal personality and prodigiously heterogeneous output of Leonardo can be best understood. His philosophical doctrines, where Frances A. Yates has recognized explicit mentions to "Ermete Filosofo" and influences of Ficinian Hermetism, in fact suggest that Leonardo may have regarded himself as a Renaissance magus.[10] Thus, in a way, it all goes back to the enigmatic *Corpus Hermeticus* manuscript, which Ficino was translating into Latin when Leonardo was a precocious twelve-year-old boy.

�֍ *imagination as magic of the mind*

Today we know that, far from having been written single-handedly by Hermes Trismegistus several millennia before the Christian era, there were in fact several authors behind the *Corpus Hermeticus*, writing it at various dates during the first and second centuries AD. This was an era when the *pax romana* was at its height, leading to the development of vast, cosmopolitan and sophisticated cities such as Rome and Alexandria, to which gravitated all sorts of thinkers from every corner of the Roman empire to create an unparalleled intellectual melting pot. Standards of life were acceptable and roads were excellent, but people's inner yearning was no longer met by the archaic pagan gods and rational philosophies. Many sought new meanings by looking inwardly through subjective and intuitive ritual experiences that gave them direct acquantaince with essential knowledge. This approach grew into a philosophy and a cognitive method called ancient Gnosticism – from the Greek word *gnosis*, meaning the kind of knowledge and deep understanding gained through direct and subjective experiences. Another popular way of looking for new responses in the Roman empire of the second century AD was to turn to the oriental brands of magic, chiefly Egyptian, Chaldean, Persian Jewish, Indian and Chinese, to which, owing to the excellent communications and trading networks in place, Roman subjects had unprecedented access. It was in this permissive and mercurial atmosphere that the *Corpus Hermeticus* was created, with its peculiar imprint of classical Gnosticism and oriental magic.

Natural magic, as Renaissance thinkers such as Marsilio Ficino and Giordano Bruno understood it, can therefore be traced back to the early contacts with a broad range of oriental doctrines that took place during the first and second centuries AD within the framework of Gnosticism and under the political sway of the Roman empire. During that time, Zoroaster, a legendary priest from Persia (forerunner of modern-day Iran), was revered by the initiated as the first magus, whose reputation surpassed even that of Hermes Trismegistus. The Renaissance magi were fully aware of this. Indeed, in his *Theologia Platonica*, Ficino gives the first place to Zoroaster in his genealogy of an unbroken tradition of ancient wisdom. Hermes Trismegistus comes next, followed by Orpheus, Aglaophemus, Pythagoras and Plato (in that order).[11] Zoroaster is the mythical author of the *Extant Avesta*, a voluminous work of which only a few fragments remain today, in which his body of thought – collectively regarded as comprising the first doctrine of magic as such – was expounded.

Avesta (*avistâk*) is also the name given to the most ancient language of the Indo-European branch, originally from Eastern Iran but extinct today as a spoken language, which gave us the term *magh* – meaning "power" – that became a root-word for many terms in the English language. The latter include not only might or dismay, but also the words magic, magician, magus, master and magister, as well as magnificent, magnanimous, machine, machinist and even imago and image. Does "imagination" – a term of uncertain etymology – also stem from the suggestive Avestan root-word *magh*? A number of arguments would appear to support this probability. On the one hand, using the term imagination to signify the human faculty for generating largely fictional mental imagery (in reference to plastic arts or to literary activity and output) is a long-established and common practice in both colloquial and scholarly speech. On the other, as has been described, the enduring ancient tradition within mainstream magical frameworks to look upon imagination as the prime cognitive power very obviously suggests a strong connection that goes beyond the purely etymological. "Good" magic was in fact regarded by ancient and Renaissance magi alike as the highest form of human activity (magnanimous), a kingly art for the wise and the initiated (magus, master, magister), who had the power (might) to see beyond the deceptive appearences of the material world (imagination) in order to grasp its essence (imago) and manipulate it at will through various physical devices (machines) and transformation processes (magic).

Ancient oriental branches of magic – whether Persian, Egyptian, Indian or Chinese – were similar in that they believed in the existence of multiple universes, all of which shared a common building block in the form of an essential fiery substance made of light and comprising archetypal words and images, which Indian magi named *Akasha*. It was by grasping and manipulating this prime substance that the magus could operate the transformational processes that gave magic its name. Startlingly, the idea of a luminous essence shared by a pluralistic set of universes is also present in other traditions, such as in ancient Peru's notion of *Illa Tecsi*, the primordial cosmic light described by Hamawtha Wiraqocha, whose profile, as portrayed by the old Andean legends, fits quite nicely with that of an ancient magus. As previously mentioned, light was also the essential fabric of the phantasms – the images that, according to Aristotle, were imprinted into our brain to form our memories. In turn, the word phantasm stems from *phaos*, the Greek word for light, which, significantly, is also the root-word for phantasia, meaning "imagination" in Greek.

To sum up, it is not difficult to sense throughout global history a persistently strong epistemological and etymological undercurrent tying the worlds of "imagination" to those of "magic", the latter understood as the mental power of the magus leading to his or her ability to harness natural forces at will. Natural magic and ancient Gnosticism shared the fundamental cognitive attitude of attempting to inwardly reflect the outside world – arguably the entire cosmos – into the mind. It is within this context that the prime importance ascribed by them to the conditioning of the imagination can be understood. By contrast, the outlook of early European scientific thinkers and philosophers of the seventeenth century such as René Descartes (1596–1650) went in just the opposite direction, by drawing the mind into the outside world. Not surprisingly, early science gradually turned its back on the conditioning of the imagination as a cognitive tool, inaugurating a tradition that regards imagination as opposed to rational thought, and that has found its way into today's colloquial speech. In fact, to deride imagination as *la loca de la casa* (the mad one in the house) is commonplace in most Spanish-speaking countries, and similar aphorisms can be found in many other Western languages.

✳ *unveiling the wisdom of the mad one*

Imagination was not totally lost in science, however. Its rehabilitation within the scientific paradigm took place during the twentieth century in two slow steps. On the one hand, there was increasing recognition by prominent scientists such as the German-born physicist Albert Einstein (1879–1955) and the Swiss psychologist Carl Jung (1875–1961) that imagination played a crucial cognitive role in the development of science. Einstein's well-known assertions have become popular adages:

 Logic will get you from A to B. Imagination will take you everywhere.

Imagination is everything. It is the preview of life's coming attractions.

The true sign of intelligence is not knowledge but imagination.

Imagination is more important than knowledge. For knowledge is limited to all we now know and understand, while imagination embraces the entire world, and all there ever will be to know and understand.[12]

Although Einstein's viewpoints on imagination must be taken as anecdotal rather than scientific, it is worth noting that they – and particularly his last quotation above – could have been taken straight from the *Corpus Hermeticus*. Jung's thoughts on the matter resonated strongly with Einstein's views, as he maintained that:

 Imagination and intuition are vital to our understanding. And though the usual popular opinion is that they are chiefly valuable to poets and artists (that in "sensible" matters one should mistrust them), they are in fact equally vital in all the higher grades of science. Here they play an increasingly important role, which supplements that of the "rational" intellect and its application to a specific problem.[13]

On the other hand, Jung did much more than Einstein when it came to securing a place for the study of imagination within modern science. He actually developed a psychological theory of Self in which both ancient Gnosticism's perspectives on imagination and his own ideas on the collective unconscious – regarded as forward-looking at the time – played a central role. According to Jung, many mental disorders stemmed from a fragmented Self, and therefore restoring its unity – namely "individuation" – was the goal of his psychological therapy. This therapy is called analytical psychology, or Jungian analysis, and it operates at various levels of a patient's unconscious dimensions, including mental archetypes (which Jung defined as primordial mental images stemming from mankind's common atavistic past), symbols (described as mental images with meanings beyond conscious or rational interpretation) and dreams. Some of analytical psychology's central tenets are deeply influenced by Jung's well-known attempt to understand and explain ancient Gnosticism – which he saw as closely related to alchemy – from a psychological standpoint. Moreover,

Jung's active imagination technique, inducing strong emotions to generate mental images of the unconscious, and stimulating the creative Self via imagination, parallels the practices of both ancient Gnosticism and natural magic for the conditioning of the imagination through rituals that heightened profound emotions.

Jung's psychological outlook on imagination regarded it as the conduit through which the unconscious Self finds its way out in the form of creative mental imagery that can drive deliberate actions. However pioneering they were, though, Jung's ideas on imagination lacked an experimentally based neurological and cognitive theory that systematically linked the formation of images in the brain to the acquisition of knowledge and skills. One of the first to move in this direction was the Harvard psychologist and cognitive scientist Stephen Kosslyn, whose theories on imagination brought the study of mental images into mainstream cognitive science, and whose pioneering use of functional magnetic resonance imaging techniques (fMRI) gave these theories an increasing experimental base. For Kosslyn, the human brain's use of mental images is a distinct – but not unique – technique for representing knowledge. These images do not necessarily stem from physical perceptions as we, in essence, can imagine anything we like independently of its actual existence. Mental images are represented at two levels: first, the image is generated in the brain; secondly, we make ourselves aware that such an image has been generated and that – although unreal – we can scan it as if actually seen with our real eyes. This two-fold, parallel representation mode is quite unique to imagination, and Kosslyn demonstrated that it works as a cognitive function because objects that are mentally visualized maintain the inherent characteristics of real objects. Thus, it is possible to mentally simulate actual and physical situations to acquire the corresponding knowledge and skills without going through the real experiences, with the associated advantages in resource-savings and the like. In addition, whereas mental images tend to be stable, Kosslyn suggests that the brain builds mental models as analogical constructions that modify these images to fit specific cognitive tasks. A mental image of a bridge, for instance, is stable, but the brain imagines a series of different mental models of it depending on whether we are about to design a new bridge, build it, demolish it or simply cycle on it.[14]

Following on from Kosslyn's early publications, a voluminous body of empirical evidence started to amass over the last two decades of the twentieth century, which built mental images into a distinct area of cognitive science. Neuroimaging fMRI evidence showed that, whereas sensory perception is unconscious, thought processing is a parallel and deliberate function involving many areas of the dorsolateral upper side of the prefrontal cortex of the brain, particularly those areas associated with recollection, imagining, attention and self-awareness tasks. Damage to the prefrontal cortex of the brain impairs a person's working memory and the ability to learn from mistakes as well as to monitor one's own performance. Moreover, the concept of working memory, developed by experimental neuroscientists such as Professor Alan Baddeley of Bristol University, shows no clear dividing line between a memory and a thought. The brain's working memory, far from functioning as a simple library for short- and long-term storage of material, actually consists of a central executive co-ordination function that retrieves, organizes, combines and directs attention to incoming information from two temporary storage systems: a visuo-spatial sketchpad holding images, and a phonological loop keeping acoustic and speech-based information.[15]

Cognitive neuroscience has exposed the brain's cortical and subcortical mechanisms that are activated in both imagined and physically executed actions, demonstrating that memories and imagination are created by the same neural circuits that are turned on when things really happen. One cognitive theory, known as the common coding hypothesis, posits that these results are possible because of the existence of physiological mechanisms in the brain that are able to couple perceptions of actions to actual actions. This theory was given support by the discovery of mirror neurons in monkeys that fired both when the animal acted and when the animal observed the same action performed by another animal (especially from the same species). Brain activity consistent with mirror neurons has been found in humans, particularly in the premotor cortex and the inferior parietal cortex.[16]

All these discoveries have started to unveil the cognitive function of imagination as a holistic process deeply rooted in both mental and actual bodily experiences as well as in social interactions, a view that is in sharp contrast with the traditional mentalistic and dualistic (mind/body) perspectives of cognition. The empirical psychological and neuroscientific record provides support for this new outlook. On the one hand, a series of well-documented studies shows that the use of imaginary simulations and mental practice enhances performance in sports by increasing motivational skills during performance in stressful situations and by actually increasing muscular activity – although the latter was limited to the muscles relevant to the imagined motor movements. Similarly, imagined motor movement techniques are widely used to rehabilitate patients whose motor control has been impaired by a stroke, as well as to train surgeons in complex surgical procedures and to teach pilots how to fly aircraft.[17] The learning effects of motor imagery are not limited to skills with explicit action components; experimental psychologists actually found that when first- and second-grade schoolchildren mentally manipulated or acted on the objects described in the text they were reading, they showed significantly better retention and understanding of the text compared with children who merely read the text without mentally simulating its content.[18]

On the other hand, mirror neurons are believed to be crucial for social understanding and interaction, because empirical studies show that people gain significant empathic acceptance from others by unconsciously mimicking others' postures, vocalization, mood and mannerisms, and by synchronizing their own behaviour with them. Furthermore, experimental psychologists suggest that people possess the ability to create images of the Self as distinct from others, and that this ability can be extended to recognizing other people's mental states as distinct from their own – and experiencing them. Exercising this ability – namely, perspective taking – allows people to dwell temporarily in another person's thoughts, feelings and internal mental states, and to use the resulting understanding for various purposes. Significantly, however, these empirical researchers warn that possessing perspective-taking skills is very different from being able actually to use them. A series of common mental barriers significantly impairs most people's ability to seriously and effectively engage in perspective taking.[19]

✳ *capricious imagination*

In *La donna è mobile* ("The lady is flighty"), the catchy aria from Giuseppe Verdi's opera *Rigoletto*, the womanizing Duke of Mantua sings about a lady's changeable nature as he ironically reveals that the opera's flighty character is in fact himself. Since its 1851 debut in Venice, this aria has become a showcase for the world's outstanding tenors, ranging from Enrico Caruso to Luciano Pavarotti, Plácido Domingo and Juan Diego Flórez. If you are like me, mental images of your favorite tenor singing *La donna è mobile* might help you recall the early 21st-century scientific evidence on imagination, portraying it as a changeable mental faculty capriciously fluctuating between the worlds of rationality, emotion and character.

Thus, on the one hand, in her provocatively entitled book *The Rational Imagination*, Irish cognitive scientist Ruth Byrne demonstrates that the way people imagine alternatives to reality – namely "counterfactual imagination" – actually follows the same rules as rational thinking.[20] According to Byrne and her colleagues, counterfactual imagination includes conditional thoughts (that is, "what if" speculations such as "What if Columbus had not reached America in 1492?") as well as thoughts leading to the creation of new instances of a category through new concept combination and insight. She found that when people imagine possibilities they rarely focus on remote alternatives or "miracle counterfactuals" such as "What if the Incas had been armed with fighter planes when the Spanish invaded in the sixteenth century?" Rather, they follow a number of fairly reasonable principles and heuristics.

For example, people tend to imagine a few true alternatives to actions rather than alternatives to inactions, and these are often limited to just a couple of possibilities that once may have been real but can no longer be true. If, for instance, Patricia decides to vaccinate her child and the infant becomes seriously ill from an allergic reaction to the vaccine, whereas Brigid doesn't vaccinate her child and he becomes very sick from contracting the new illness, most participants in Byrne's experiments judge that Patricia will regret her decision to vaccinate her child more than Brigid will regret her decision not to vaccinate her infant. Byrne also discovered that the way people imagine alternatives to reality is bounded by their moral and ethical beliefs, and follows their rational understanding of obligations and causal links. Thus, when considering the story of someone who missed being at home when his wife suffered a stroke because, subsequent to going for his usual beer after work, he had a minor car accident at an intersection, most people would tend to imagine "If only he hadn't stopped for a beer," rather than focus on the exceptional event of another car coming through the intersection at just that time. Byrne also found that when people imagine new instances of a category, some aspects of reality are more readily modified than others and along similar fault lines. This is because people tend to think about some characteristics in terms of multiple possibilities, whereas others are thought of as single possibilities and therefore remain immutable. When challenged to imagine a fantastic bird, for example, most people tend to make variations in size, shape and colour, but rarely imagine birds without eyes or birds that swim rather than fly (although penguins do). Similarly, people usually combine concepts by mixing the most mutable aspect of one concept with the most immutable characteristics of the other one. Thus, "robin snakes" tend to be imagined either as snakes with red breasts or as snakes that eat robins, a "cactus fish" is usually seen as a fish that has prickly spines, and so on.

On the other hand, however "rational" it may seem from one perspective, Byrne and her colleagues also found a two-way link between counterfactual imagination and emotions. First, what people actually imagine may depend on strong feelings – such as gratification, blame, fear or guilt – stemming from the social judgements ascribed to possible alternatives. People fantasize about their mothers winning next month's lottery prize rather than imagining themselves as voluntary guards at a Nazi concentration camp in 1944. Secondly, thoughts about what might have been seem to amplify certain emotions such as hope, anticipation, sorrow, shame or relief, which are regarded as counterfactual emotions.

More pointedly, emotions can also help you travel mentally into the future. Imagine yourself spending time with a stranger and with a romantic partner. In which situation would you expect to feel happier? In this experiment, the social psychologist Elizabeth W. Dunn found that most people expected to be happier after interacting with a romantic partner rather than with someone they had just met. But the opposite actually happened in reality, because the subjects tried harder to be really charming and pleasant with the stranger, and this made them feel at their best.[21] This line of experimental research has led psychologists to posit the existence of the experiential and rational systems as two distinct human information-processing systems operating in parallel. Whereas the rational system is highly analytical, flexible and efficient in processing abstract ideas and numbers, the experiential system is older, emotions-oriented and holistic in integrating primarily concrete information stemming from even minor events.[22] Dunn found that the experiential system is able to accurately predict how people will feel in imagined future situations, which can have an obvious impact on their decision-making. The problem is, people often let their rational systems get in the way of their effective forecasting, taking a highly analytical approach in imagining their emotional responses to future events. Only when subjects are reminded to take a more contextualized and holistic approach – preventing even minor details from fading into the background – do forecasts and actual experiences converge.[23]

University of Pittsburgh psychologists William Klein and Laura Zajac highlight personality traits as another important factor in how people imagine the future. It is well known that inherently optimistic people – what Klein and Zajac call dispositional optimists – tend to imagine the future more positively than pessimists, and this holds important consequences for mental and physical health, individual productivity and decision-making. However, some people have been found to show simultaneously high levels of optimism *and* pessimism towards different sets of issues, suggesting that these traits are not necessarily opposites but simply reflect high levels of emotional engagement. Dispositional optimism also varies depending on context. For example, people are generally less optimistic after a terrorist attack, and become more pessimistic in the presence of verifiable data and threatening feedback, such as when facing the results of an HIV test following unprotected sexual relations with a relative stranger.

Can people develop or increase their dispositional optimism over time? Studies show that this is a stable dimension of personality, difficult to change and probably hereditary. Even when optimists are educated and asked to form mental images of people facing a high risk of health hazards (such as those stemming from heart attacks, being overweight, drinking problems and the like), they often maintain and sometimes even increase their optimistic views on those issues.[24] Although empirical research aimed at changing dispositional optimism in a healthy population was still in its infancy in 2009, attributional training is regarded by practising psychologists as a promising way to foster realistic optimism within organizations. By altering pessimistic beliefs and attributional patterns in employees' minds while developing their ability to provide and accept realistic feedback about what works and what is repeatedly failing, leaders can generate contagious optimism within the organization without falsely or superficially raising performance expectations.[25]

Overall, despite the regularities observed in how we imaginarily travel to the past and into the future, experimental psychologists point out that people do differ widely in the way they imagine alternatives to reality. Individual emotional states and levels of motivation, and specific personality traits as well as cognitive differences in people's spatial, linguistic, observational and working memory abilities, all of which stem from people's natural predispositions and life experiences, lead some to imagine alternatives to reality in ways that are radically different – sometimes opposite – to most people's approaches. Thus, for instance, a minority of individuals tested in social experiments was consistently found to be adept at imagining remote possibilities and unlikely future scenarios; generating insightful and unexpected concept combinations; extracting deep understanding from plunging into others' perspectives; accurately forecasting their feelings in future situations; and remaining optimistic in the face of distressing events, verifiable data and threatening feedback, and so on.

✳ *imagination reigns*

Not surprisingly, as a result of the groundbreaking psychological and neuroscientific research started in the mid 1970s (which I have only briefly summarized here), any 21st-century scientific definition of imagination is firmly rooted in a cognitive framework. No longer "the mad one in the house", most contemporary psychological definitions of imagination typically describe it as one of the "higher mental functions" that "involves the synthetic combining of aspects of memories or experiences into a mental construction that differs from past or present perceived reality, and may anticipate future reality". More pointedly, the same definition also recognizes that "[mental] imagery plays a significant role in emotion, motivation, sexual behavior, and many aspects of cognition, including learning, language acquisition, memory, problem-solving, and perception." [26]

In addition, more popular scientific definitions of imagination portray it as "the ability of forming mental images, sensations and concepts, in a moment when they are not perceived through sight, hearing or other senses," or tend to further characterize it with statements that read like Einstein's popular aphorisms on imagination:

Imagination is a fundamental faculty through which people make sense of the world, and plays a key role in the learning process.

Imagination helps provide meaning to experience and understanding to knowledge.

Imagination is the faculty through which we encounter everything...[27]

Modern scientific definitions of imagination distinguish two broad categories of mental phenomena – a taxonomy that had already been recognized by ancient philosophers such as Plato. On the one hand, there is what can be termed fanciful imagination, largely involving the generation of imitative mental images of past events. On the other, there is creative imagination – a faculty we exercise whenever we daydream about the future, for example – which involves the mental restructuring of sensory impressions that may differ from reality to a greater or lesser extent.

It is clear that the study of creative imagination will continue to evolve within modern science, shedding new light on the human capacity to produce conscious meaning. Although this area is crucial to understanding our ability to imagine the future – and more generally our capacity to deal with the external world the way we do – it attracted relatively little attention during the twentieth century. Then, on the eve of the 21st century, researchers such as the Harvard psychoanalyst and psychiatrist Arnold Modell argued that cognitive research must move beyond the classical representational explanations to account for the deeper biological sources of imagination that are found in embodied metaphors of unconscious meanings.[28] As a cognitive mental function, metaphor involves the dynamic transfer of meaning between dissimilar domains, allowing us to achieve balance within a constantly changing external world as well as to engage in creative thinking, deal with emotions and overcome psychic traumas. Thus conceived, the psychic process of metaphor may be at the core of our ability to imagine mental futures. Modell finds support for his views by drawing from an eclectic array of scientific disciplines and describes how imagination is enhanced by empathy and by actually provoking in others the kinds of behaviours we imagine for them.

With imagination firmly assuming a visible role within the realms of mainstream science, our historical quest for it seems likely to come to a close. For well over two millennia the outlook on imagination has shifted dramatically, from ancient Gnosticism and natural magic to modern science, engaging the minds, hearts and efforts of an unlikely cast of characters ranging from ancient philosophers and Renaissance magi to artists, social dissenters, power players and experimental scientists of every kind and era. Yet, in spite of such a broad and disparate collection of sources, a consistent pattern emerges throughout global history, connecting the remarkable human ability to form mental images to its decisive impact on shaping our destiny through arresting pictures of the mind that grip our emotions, enhance our understanding and inspire our actions. Not surprisingly, ancient philosophers, Renaissance magi and modern scientists alike have all been enticed by imagination's captivating power to breed incredible mental futures and help us to actually deliver them. In finding out how to positively unlock this power, I discovered that extraordinarily successful individuals and organizations more or less deliberately enact a unique process of imagination that interweaves natural magic threads with scientific strings and that can be explained in terms of either. In the next chapter, we will examine just how this process is brought to life.

✳ unleashing the wizard within

....

The most beautiful world is always entered through imagination.
Helen Keller (1880–1968)

EDUARDO AND MIRTHA AÑAÑOS could not believe
that the ruthless *Sendero Luminoso* (Shining Path) terrorists had
razed their family hacienda to the ground. Even as they con-
templated the wreckage of a lifetime's work, Shining Path was
besieging the Añaños family's home town of Ayacucho, after
asserting control over most of the surrounding areas in Peru's
rugged central Andean region. The entire city had become an
open wound in that fateful year of 1988. People were being killed
every day, and the survivors were on edge. Food and medicines
were in short supply. Lima – Peru's capital, and the country's
largest city – had never felt so far away, with access to it now cut
off by the deadly terrorist forces and by the forbidding heights of
the majestic Andean *cordillera*. The future was bleak.

Ayacucho was, in 1988, an unlikely place in which to discover
the positive power of imagination at work. Yet, like everyone
else that year in the besieged city, Carlos Añaños, a chemist
and the youngest of Eduardo and Mirtha's six children, had
noticed among the general shortages the total absence of soft
drinks as Shining Path had forced Coca-Cola and all the other
big brands to leave Ayacucho. He talked to his parents and to
Jorge, his eldest brother, who worked on the distribution of a

local beer, and together they spotted an opportunity. Eduardo told them: "We must dream big: to create Peru's greatest soft drinks company." The family decided to stay on in Ayacucho to live their dream. Eduardo sold his agricultural equipment for US$8,000 and mortgaged his land to obtain a further US$22,000 from a local bank. With that money, Jorge set up a rudimentary bottling facility in their new house's back yard, and Carlos went to work on developing a "secret formula" very similar to Coca-Cola's.

When it hit the market by the end of 1988, Kola Real was an instant success. The new soft drink came in recycled beer bottles delivered to the stores by cash-hungry *ayacuchanos* anxious to make a living in those uncertain times. No advertising expenses were needed (nor could be afforded), so the new drink relied on word-of-mouth publicity. It worked. However, the decisive factor was the slogan, *"calidad a precio justo"* (fair-priced quality), printed on the label. Kola Real offered a two-litre bottle of a high quality soft drink at half the price Coca-Cola charged for a smaller bottle. The customers loved it. Carlos observed:

> Most of our customers had never tried a soft drink before. They could not afford to buy the big brands, but they were the majority of the population. With our products, they became part of the market. Our mission was to expand the market, not to fight against anyone or become number one. Everyone was a winner with this approach, even the big brands.

A decade of spectacular growth in Peru's local market followed, but then Coca-Cola started to pay closer attention. Together with its recent Inka Cola acquisition – which gave it 80 per cent of the Peruvian market – it declared a "hundred days war' against Kola Real in early 1999, aiming to asphyxiate it through aggressive advertising and price cuts. When Kola Real's board – by then comprising the entire Añaños family – met to address this challenge, a new Peru was emerging from its ashes, and was on the way to becoming one of Latin America's star economies. Says Carlos:

Paradoxically, this situation forced us to evaluate the internationalization of the company. We could invest in the battle for further growth in Peru, which represented less than 1 per cent of the Latin American market, or enter similar markets applying the same formula.

This time, it was Mirtha who declared, "Planet Earth is huge." Her dream of replicating Kola Real's success in foreign markets similar to Peru in fact encompassed well over two-thirds of the world's population. Her family shared her dream. In 1999, Grupo AJE, a new Añaños family-owned holding company, managed to gain 10 per cent of the Venezuelan market in its first year of operation there. In 2001 it was Ecuador's turn.

But the real test came in 2002, when the Añaños family decided to enter Mexico. At nearly US$15 billion, Mexico was the second-largest soft drinks market in the world at the time. It was also the crown jewel of Coca-Cola, which made 11 per cent of both total sales and profits there, by controlling over two-thirds of the Mexican market and dominating its large distribution channels (such as the Mexican subsidiary of Wal-Mart Stores). But Grupo AJE knew that 75 per cent of Mexico's distribution was still carried out in small mom-and-pop eateries, and decided to focus on these with the same formula of "*calidad a precio justo*" and a truly no-frills operation. When Grupo AJE's "Big Cola", produced at their newly established state-of-the-art plant in Puebla, managed to corner 5 per cent of the tough Mexican market in less than two years, the company made headlines internationally and became a textbook case study in US business schools. The company's globalization strategy and adaptation to local markets was in fact turning the tables on behemoths such as Coca-Cola and Wal-Mart, and their success continued unabated as they entered Costa Rica in 2003, Thailand in 2006 and Colombia in 2007, going on to double Big Cola's share of the Mexican market to 10 per cent by 2007. In 2008, in defiance of a global recessionary economy, Grupo AJE's overall revenue growth reached 25 per cent, making it the largest producer of low cost drinks in Latin America and the continent's second biggest beverage group. By 2009 it was difficult to foresee any end to the company's success, as big retailers were increasingly selling lower-priced B-brands and private-label carbonated drinks everywhere from Germany and the UK to Brazil, Poland and China. As in Mirtha's dream, planet Earth turned out to be a huge place indeed.

✳ *imagining the future*

When I first met Carlos Añaños in 2006 at his Kola Real factory in Northern Lima's industrial district, I suggested to him that, oddly enough, it was Shining Path that had allowed his family to live their dream. But he told me a different story. He said that when Kola Real was already proving to be a success, one of his brothers attended a business strategy course at a prestigious business school. There he learned that new ventures should analyse their "strengths, weaknesses, threats and opportunities" in advance. When the course ended, he set out to apply those lessons to Kola Real. It was easy for him to identify the initial opportunity his family had back in 1988 when Shining Path unwittingly transformed Ayacucho into the ideal market to grow all sorts of new local consumer brands. Likewise, the column labelled "threats" was promptly filled in with the names of the big soft drink brands alongside that of Shining Path. The list of weaknesses was particularly easy to complete, as when Kola Real started it had no strategic resources at all in the form of industry knowledge, financial clout, technology, management experience and the like. But try as he might he could not identify any strengths. He asked all his family members for help, but to no avail. The column labelled "strengths" remained stubbornly empty. Frustrated, but "just to prevent it from remaining empty", said Carlos, the siblings wrote the following strengths: "capacity to dream" and "determination".

Chance events and fortuitous circumstances undoubtedly gave the Añaños family's new venture a head start. But others had the same opportunity. In fact, during the tragic events of the late 1980s, a broad array of local consumer brands ranging from toiletries to groceries sprang up in Ayacucho. Some of them could still be found in the city's shops in 2009. But none of these brands made it to Lima, let alone the international markets. What makes Kola Real such an extraordinary showcase for the power of imagination at work is that it demonstrates the difference between determined individuals with the "capacity to dream" – that is, the ability to create the future – and the rest. This is a difference that I have found repeatedly in many other extraordinarily imaginative and successful individuals and organizations all over the world.

First, the capacity to dream means cherishing a dream so obsessively and so fervently that it motivates you to act positively, daringly and consciously to realize that dream. This is sharply different from the fanciful daydreaming we sometimes engage in, that either does not translate into positive actions, or leads to inconsequential ones. Instead, what Carlos Añaños clearly had in mind when he identified his family's capacity to dream as a crucial strength behind Kola Real's unlikely success was the ability to imagine a new future so passionately that it could inspire a group of people to courageously remove any barriers and find creative ways to transform their mental images into reality. In June 2008, almost exactly twenty years after Kola Real was started in their back yard in Ayacucho, Carlos's brother Ángel Añaños, as president of multinational Grupo AJE, shared with a group of Peruvian entrepreneurs his belief in the real power that this capacity to dream had to create unthinkable futures:

 I wish that today all of us leave this room with a dream. Or if we already have a dream, I wish that all of us work harder to achieve and accomplish our dream. Leave this room with a dream; if you do not yet have one, work hard to get the biggest and the most beautiful dream you could have and build. Not just for you, but also for your children, the best thing is to cherish a great dream.[1]

And in March 2009, speaking to 1,200 graduates at a leading Peruvian business school, Ángel Añaños again insisted on the crucial importance of this capacity to dream:

 The mind generates the seed, the dream is like the tree that stems from it, and the roots of the tree are your passion that takes its nourishment from the land. Dare to take the first step just thinking of the next one, dare to accomplish your dreams.[2]

Secondly, the capacity to dream means being able to courageously condition your imagination to shape hopeful images of the future even in the face of extraordinary adversity. If you lived in Ayacucho in 1988, and you took a hard look at what a disaster the past decade had been, your mental pictures of the future would probably have developed into vivid images of a swift escape. Indeed, most *ayacuchanos* simply took flight to Lima during the late 1980s, turning vast areas of the city into refugee camps. The Añaños family were different. They could have left Ayacucho in 1988 and started their lives again in Lima or elsewhere with the US$8,000 that Eduardo obtained from selling the family's agricultural equipment. Instead, they decided to share their dream to create Peru's greatest soft-drink company. And they saw an ideal opening in Ayacucho to live their dream by starting up a new kind of soft drink: one that the entire Peruvian population could enjoy. It isn't so much that they insulated themselves from their country's troubles – they couldn't and they didn't. It is just that, in 1988, the Añaños family courageously prevented bleak emotions from overwhelming their thoughts. Instead, they let the positive images of an entirely new soft-drink company capture their imagination. Eduardo Añaños's ability to keep his head cool on despair but hot on perceiving the real opportunities was to prove particularly decisive for his capacity to dream and to share a dream with his family.

Thirdly, the capacity to dream is "dreaming big" with a sense of urgency attached to it. In Ayacucho in the late 1980s, it is easy to see that the sheer struggle to survive was providing both the Añaños family and many other improvised entrepreneurs with the motivation to swiftly live their dreams by launching immediately into the marketplace an array of products that were desperately needed by the local population. Here, the main difference between the Añaños family and the rest was that their dream turned out to be, from the outset, a much bigger dream, born not just of the will to survive, but also of the aspiration to create something entirely new. So they had a different sense of urgency and a multiple set of deadlines attached to their dream. As a result, in 1991 Kola Real opened a second plant in Huancayo, a neighbouring city in the Peruvian central Andes; in 1993 it opened a third factory in Bagua, in the Amazon jungle; in 1994 it was the turn of Sullana, in northern Peru's tropical coastal regions; and in 1997 Kola Real reached Lima, the big city. When they were challenged head-on in Lima by the big brands, the Añaños family characteristically responded to adversity by dreaming even bigger, this time on a "planet Earth" scale. But most of the other ventures that a decade earlier had launched new consumer brands simultaneously with Kola Real had by then faded away or had never made it outside Ayacucho to start with.

Fourthly, the capacity to dream means keeping the mind free from broadly shared causality biases that – either genuinely or only apparently based on logic – do filter most people's mental images out, allowing the passage of only narrow pictures that are slim projections of the past into the future. The appalling socio-economic scenario in 1988 meant Peru simply wasn't a country fit for new consumer goods ventures. With a relatively small population even by Latin American standards, Peru's principal business had historically been based on natural resources ranging from mining and fishery to agricultural products. Moreover, with nearly two-thirds of its population living under the United Nations poverty line in 1988, Peru's market for consumer goods was small and rapidly shrinking still further. On top of this, historically the Peruvian soft-drinks market had been a long-lasting duopoly firmly controlled by Coca-Cola and Inka Cola. It is quite difficult to imagine many rational businessmen dreaming "big" in such scenario. However, the Añaños family's capacity to dream turned all this supposed rationality on its head. They were simply able to see that, even with a distressed population with shrinking incomes, a low-cost, low-priced and high-quality soft drink was bound to achieve spectacular growth in Peru – and even beyond. This is a very important point. In 1988, the Añaños family could have simply and opportunistically skimmed the depressed market of *ayacuchanos* by pricing their soft drinks at the same levels as the absent Coca-Cola and Inka Cola. Many other first-time entrepreneurs from Ayacucho did just that across other sectors, making big short-term gains. But the Añaños family didn't. From the start, they set out to build Peru's greatest soft drinks company, one that would expand the market because everyone could afford to buy its products. Their dream was, in fact, about creating a new future – a big long-term shift – rather than surviving opportunistically by living a narrow dream within a "rational" projection of Peru's 1988 status quo.

Finally, the capacity to dream means using your own eyes and your own imagination to observe what already exists around you and to create the future as a result, rather than attempting to objectively predict it. In 1988, and again in 1999, rather than falling for the contagious pessimism underlying most expert predictions of the future, the Añaños family visibly acted upon their subjective observations and strongly imprinted their own personal values, character traits and lifelong experiences on their dreams of the future.

The son of Nivardo Añaños, Eduardo grew up in Patibamba, the family hacienda located in Ayacucho's temperate areas of the San Miguel province. Eduardo's sister-in-law had married Amaniel Castro, a colourful character who had started San Miguel's first bottling company. It was as a result of meeting Amaniel, during the 1970s, that Eduardo acquired an interest in the soft drinks business. During the same decade, the Añaños family showed the old-style values of resilience typical of a certain class of Peruvian landowners when, following an agrarian reform by the authoritarian regime of General Juan Velasco Alvarado, Nivardo refused to abandon his land and instead distributed it in smaller parcels amongst his children. This was how Eduardo got his land – and probably his sense of determination as well. Being thoroughly provincial landowning *ayacuchanos*, the Añaños clan also had a lifelong interaction with the lower-income rural population, unlile most educated managers and entrepreneurs from Peru's urban areas, who neither had this contact nor had any real interest in developing it. Therefore, in 1988, the Añaños family's idea that the country's lower-income rural population was ready to become actual customers was something they knew from experience, but that was unimaginable to Peru's urban businessmen. Later on, in 1999, the Añaños family once more defied conventional business wisdom by successfully acting upon the unthinkable idea that a soft drinks company that had come from a ridiculously small market by any standard could grow swiftly to international status on Coca-Cola's own turf.

✳ *creating the future*

It is quite obvious that even the most arresting dream has no real value beyond the dreamer's own individual emotions. What gives our capacity to dream the power to create the future is, to use Carlos Añaños's word, determination. Here, the meaning is clearly the "unshakeable will and firm resolution" that you will find in your average English dictionary. Let us now take a closer look at the root of the word "resolution", as it highlights three central characteristics of the process for creating the future that I have found at work in successful imaginative individuals and organizations across the globe.

The word resolution stems from the Latin verb *resolvere*, which in turn bring us to the root word *solvo*, meaning to untie, unbind or loosen. The English words solution, absolution, solve and dissolve all derive from this root, in the sense of untying a problem or loosening a situation or a substance. Now, when the ancient Romans attached the prefix *re-* to a verb they did it – much as we do – in order to strongly accentuate the action. In other words, the verb *resolvo* meant "to untie again and again", and the related Latin word *resolutio* signified – usually within mathematics – the breaking down of the elements of a problem into simpler parts again and again until the problem was solved.

Likewise, the underlying process for creating the future is a showcase of individual resolve and organizational resolution in three main ways. First, I found that the process is iterative and openended over time. Second, the process has elements that provide continuous feedback at each step and in every iteration until all problems are resolved, making the team or the organization ready for the next cycle. Third, throughout the open-ended and iterative process, it is the steady will of the individuals and team members carrying it out that gives the process a clear sense of direction towards the future that has been dreamed in the first place.

The process for creating the future is unfolded by the seven keys to imagination that were introduced in the prelude to this book, providing an orderly sequence of stages. The whole process can be divided into three phases.

Firstly we find *imagining*, or the applied capacity to dream the future. As has been illustrated in the previous section, a big dream is usually evoked at first by a single individual – or just a few people – who will turn it into a purposeful mission.

Secondly, the mission is shared with others to form a team that carries out the *nurturing* phase of their big dream. This is achieved through a more deliberate creative process, introducing specific commitments to generate an infant prototype of what has been up until that point no more than a common mission and a shared mental image of the future. Overall, nurturing is a team-based, iterative and hybrid process of creative experimentation combining a sheer imaginative mode with concrete technological applications and well-defined economic parameters in order to generate this prototype of the team's big dreams. (By "sheer imaginative mode" we specifically mean an applied trade-on mindset, in other words, the team's mental predisposition to imagine ideas leading to a radical prototype that generates vastly superior customer value at a reduced cost.)

Finally, the *transforming* phase of the process allows the new infant prototype to grow into maturity on a much larger scale. At its heart, transforming is a results-oriented innovation phase, typically involving an array of organizational functions working systematically under a clear technological and economic approach that is capable of releasing successive generations of the new prototype at appropriate times and on a large scale. When it soundly follows up on a big dream for the future and its associated prototype, a functioning transforming phase is the milestone indicating that a new future has been created by the team or by the organization (or both), making them ready for another iteration of the entire process (see Figure 2).

The process for creating the future is holistic in the sense that the whole is more than the sum of its three component phases (imagining, nurturing, transforming), "more" being constituted by a continuous stream of new futures actually delivered by the team or by the organization. The process is also holistic in the sense that the harmonious interplay between the crucial capabilities and resources required to effectively create the future – capacity

FIGURE 2 : The process for creating the future

to dream, creative process, innovation process – is much more powerful than each of them playing solo.

The challenge for imaginative individuals and organizations is of course how to keep the process for creating the future functioning smoothly as an integrated whole, given that the inherent spirit and operating dynamics of its component phases are so very different. On the one hand, the capacity to dream is an imagining exercise stemming from a few people's ability to use imagination, heightened by inner experiences of emotions and perspective taking, in order to visualize radical mental images of the future. On the other hand, the creative process is about nurturing an environment in which a group of individuals are trustful, motivated and capable enough to reveal their insightful ideas – even "wild" ones – to each other and to work together on building a radical new prototype. A crucial enabler of this nurturing ability is the skill to develop a common language and clear conversation rules that are shared and practised by the whole team. This allows for insightful and creative conversations to take place routinely within the team, turning it into a great and powerful team. Finally, the innovation process means implementing the organizational capability to systematically release new offerings on a large scale – in other words, the consistent ability to make generations of new products and services widely accessible to people, thereby shaping the future around us to some extent.

In the remaining parts of this book – particularly in chapters 4 and 7 – we will look in detail at how successful and imaginative teams and organizations develop the *common glue* to keep such a heterogeneous and multi-phased process together. At this point, we need only highlight two crucial enablers for the achievement of that elusive aspiration. On the one hand, it is important to recognize two steps of the process for creating the future as particularly relevant to the team because they signal transitional stages between its component phases. First, *purposeful missions* – that is, missions that radically break with the prevailing status quo and resonate strongly with the team members' core emotions – turn a purely imagining phase into a more deliberate, nurturing one aimed at creating a radical prototype. Secondly, the establishment of *gentlemen's promises* – in other words, specific promises to release the radical prototype on a larger scale and within tight deadlines – signals the transition of a nurturing phase into a transforming one, where the central endeavour is fully fledged organizational innovation. On the other hand, throughout the process for creating the future it is essential to practise *Wiraqocha leadership* – in other words, purposeful guidance that combines an imaginative mindset, the ability to nurture strong leadership cohesiveness, and a passion to deliver.

✳ *making the future*

When it comes to applying the process for creating the future, I found that successful imaginative individuals and organizations apply it with an ongoing rhythm over time rather than approaching it as a one-off exercise. In certain cases, like the Italian San Patrignano community, there is a high-frequency rhythm, meaning that the organization constantly reinvents itself. A world-class drug rehabilitation community that self-supports itself financially through its own business activities and private fund-raising, San Patrignano has continued to transform itself dramatically since its foundation back in 1978. The community's drug rehabilitation aims and most of its initial businesses have remained, but the constant addition of entirely new activities keeps transforming San Patrignano into an increasingly sophisticated place. The change has also been physical. If you had visited the community in 1999, and then again in 2009, you would barely have recognized it as the same place.

Similarly, Zara's radical reinvention of women's fashion on a global scale over the 1990s – turning it from a seasonal experience to a weekly one – has increasingly crossed over to other areas. Thus, during the first decade of the 21st century, the world of men's fashion, children clothing and home accessories has been transformed by Zara's revolutionary approach to inexpensively move fair quality and fashionable products across more than seventy countries every week, making all sorts of fashion items highly accessible to the global masses. The fact that in 2008 Inditex – Zara's parent company – established Europe's largest logistics complex, just outside Zaragoza, was proof of the company's further plans to dramatically grow its global business, both in volume and by venturing into new markets that can be thoroughly reinvented by Zara's winning formula.

In Peru, the Añaños family nurtured their unusual capacity to dream the future in their back yard. Together with just fifteen employees, in 1988 they developed a rudimentary bottling machine, code-named Atahualpa, after Peru's sixteenth-century Inca leader. This was their infant prototype, and their testing experiences in Ayacucho turned into a steep learning curve over the ensuing couple of years. By the end of 1990, they had perfected the powerful approach of high quality at a fair price and were ready for larger-scale dreams. Remarkable success followed, turning Grupo AJE by 2009 into a 7,000-strong multinational organization that controlled significant markets in Latin America and parts of Asia with a highly diversified portfolio of brands that included not only soft drinks, but also mineral water, sports drinks and beer. And unlike their soft drinks, which characteristically tapped into the lower-income populations, the group's forays into mineral water, sports drinks and beer were from the outset successfully positioned to encompass the whole market, from the sectors of lesser affluence up to the highest earning areas. In doing so, companies like Grupo AJE remind us that, after all, fairly priced quality is a near-universal dream.

Organizations such as US-based Medtronic – which in 2009 ranked as the world's largest medical technology company – apply parallel processes to create the future. Founded in 1949 by Earl Bakken and Palmer Hermundslie after their invention, in a domestic garage, of the first wearable artificial pacemaker, Medtronic's innovation process became so effective that by the mid 1990s 70 per cent of the company's annual revenues came from new products launched within the previous two years. These results constituted an unprecedented improvement over the previous global innovation "best practices", such as those at 3M or Hewlett-Packard, about 30 per cent of whose annual revenues stemmed from products launched within the preceding five years. As a result, Medtronic's market value soared from US$1.1 billion to US$60 billion during the 1990s, in the process transforming the medical device industry beyond recognition. Bill George, as CEO of Medtronic from 1990 to 2001, presided over this extraordinary transformation. As he explains:

 We managed in a differential way; it was really one company, two cultures. One culture was the disciplined, engineering, bring-it-out-on-schedule. And then there was a whole group of people over here that are working in small teams – ten to fifteen people – doing really innovative things, very, very creative things. That's where the new ideas came from, and then they would have to be worked back into the mainstream system. We gave them a lot of freedom, kept them out of the disciplined system since [our new product release cycle] had to be sixteen months. So, they could be working on an invention that could take a month, it could take ten years.

In addition to their outstanding process for creating the future by releasing a new generation of products every sixteen months, Medtronic applied a different version of the same process to reinventing itself every five years. These parallel processes were fairly different in content, but both of them relied upon the same underlying capabilities – capacity to dream, creative process and innovation process – and involved the same key leadership group sharing a common mission and values. Bill George observes:

 Shortly after I became CEO I wrote a paper called "Reinventing Medtronic" that said we will be a totally different company every five years, but what will never change is the mission and the values [of the company]. So that gave people a certain confidence that, yes, the strategy may change, the businesses may change, we may do things differently, but we know it's Medtronic.

Medtronic launched a new iteration of this reinvention process at its January 2000 Global Strategic Direction meeting. Baptised "Medtronic Vision 2010", this company-wide initiative aimed at radical transformation from a medical device organization offering innovative products every sixteen months, to the world's leading medical technology company providing lifelong solutions to patients with chronic disease. The company's lifelong solutions were designed to improve the quality of life of vast numbers of patients around the world, while significantly reducing healthcare costs. All of the Medtronics leadership group – from CEO Bill George to the heads of the key businesses and global functions – were personally involved in the implementation of Medtronic Vision 2010, working within five cross-functional teams. These teams identified the disease states that would have the most impact in the world's health and economic welfare; mapped the emerging new experiences in the healthcare delivery system from the point of view of all stakeholders (in other words, not just the patients but also their families); and spotted the revolutionary effects of the emerging medical, information and communications technologies on the company's future business. Next, the teams articulated in detail how Medtronic would stay on top of the new medical businesses and technologies that had been identified, by releasing lifelong solutions that would radically change the industry by 2010. George had encapsulated all this in his January 2000 speech for the launching of Medtronic Vision 2010:

 You can now see why I said that we stand at a major inflection point in Medtronic's history. Over the next decade, Medtronic will reinvent itself once again by providing a more complete range of products and services to a broader set of customers:

physicians, healthcare institutions, and patients. Our patient management solutions will result in better quality of life for those suffering from chronic disease, lead to a reduction of overall healthcare costs, and provide Medtronic with new, ongoing revenue streams. The rapidly increasing complexity of our business enviroment will demand new capabilities that do not reside within Medtronic's traditional strengths. Creating business partnerships will expand our capability and leverage what Medtronic does uniquely well. [3]

Creating partnerships or making outright acquisitions to boost their own capabilities to create the future around us is something that organizations like Microsoft have also done consistently. Since its first acquisition in 1987, of Forethought – whose presentation program would later become Windows PowerPoint – Microsoft acquired an average of six companies a year between 1988 and 2009. Nearly all of those acquisitions have tended to fit quite nicely in specific niches that helped Microsoft evolve to maintain its position as the world's leading software organization. Interestingly, when it comes to the endeavour of creating the future, Microsoft's 1987–2009 acquisition strategy portrays it as an early mover rather than a first one, but a mover of unmatched effectiveness nevertheless. Its 1997 US$500 million acquisition of Hotmail, the free webmail service founded the year before by Jack Smith and Sabeer Bhatia, made it a leading player in the global e-mail revolution that over the ensuing years completely reshaped the way we communicated. Likewise, its 2007 US$6.3 billion acquisition of aQuantive (a leading web advertising specialist) and its 2008 US$1.9 billion purchase of Norwegian Fast Search and Transfer (a web search technology firm) boosted Microsoft's capability to share with Google in transforming the Internet into a truly global connectedness resource, with applications ranging from web search to online mapping, social networking, video-sharing and office productivity.

Other players have turned their ability to create the future into a core service for their clients. This is the case with Silicon Valley's industrial design champion IDEO. Over the 1990s and the first decade of the 21st century, this firm created mainstream products and services that were radical departures from previous customer experiences, for a broad array of leading clients ranging from automotive organizations and high-technology firms to banks and movie studios. It is not an exaggeration to say that these clients in fact outsourced to IDEO essential parts of the imagining and nurturing phases of their own processes for creating the future. In addition, captivated by IDEO's smooth ability to bring previously unthinkable customer experiences to life, many of its clients routinely turned to it for help in developing a culture and a set of processes to unleash their own powers of imagination and creativity.

Apple is, of course, an example of a highly imaginative organization that over the late 1980s and 1990s lost its trademark capacity to dream the future, only to recover it spectacularly at the dawn of the 21st century. As a result, in 2009 people of all ages and geographies were engaging in a lifestyle that in many ways – from iPods to iTunes and iPhones – was a future which Apple and a few others had created just a few years earlier. Organizations such as Apple – and mercurial characters such as its company founder Steve Jobs – illustrate the capability and the process of creating the future as something that individuals, teams and organizations can decide to develop from scratch, let fade away, or revive – or even experience all three over time.

I also examined plenty of teams and organizations that were missing at least one phase of the process and were therefore unable to create the future effectively. This highlights once more the fundamental importance of applying all three phases of the process for creating the future – imagining, nurturing and transforming – as a holistic, integrated totality.

On the one hand, organizations such as Motorola and Sun Microsystems demonstrated during the 1980s an extraordinary ability to create the future through the introduction of, respectively, a leading array of new wireless communication devices, and ingenious UNIX-based servers that powered computer networks and websites. However, over the 1990s these companies seemed to lose their imagining capacity to dream the future, and consequently missed out on breakthrough innovations. As a result, during the first decade of the 21st century they became followers that let others such as Google, Nokia, Microsoft and BlackBerry create the future of global connectedness around them. The time-cycle over which this particular type of situation unfolds continues to shorten dramatically in every industry, owing to the combined forces of globalization and swift scientific and technological development worldwide.

On the other hand, during the 1980s a number of highly imaginative organizations such as Philips, Xerox and IBM had individuals and teams with a strong capacity to dream the future (imagining) together with outstanding creative processes to support those dreams (nurturing). However, these organizations either lacked a sound innovation process to follow up on their new prototypes of the future, or their innovation processes were functionally disconnected from the organization's key imagining individuals and creative teams. As a result, over the 1980s these organizations continuously generated extraordinarily useful new technologies and even invented entire categories of breakthrough products – ranging from personal computer operating systems to the initial digital recording technologies – only for others such as Microsoft and Sony to seize the advantage and build new futures based on them.

✳ *predicting the future*

I often think of my old college classmate Pedro Cabredo – a thin and perennially smiling figure, with the broad forehead and general air of a precocious intellectual – who once suggested that one could forecast anything except the future. At the time, I thought of this as nothing more than a clever remark. Five years later, as I was in the US studying statistical forecasting methods on the best doctoral programmes that money could buy – and growing doubtful of their real power to say anything really insightful about the future – mental images of my good friend Pedro would come back from time to time. You can easily imagine my nostalgic smile when, many years after that, I came across the following words by legendary management author Paul Drucker:

The probability of any prediction coming true is no better than 2 per cent [...]. The only way to successfully predict the future is to make it new [...]. The future has already happened. The task we must take up is to look at all that has already happened, but has yet to have an impact.[4]

To slightly paraphrase Drucker, creating the future is the only way to successfully predict it. More pointedly, the extraordinary stories we have just examined suggest that the process for creating the future is a capability that can be – and ought to be – developed by individuals and organizations alike. Creators of the future make positive things that have a radical impact happen, and reshape their surrounding contexts beyond recognition. They are able to do this time and again because they see things in their surroundings that others keep missing, build courageous dreams of the future based on what they see, and move resolutely to transform their dreams into reality through an orderly process.

An organization doesn't need to build in-house all the pieces that are required to create the future. As mentioned, players such as Microsoft regularly purchase specific imagining or nurturing capabilities when moving to create new futures. On the other hand, organizations such as IDEO use their creativity and capacity to dream to contribute to others' innovation pipelines. However, what creators of the future do maintain is their leadership over the entire process of creating the future. Even if, from time to time, other players are invited to participate in specific parts of the process as partners, targets, customers or allies, the endeavour for creating the future invariably calls for a strong leadership capable of running it as a holistic process. The latter is a sort of higher capability that gives its holder the upper hand in the astonishing performance results and economic value that are generally achieved by the creation of a radically new future.

✳ *lucrative economies of imagination*

Individuals and organizations like San Patrignano, Zara, Medtronic or the Añaños family regularly reinvent themselves in order to create the future around them, making radical internal changes an integral and harmonious part of their experiential journeys. Unlike them, most organizations I have examined move to profoundly change or reinvent themselves only as a one-off response to traumatic crises or life-threatening competitive menaces. Often the latter stem from creators of the future who have radically transformed the playing field, suddenly turning former leaders into followers and previously fit organizations into obsolete also-rans.

The extraordinary stories we have examined also make clear that a few things must stay unchanged over many decades, in order to allow the rest to radically, constantly and regularly shift around. This fixed core is constituted by the original dream of the future, the captivating child of an individual's – or a small group's – imagination. This original dream, articulated in both a purposeful mission and a trade-on customer formula, stays stubbornly fixed, with the organization tightly holding on to it throughout radical changes and countless reinventions. Thus, no matter how radically different are the new additions to San Patrignano's portfolio of world-class businesses, its initial commitment to train marginalized people and bring them to achieve extraordinary things has remained unchanged over a period of three decades. And throughout the same period, San Patrignano's formula was to achieve the world's highest drug rehabilitation rate at half the annual cost per person compared with similar institutions. Over a similar timespan of thirty years, not only did Zara remain faithful to its original mission of democratizing fashion, but it also, during the first decade of the 21st century, increasingly expanded its formula of fast-changing and inexpensive designs across many other sectors such as men's clothing, children's fashion and home accessories. Likewise, when Grupo AJE's Big Cola was launched in Mexico in 2002 it was produced at a highly automated factory that was a far cry from Atahualpa, their first rudimentary plant established in Ayacucho back in 1988. After barely a decade in business, by 1999 the company had been forced to dramatically scale up its original dream of allowing most of the population to become part of the market for soft drinks. This was because of Coca-Cola's aggressive price war, aimed specifically at eliminating Kola Real, and clearly a strategy to maintain its market dominance in Peru rather than to pursue any radically new dreams about the future. Nevertheless, Grupo AJE's forays into the Mexican market in 2002 still kept to its initial "fairly priced quality" customer formula, as Big Cola's 3.3 litre bottle retailed for 12 pesos against Coca-Cola's 2.5 litre bottle priced at 15 pesos. But in 2007, when Grupo AJE carried out its hugely successful launch of Big Cola in the Colombian market, the slogan tagged to each bottle had changed – both slightly and significantly – to *calidad internacional a precio justo* ("international quality at a fair price"), reflecting the company's bold new dreams in the global arena.

Interestingly, when Medtronic launched Medtronic Vision 2010 in January 2000, it did change its core mission from "restoring people to full health and life" (which had remained unchanged since its foundation in 1949) to "providing lifelong solutions for people with chronic disease". The winning formula behind Medtronic's solutions was to aim at simultaneously improving quality of life and reducing healthcare costs. The company's epochal change of mission reflected the fact that, at the dawn of the 21st century, a few Medtronic leaders had – in Drucker's words – looked at "all that has already happened, but has yet to have an impact", and decided it was time to dream big once more. Among the main things that had already taken place by 2000 but had yet to realize their full impact were the global connectedness revolution and the epidemic growth of impairing chronic conditions such as heart disease, arthritis, emphysema, diabetes, cancer and AIDS, which together affected over 100 million people and represented 80 per cent of direct medical-care costs in the US alone. Against this background, Medtronic's leaders envisioned their organization becoming by 2010 a world leader in the application of leading-edge medical, informational and communications technologies to chronic disease states that would continue to have a profound impact in the future social and economic welfare of the entire world.

The fact that the same radical dream of the future together with an associated purposeful mission and trade-on customer formula can be applied over a very large time-span and in entirely different environments, there to be transformed beyond recognition, was one of the pivotal findings of my discovery journey. When there is a single organization behind these multiple transformations, it drives astonishing performance results over the long term and in nearly any way you care to measure it, ranging from the social and motivational (think of San Patrignano), to fast innovation and market value creation (think of Medtronic), explosive and profitable revenue growth (think of Zara and Grupo AJE), and the creation of extraordinary value to customers at low cost to the organization (think of all four).

These performance results lead to the idea of economies of imagination – or imagination economies – as distinct from and complementary to economies of scale and scope. Whereas economies of scale result from the reduction of unit costs as production volumes increase, and economies of scope stem from a broader application of certain knowledge-based assets (such as brands or technological know-how), economies of imagination are about bringing powerful mental images of a radical new future from their original breeding grounds to different environments where they may flourish vigorously and drive extraordinary economic results. Players such as Zara, Medtronic or the Añaños family can deliberately exploit economies of imagination over a large time-span of many decades, because their radical dreams about the future are backed up by purposeful missions and trade-on customer formulas, all of which can be smoothly transferred on a global scale across entirely different environments.

❖ *unleashing the wizard inside you*

As suggested in the previous chapter, the process for creating the future can be described fully in scientific terms, particularly by the experimental psychology, neuroscience and management disciplines. Thus, neuroscientists and psychologists have linked our capacity to dream the future to the cognitive faculties of imagination, which are able not only to grasp current reality, but also to generate radical mental alternatives to it. Individual emotions, dispositional optimism and socially shared values can strongly condition this process by influencing the kinds of things people will – or won't – daydream about. A creative process relies on group creativity, which has been shown to be particularly effective when carried out within trustful teams sharing a clear commitment, a common language and a single set of behavioural rules. Innovation process – in other words the organizational capability to systematically release new products or services on a large scale – is a classic subject of study in both economics and management sciences, stressing the importance of smooth cross-functional links throughout the process in order to leverage the innovative strengths of the entire organization.

However, crucial aspects of the process for creating the future, particularly imagining and nurturing, can also be properly described through the prism of Renaissance natural magic. This isn't surprising: there *is* something magical in the endeavour of creating the future anew. As previously described, Renaissance magi carried out verbal and musical rituals to condition the imagination into visualizing a specific outcome they had obsessively set their eyes on. Next, they created a physical image or a smaller scale model of the outcome they had mentally envisioned and endeavoured to turn it into a larger-scale, functioning mechanism. Unlike those conducting scientific experiments, participants in the magical process were not expected to remain objective or to rely upon previous experience. Quite the contrary; natural magic operated through a distinct social communication approach that used specific, ritualized language in order to arouse the participants' emotions to positively imagine and believe in the final outcome. At heart, Renaissance natural magic was subjective optimism and positive imagination underpinned by faith in the attainment of a successful outcome, all carried out through ritualized linguistic formulas for group work.

Natural magic is, in essence, an approach quite similar to the process of creating the future through imagining and nurturing, with a couple of important differences. First, the obsessive focus of individuals like Muccioli, Ortega or the Añaños clan is invariably on a specific customer experience, such as drug addicts missing family love, women longing for fast-changing and accessible fashion, or masses yearning to be included in the consumer goods markets. Secondly, the strong emotional components conditioning the imagination in natural magic are also very much in place in the imagining process, but they are triggered by direct interactions with real people rather than by ritualized experiences. It was strong emotions activated by direct contact with actual people that fuelled Muccioli's imagination to envision a large and successful family made up of drug addicts in rehabilitation, that encouraged Ortega's dreams about the democratization of fashion, and that induced the Añaños family to imagine a world-beating new cola that everyone could afford to buy and enjoy. Once it is clearly visualized, the dream of the future is linguistically ritualized in a purposeful mission that both inspires and guides a group's actions. Next, a small-scale model of the new future is created in the form of a radical prototype that is built and nurtured by the group. Throughout this journey, just as in natural magic, it is all about a group of highly committed people working with optimism and unshakable faith to live its shared dreams and fulfil its common mission.

Thus, from one perspective, positively creating the future is a rational endeavour leading to extraordinary performance results for all players involved. However, from another standpoint, dreaming about a radical new future and moving resolutely to deliver it means nothing less than unleashing the wizard within. As a minimum, creating the future rather than predicting it requires its protagonists to move optimistically between technological certainties and the magical realms of that which we believe in but which remains unknown. It is to help us enter those territories and unlock those possibilities in our minds that I have articulated the seven keys to imagination. Let us now examine them in closer detail.

part two

....

the seven keys

1

the first key:
trade-on mindset

....

En este mundo traidor
nada es verdad ni es mentira
todo es según el color
del cristal con que se mira.

(In this treacherous world
nothing is true nor a lie,
all depends on the colour
of the glass you look through.)

Ramón de Campoamor (1817–1901), Spanish poet

WHEN THE RESIDENTS of the sophisticated northern Italian city of Turin describe their metropolis as a "magical
city", they really mean it. For some reason, Turin has always been
regarded as one of Europe's capitals of magic. Every day crowds
of visitors eagerly join guided tours offering to unveil the city's
mysterious landmarks, ancient underground galleries and secret
topographical orientations that supposedly define immense,
open-air magical talismans that puzzle the imagination. But
in 2009 all of these tours were systematically missing Settimo
Torinese, one of Turin's industrial suburbs and the site of the
rechargeable house experimental project, an initiative that felt
decidedly magical to those involved in it.

The rechargeable house was the fruit of the imagination of Mario
Cucinella, an Italian star architect whose personal motto, "more
with less", permeates his life and work. In 2007, he surprised the
Italian establishment with his radical layout of a 100 square metre

house that stored rainwater in underground tanks and could be recharged like a cell-phone through solar panels, wind power and high-tech materials. The house was priced at €1,000 per square metre, compared with the average €2,636 per square metre then prevailing in Italy. Moreover, prospective owners would qualify for government subsidies as a result of low CO_2 emissions. Not only did Mario Cucinella's rechargeable house have zero carbon emissions and virtually eliminate water, electricity and heating bills from its fortunate owners' monthly expenses; it also produced an energy surplus that could either be sold to neighbours or used to power an electric car. Just two years after the initial design was publicly presented, the first 50 rechargeable houses were being built in Settimo Torinese, heralded as the new housing for the future. Cucinella observed:

 My idea is to propose a house Ikea style: with high levels of design at low cost, accessible to all. I am convinced that it is a great expression of democracy to bring design to our daily lives. We shouldn't make our work so exclusive.[1]

Ikea, the organization that inspired Cucinella's rechargeable house vision, had epitomized the idea of doing more with less ever since it started business in 1943. By 2009, Ikea was the world's largest furniture retailer, with about 300 stores in over 40 countries. It had completely reinvented the way in which people all over the world used and shopped for furniture. Its gigantic stores, where well-designed, inexpensive furniture was picked up, transported and assembled at home by the customers themselves, offered a unique shopping experience, complete with childcare playgrounds, coffee-shops and restaurants. From the outset, Ikea's pioneering use of global sourcing, customer self-service and store layout led to a low-cost operation that allowed the retailer to offer superior value for money to customers and enjoy double-digit annual margins and revenue growth in the process.

In their seminal book *Co-opetition*, first published in 1996, authors Barry Nalebuff and Adam Brandenburger coined the expression "trade-ons" to account for the notion of pursuing high quality and lower costs at the same time, within the context of negotiations strategy and game theory.[2] Trade-offs on the other hand are about getting high quality by means of higher costs (or vice versa). Both the rechargeable house and Ikea's products offer clear examples of trade-ons. However, individuals like Mario Cucinella or Ikea's employees do not just pursue trade-ons in the transactional sense of "high quality at lower cost" outcomes that Nalebuff and Brandenburger intended. To describe the rechargeable house project or the Ikea customer experience as merely superior value for money hardly does justice to the unusually broad range of positive transformations, useful applications and emotional responses that these innovations create in customers, stakeholders and entire societies alike. When they started, every detail of the rechargeable house or the Ikea experience was about doing, gaining and experiencing much more with a lot less within a radical concept of the housing of the future, which made everyone coming into contact with them just a bit closer to sharing the same new philosophy. In other words, rather than occasional transactional trade-ons, it is a far-reaching *trade-on mindset* that stems from individuals like Mario Cucinella or the Ikea organization, pervading every aspect of their existential journeys and their surroundings through contagious new ideas, emotions, creations, offerings and experiences.

Cucinella's rechargeable houses are actually four-storey blocks of flats where individuals or families live side by side. There are high ceilings, huge windows and glass doors everywhere, with a colour scheme predominantly of light green and white adding to the prevailing sense of lightness, simplicity and serenity. Contiguous blocks of flats are connected by wide walkways with transparent rails that can be accessed either from the street via well-designed stairs or directly from the apartments' main entrances. The technological devices that power the rechargeable houses are discreetly integrated into the aesthetics and the functionality of the houses themselves. The transparent green ceilings protecting the terraces of the buildings from rain and excessive sunlight are in fact solar panels. The huge tanks storing rainwater for consumption and for the generation of hydrogen gas are concealed underground. Even the strikingly designed blades that revolve with the wind on top of 15-metre-high columns, looking like modern

aerial sculptures, are actually wind power systems. The large veg-
etable plot in front of the buildings and the well-equipped set of
garden appliances are the shared property of all tenants. Emiliano
Cecchini, the Italian physicist who designed an electrolytic device
the size of a small box that is powered by solar energy, and that
extracts hydrogen gas from water to generate electricity for the
rechargeable house, observes:

> Literally speaking [the rechargeable house is] off-grid. And by
> "grid" we mean the private or public utilities that supply [water
> or] energy for money. Think of a farmer who lives off the land:
> the off-grid system follows the same logic. The condominium
> of flats live from the energy that they themselves cultivate, in a
> totally clean way.[3]

It isn't just that Cucinella's and Cecchini's rechargeable off-
grid house is staggeringly good value for money. By living in it,
tenants, their visitors and the surrounding community inevitably get strong mental stimuli stemming from the radical ideas
embedded in the new housing environment. As a result, their
lives and work are likely to adapt to the "doing more with less"
mindset characteristic of 21st-century energy farmers. You don't
actually need to visit a rechargeable house or meet its tenants
to feel the powerful effects; just getting in touch with the idea
is enough. As I was looking at pictures of Cucinella's wonder
houses during a flight back home to Peru, new images of my
not-for-profit project for a contemporary Andean art museum in
Lima suddenly captured my imagination. I saw it was going to be
just like Cucinella's rechargeable house: an off-grid, totally zero-
emission, beautifully designed building, the first of its kind in the
world. I instantly felt that my new vision was bound to be very
much in tune with both the 21st century and the ancient Andean
mindset of going with nature rather than against it.

Cucinella and Cecchini's visions for the housing of the future
encapsulate what a *trade-on mindset* is all about: the pervasive,
deep-rooted predisposition to perceive and interpret reality with
the mental eyes of being, doing and gaining much more with a
lot less. When a trade-on mindset is applied to imagining new
and positive futures, it unleashes radical mental images that are

unthinkable to most people, but instantly unlock their imagination to think and act in the same beneficial direction of being, doing and gaining much more with a lot less.

My visits to the Ikea store outside Geneva with my infant son Leonardo during his school vacation will always be among my most cherished memories. It was the perfect way for me to successfully combine a professionally productive morning with spending time with my son. The sweet spot was a very large, U-shaped table just beside the restaurant area with all sorts of video games and colourful toys scattered inside the U. Children would flock there to play for hours. I would sip coffee and work on my laptop while Leonardo played right in front of me with his new-found friends. From time to time, he would approach me to say, "Have you seen they are playing a brilliant movie, Dad?" or, "Dad, meet my new friend Eric!" After a few hours, we would eat at the noisy and playful restaurant, and then we would head back home. There was a carefully designed circuit you had to follow to reach the exit, though, which forced us to walk through most of the store and gaze at all sorts of new Ikea products. Leonardo would always come and ask me to buy a new lamp, a monster chair or a drawing kit. Often I would also buy something else that we needed at home. After all, the products were just fine, the prices were quite low, and Leonardo and I felt very happy together.

After about a year and a half, our home looked a bit like one of those interiors displayed in Ikea catalogues or exhibited in the store itself: playful and nurturing for the kids, sober, simple, balming and very functional for the entire family. From the interior design of our Swiss home, Ikea's underlying philosophy slowly made its way into my mode of thinking and acting in a broader context. I found myself increasingly adept at embracing simplicity as an intrinsic value, and developed a zest for avoiding all sorts of clutter – physical, digital, intellectual or emotional. I was not the only one. Over the last two decades of the twentieth century and across every major European country, an entire "Ikea generation" grew up under analogous influences. Just think of Mario Cucinella's and Emiliano Cecchini's architectural visions which – like the Ikea experience itself – represent the very essence of a *trade-on mindset*: the infectious predisposition to go about life with the intention of being, doing and gaining much more with a lot less.

❋ *the key to a magical mindset*

Psychologists studying "mindset" define it as a self-conception people use to structure the Self, guide their behaviour and interpret reality. Carol Dweck, a leading expert in mindset and personality psychology, maintains that our mindset develops over our childhood and adulthood, shaping our personality, forming our entire mental world and driving every aspect of our actions, from family relationships to work and sports.[4] There are also shared mindsets and collective self-conceptions that help explain why certain groups, organizations and even entire societies differ from one another in their common reasoning, character traits and performance results over time. Dweck suggests that every individual has either a fixed or a growth mindset. A fixed mindset is the belief that your talents and abilities are a given and stable quantity that won't change over your lifetime: either you have them or you don't. If you want to prove yourself smart or talented, you have to do so at the risk of discovering you are not – and paying the price for it. On the other hand, a growth mindset means faith in the idea that exceptional talents and rare skills can be developed over time. You are not limited to the cards you have been dealt. You can keep those but acquire some more and end up with a much stronger hand that you ever imagined. The upper limits for your growth possibilities actually are unknown; it is up to you to discover what they are over your lifetime.

Whereas a trade-off mentality can be described as fixed mindset at work in personal behaviour as well as in decision-making, both a *trade-on mindset* and a growth mindset are based on the same underlying self-belief in boundless opportunities and inner optimism that sets individuals like Mario Cucinella and organizations such as Ikea on the path to success. Beyond this, a *trade-on mindset* – the predisposition to be, do and gain much more with a lot less – has a number of specific qualities attached to it.

Simply put, a *trade-on mindset* is the state of mind of having positive beliefs about Self and Nature. It leads to seeing the world from a courageous and self-confident perspective, where the excitement of natural curiosity has long vanquished the innate fear of the unknown. It relies upon the deep-seated belief that, whatever is it you are looking for, in the end it's bound to be extraordinarily good news. It stems from faith in the forces of Nature being inherently positive for all creatures. It is a deep-down trust in the nourishing power of positive emotions, even in the face of seemingly awful-looking surroundings out there – as all storms are, for trade-on minded people, just temporary conditions invariably followed by sunshine. It is the mindset that we all probably had as small children.

It is also the underlying mindset of magicians. In his classic volume *Magic, Science and Religion*, first published in 1948, prominent anthropologist Bronislaw Malinowsky (1884–1942) pioneered the ethnographic, field-work based study of the different world-views of native cultures, including what he called the "sacred" domains of magic and religion, as opposed to the "profane" domain of science. According to Malinowsky there were no peoples – however primitive – without religion and magic. Within any society, Malinowsky saw the "magical function" as the ritualization of human optimism and the expression of faith in the victory of hope over fear, of confidence over doubt, of stability over uncertainty, of positive emotions over pessimism.[5] Malinowsky's observations fittingly characterize the frame of mind of proponents of natural magic – ranging from Marsilio Ficino and Pico della Mirandola to Giordano Bruno and Athanasius Kircher – whose works and approach blossomed in Italy and many other European countries over the Renaissance period (that is, from the fourteenth century to the seventeenth). Theirs was a mindset featuring clear trade-on characteristics and, in addition, their lives and careers certainly offer an example of what Carol Dweck terms a growth mindset.

Most people have, at certain points in their lives, let their trade-on neurons prevail within their mental territories. However, many of them slowly acquire a distinct trade-off mindset – often from a very early age – that gradually closes off their ability to think and act from a trade-on perspective. For these people to realign their "mindset balance", I have found two simple – but not simplistic – approaches that can reactivate their trade-on neurons, with a positive effect on how they imagine their futures, both personally and professionally. I call the first approach "emotional rotation" and the second "emotional storming". As the names suggest, both approaches are based on positively using the emotional key to unlock a torrent of positive feelings that may have been contained and repressed by some people.

Contrary to what you may expect, the real bad news here is *not* that you are a "born pessimist", which often translates as people becoming exceedingly trade-off minded. Psychologists have found that the same people can simultaneously show high degrees of optimism and of pessimism in the way they assess their choices, suggesting that optimism and pessimism are just two ways of expressing high levels of emotional engagement. And as we saw in the "Magic of Imagination" chapter, modern scientists and ancient magi alike found that heightened emotions could drive our imagination both powerfully and positively. So if you find your general outlook leaning towards the pessimistic side, this means you are already highly engaged emotionally and you may just need to make a 180-degree turn in your emotional core (an "emotional rotation") to start seeing the world – and imagining the future –more optimistically. The real bad news is in fact if you find yourself to be emotionally flat, which frequently leads to an unnecessarily cynical way of seeing the world in general. If that is your case – and you want to re-engage yourself emotionally in order to unleash your imaginative powers – you may be ready for an emotional storming experience to suddenly switch your trade-on neurons back on.

Emotional rotations work best – and lead to quickest results – with either optimistic people or relatively pessimistic individuals who are nevertheless both open minded and good observers. The system consists of relentlessly challenging yourself and/or your team to engage your minds with images eliciting positive emotions, and then to observe your entire surroundings with new eyes in order to identify excellent examples of trade-ons. If you are working individually, you will then challenge yourself to increasingly identify trade-on options in your personal as well as your professional decision-making. If you are doing this exercise with your team, you will challenge your teammates to present their trade-on examples to each other and discuss them. If you do this continuously over a period of time you will find yourself and your team suddenly and naturally coming out with increasing numbers of ideas, options and choices from the perspective of offering much more and much better results while requiring a lot less resources.

As a professor, I like to make emotional rotations amongst the classroom participants in my courses. After talking about trade-ons and getting them to focus on positive emotions, I challenge them to evoke mental images of everything they have experienced from the time they woke up that morning. Then I give them just a few seconds to identify a few trade-ons. As the participants present their examples to the whole group, one can typically organize their work into three basic categories. A first group of participants – usually a minority – very quickly come up with great examples of trade-ons they actually observed, ranging from the self-service breakfast experience they had in the hotel restaurant and the USB technology some of them use to digitally manage their client presentations, to their favourite e-commerce sites. A second and larger group of participants either bring in trade-on ideas they have invented on the spot rather than observed that morning, or present examples of trade-offs rather than trade-ons. Finally, a third group of participants typically come up with no trade-ons, complaining instead that it is either too difficult or that the very notion of trade-ons doesn't follow any logic at all. The first two groups normally comprise people who already display sound trade-on mindset characteristics and individuals who need just a bit of training in trade-on thinking. It is the third group that poses the greater challenge to mindset change, because it typically includes exceedingly cynical individuals who understand the power of imagination fully, but struggle to develop it. This is where emotional storming comes in.

The idea of emotional storming as a way of unlocking people's imaginations in a trade-on direction is based on the fact that mindset turns out to be a pervasive and quite contagious thing. Everyone who has tried living for any time with a group of pessimists or a group of optimists has doubtless found some of the prevailing attitude rubbing off on them. We also know that one of the best ways to turn a cynic into a believer is to face them with the overwhelming physical evidence of something whose very existence has been stubbornly doubted. Emotional storming shakes the hearts and minds of doubters and cynics alike, as a result of their being plunged into an environment where real people do extraordinary things with very little and against all the odds.

My favourite emotional storming place is, without any doubt, the San Patrignano community. I will never forget the first time I took a group of twenty stern-looking, deeply cynical and quintessentially trade-off minded corporate executives there. The night before the visit I announced that we would spend the next day at a drug rehabilitation community, and asked them to say one phrase that came to mind to describe a hard-core drug addict. The words "human refuse", "garbage of society", "sick people", "out of control slaves", "disgraced losers" and so on were uttered and promptly written up on a whiteboard.

The next morning they visited the immaculately clean community where 2,000 people live and work as a family, in a place that looked more like a five-star vacation resort than a hospital. They were surprised to learn that two-thirds of the smiling and healthy-looking men and women they met everywhere within the community actually were HIV positive. They were also amazed to realize that San Patrignano routinely achieves the world's highest rate of drug rehabilitation at half the cost per person compared with its peers, using neither drug substitutes nor physicians. They were even more astounded when they saw the state-of-the-art businesses and the world-class output these individuals produced and sold, all by themselves. San Patrignano's superb wine-producing facilities, which had swept the Italian top prizes for wines over the previous four years, particularly overwhelmed them. But the real punch was the horse-jumping area and the double gold medals San Patrignano had won in the 1994 World Championship at The Hague, just five years after starting up the activity from scratch with an initial group of horses saved from the slaughterhouse. One executive shyly asked whether the gold medals were "actually from the 'real' world championship, or just from a kind of 'special Olympics' championship"? The head of the horse jumping team, himself a former drug addict rehabilitated in San Patrignano, smiled broadly when he replied that "Of course the gold medals come from the 'real' World Championship," adding that "We haven't won the Olympic gold medal yet, but we are working hard to win it soon." For some reason, only the former drug addict laughed heartily. The executives were not amused at all; they just stood silent and mesmerized, watching every detail attentively and quite respectfully.

That evening, after the one-day visit was over, we all went back to the same classroom we had shared the night before. The words "human refuse", "garbage of society", "sick people", "out of control slaves", "disgraced losers" and many more were clearly visible on the whiteboard. I asked three questions. First: "How many of you have won gold medals in the world championship of any Olympic sport?" It turned out that just one of them had won a bronze medal, at a college championship. My second question was: "If you see drug addicts as sick people, what do you build to solve that problem?" A chorus of voices replied, "A hospital!" My last question was: "If you see drug addiction as an educational problem – mainly the result of people missing a supporting family for a variety reasons – what do you build to address that issue?" This time, the answer came more slowly: "A loving family." An uneasy silence followed. I could see many of them struggling to contain their own tears. We called it a day and went to bed. The next morning the class went fast – really fast. These executives already knew about trade-ons somehow. For them, it had become more than just another clever concept; it was an unforgettable experience they had lived together. And they were all smiling.

A few months after that I found a way to create and produce a video of the San Patrignano community. Since then, I have shown this video to countless people across many countries, so that anyone who wants to experience trade-on mindset and the boundless power of human imagination – rather than just learn theoretically about it – can visit the San Patrignano community, at least virtually.[6] And it has never failed to induce in all kinds of people the same emotional storming I saw with the first group I brought to the community. Emotional storming that, for many of the other trade-on champions portrayed in this book, stemmed from a variety of sources and personal experiences, but brought the same radical and transforming effects in the way they saw their world and imagined their future.

The story of Stelios Haji-Ioannou, founder of easyJet – the air carrier that was ranked as one of Europe's largest airlines in 2009 – offers another remarkable example of how emotional storming can drive a *trade-on mindset* that will shape the choices we will (or won't) imagine for our own futures, at both the personal and the organizational level. Strategic choices that we first conceive in our mindset-driven imaginations, but which will ultimately – and strongly – influence our lifelong performance in very concrete ways.

✳ *imagining new futures with trade-on eyes*

The son of a Greek Cypriot shipping tycoon who was, back in the 1980s, one of the world's largest independent oil tanker owners, Stelios Haji-Ioannou – whose orange business card describes him as a "serial entrepreneur" – achieved much more, much earlier, than any of his peers. He was young when he attained major international success – founding easyJet in 1995 at age 28 – but younger still when he tasted real failure. Tragedy struck his family in 1991 when one of his father's ships – the *Haven* – exploded off the Italian port of Genoa, killing five people and spilling 50,000 tons of crude oil in what was to be the worst ecological disaster in the Mediterranean up to that date. Stelios and his father Loucas were jointly charged with corporate manslaughter and accused of attempting to bribe witnesses. The Haji-Ioannou name was dragged through the mud before the Italian Supreme Court finally acquitted them in 1999. Many years later, in 2006, Stelios spoke about this experience in an interview with Jane Martinson for the *Guardian*:

> [I am still haunted by this] traumatic experience in my youth. It was enough to make anybody think twice about what they want to do in life. It was a life forming experience. The worst thing was being unable to prove the allegations wrong until the court case. The facts are irrelevant to the public. At that stage I was the enemy, I was the villain. That's what I hated. I couldn't explain that I wasn't. They didn't care.[7]

Halfway through this testing experience, Stelios decided he would bring about a radical change in his life. Instead of working as his father's partner in the family oil shipping business, he would go out on his own and devote his life to becoming popular with people by making out-of-reach consumer products and services accessible to the masses:

> I decided [...] that the way to make a difference in my life and in other people's lives was to give them services and products that are actually for the many and not for the few. Because it makes you more popular. [...] Because it's better than being unpopular. Better than being hated.[8]

It was during this trying period that Stelios, on a flight to London, sat next to a school friend who offered him the chance to buy shares in a Greek company that was flying a franchised route for Virgin Atlantic, the innovative airline founded by Richard Branson. Stelios declined the offer, but met Branson, a larger-than-life character admired by both the public and the media. And it wasn't long after that, during a flight with Southwest – the US airline that based its success on friendly service and flying point-to-point routes – that a mental image of a "bus in the air", flying point-to-point and easy to access, use and enjoy by everyone, suddenly hit him. Said Stelios:

> [In 1995...] I was going to build a brand that I would be proud of ... identify myself with it and take the good with the bad. I can't just go in and out. I'm a long-term investor.[9]

This was how Stelios came to imagine the "easy" concept, as a brand name that stood for doing things that the masses would find popular and friendly, such as making out-of-reach products and services accessible to all. A point-to-point "bus in the air" type of airline offering unmatched value for money seemed like an obvious first step to Stelios, owing to the liberalization and deregulation of the skies that had been sweeping Europe since the early 1990s. Stelios explained how the name "easy" actually came about:

 I think I was in a bar one evening [laughs]. Actually the working title was StelAir, but I thought it was too egotistical. So I started looking for something that would suit the position that I intended for the airline, which was value for money. Eventually I came up with the name easy.[10]

Stelios started easyJet with a mental image of a friendly "bus in the air", his experience as an airline customer himself, and £5 million from his father. Fourteen years later, in 2009, he was chairman of EasyGroup plc, an investor group that owned the brand "easy" and that made scores of products and services accessible to all through dozens of business ventures, ranging from easyJet to easyCar (a rental car operation), easyCruise (a boutique line of cruise ships), easyMoney (a credit card business), easyInternet (a chain of cyber-cafes) and easy4men (a range of no-nonsense male toiletries). His 2005 US$1.3 billion sale of Stelmar Shipping – Stelios's first venture, created in 1992 – turned him into one of Europe's wealthiest individuals. Beyond business success, at the age of 42 Stelios had become one of the UK's most influential personalities, with a knighthood and four honorary doctorates, and a growing reputation as an outstanding European philanthropist. Loucas, Stelios's father, was quoted as saying, just before he died in December 2008:

 My Stelios is ten times better than I was. He single-handedly did the unthinkable.[11]

Believing, like Stelios, that, even in the face of extremely testing experiences, you can do more than it seems with the cards you have been dealt, and, very early on in your life, actually setting out to do the unthinkable is the trademark of a *trade-on mindset* on a personal level. In addition, easyJet and the scores of revolutionary ventures started up by Stelios under the easy brand demonstrate how such a mindset can be shared and turned into a collective trade-on mindset within organizations.

✳ *double-trade-ons*

From the outset, easyJet was about creating a radically different, "no-frills" flying experience that offered unmatched value for money to customers. The fact that the company ensured that lots of double-trade-ons were built into their customer experience not only made it unique, but also gave it tremendous advantages in terms of both value to customers and cost efficiency. A double-trade-on is anything that simultaneously represents higher value for money to customers and lower costs to the organization. In 1995, when many of them had only just heard of the World Wide Web, some customers could at any time buy easyJet tickets within their own homes on the company's easy-to-use e-commerce site. For these customers, it meant eliminating the hassle of driving to the nearest travel agency and asking the agent to recommend a route or a carrier through a complicated process. For the company, it completely removed the travel agencies' double-digit mark-up on the ticket price.

The company's e-commerce site was a trade-on for both the customer and the organization: a double-trade-on – but it was far from being the only one. Because you could check in at the airport with a code reservation number generated by the easyJet website – or just by showing your ID in case you forgot it – customers didn't have to worry about keeping tickets safe and the company didn't have to print them at all: another double-trade-on. At the boarding gate customers realized that no pre-assigned seats were given, so they would show up earlier to get the best seats, which in turn helped easyJet develop a world-class airline punctuality record from the outset: another double-trade-on. Customers also realized that easyJet fares systematically went up nearer to departure dates, so they booked earlier to get unbelievably low prices. Once they found there were no more cheap seats available, customers would buy easyJet tickets anyway as the company's highest fares were still considerably less expensive than its competitors. This, together with the point-to-point route structure and the fact that the company initially used just one type of aircraft, meant that easyJet could, from the outset, boast some of the highest load factors in the airline industry and fly each plane for eleven hours a day instead of the industry average of six. Thus, easyJet's yield, aircraft and route management generated another, quite massive, double-trade-on for both the customer and for the organization.

Once inside the aircraft, customers could see that the plane was new, that the flight attendants were smiling, and that they could buy at a fair price any meal or beverage they wanted from easyJet's on-board menu. No more putting up with food that somebody else had decided in advance you wanted to eat during your flight. And for the company, this meant turning a cost item (in-flight catering) into a profit centre: another double-trade-on. Since a lot of people were happier without ordering any drinks on a two-hour flight, easyJet could install only two toilets instead of four in their Boeing 737–300 planes, with the additional space being filled with more seats: another double-trade-on. Because easyJet's "no-frills" flying experience was built on such big and small double-trade-ons throughout, from the very beginning the company could obtain high levels of customer satisfaction while charging prices that often were well over two-thirds cheaper than its competitors, and at the same time generate profit margins and returns on assets far superior to the airline industry average. That really was, without a doubt, a case of multiple double-trade-ons.

Stelios's trade-on mindset migrated naturally to easyJet first, and to all of his "easy" ventures next, largely because he attracted and recruited talented people with similar mindsets and the same passion: to create a very popular brand that made out-of-reach products and services accessible to all. Even within the context of the increasingly environmentally conscious 21st century, easyJet grabbed the headlines at the 2007 Paris Air Show by unveiling its "ecoJet" prototype, a radical design concept that could transport the same number of people and cost the same as the Airbus A320 while setting new, dramatically low emission standards – another double-trade-on. Surprised aircraft manufacturing executives present at the air show visibly struggled to fit easyJet's unconventional "ecoJet" into their delivery plans for the next generation of commercial airplanes.

✳ *seeing the world through trade-off lenses*

I continue to meet friends displaying clear *trade-on mindset* characteristics, especially amongst creative professionals such as performing artists, novelists, architects, entrepreneurs and designers. On the other hand, I have been amazed to find that most executives in large and small companies everywhere not only apply a one-sided trade-off mindset quite thoroughly and deliberately in their professional careers, but also choose to attract similar trade-off minded people to join their teams. Often this is an acquired taste encouraged by a surrounding context that includes conspicuous parts of the scientific and expert literature – especially within certain areas of the management field. After all, as psychologists like Carol Dweck have suggested, our mindset determines what we will or won't imagine, and this may be true also for social scientists. Consider leading management strategy pundit Michael Porter, whose 1980 notions of "generic strategies" suggested that all companies competing in the business arena could adopt a strategy of either differentiation – that is, providing very distinct offerings that entail higher costs – or cost leadership at the expense of offering undifferentiated products or services to customers.[12] This way of thinking clearly suggests a trade-off mindset at work that, in Porter's particular case, was to deeply influence an entire generation of management executives, academics, students and consultants. Sixteen years later, in an influential article entitled "What is strategy?", Porter insisted that "trade-offs are essential to strategy. They create the need for choice and purposefully limit what a company offers";[13] adding that: "a sustainable strategic position requires trade-offs".[14] Porter's self-assured prescriptions in support of trade-offs lying at the very heart of management strategy were illustrated with examples that actually included the airline industry:

 Simply put, a trade-off means that more of one thing necessitates less of another. An airline can choose to serve meals – adding cost and slowing turnaround time at the gate

– or it can choose not to, but it cannot do both without bearing major inefficiencies.[15]

In 1996 (the year of publication of "What is strategy?"), Stelios Haji-Ioannou's easyJet had already been in business for a year, and Nalebuff and Brandenburger's book *Co-opetition* – in which the term "trade-ons" was coined – was published. All three would probably have begged to disagree with Porter's example.

✳ *strategic mindsets to imagine the future*

It isn't so much that any particular management theorist should be heralded as "right" or "wrong" in his or her outlook on corporate and business strategy. It is more that we should recognize the widespread logical biases favouring trade-off thinking throughout the 1980s and 1990s that condemned its natural complement – *trade-on mindset* – to near oblivion in certain circles. Nalebuff and Brandenburger's view of "co-opetition" as the simultaneous play of both competitive and cooperative strategies, as well as of trade-off and trade-on schemes as ways of gaining transactional business advantages, takes a broader view that goes well beyond Porter's one-sidedly trade-off competitive perspective. Similarly, W. Chan Kim and Renée Mauborgne's 2005 notion of "blue ocean strategy" as the simultaneous pursuit of differentiation and low cost in order to create uncontested market spaces clearly suggests mental approaches other than trade-off thinking to imagine strategic choices for the future.[16] Indeed, both trade-ons and trade-offs are essential parts of everyone's portfolio of mental tools that help us chart the entire field of possibilities we can imagine unfolding in front of us. Let us apply this all-encompassing perspective to the issue of how people out there can go about imagining future strategic directions for both themselves and their organizations. In over two decades spent examining this issue, I have found striking similarities as well as profound differences at play in the way people imagine the future strategically.

Let us start with the similarities. I have found that most people and organizations active within reasonably open societies and economies share two transactional obsessions when pondering how to turn their newly imagined ideas of the future into reality. On the one hand, they worry about the value that those new ideas will bring to their future clients in the form of new products and/ or services that will drive certain customer experiences. We can think about the value of any customer experience in terms of the assessment that people like you and me make when we consider all the positive or negative happenings we went through when consuming a particular product or service, and compare this with the price we paid for it. We can express this value assessment as a ratio, where the sum of all the positive or negative customer experiences is the numerator and the price paid by the customer is the denominator. On the other hand, people and organizations with new ideas out there are also concerned with the cost they have to incur in order to actually deliver those new ideas to their future customers in the form of new products and/or services. By "cost of delivering the customer experience" I mean the comprehensive accounting of all costs (research, developmental, manufacturing, logistical, inventory, advertisement, marketing, sales, financial, etc.) incurred from the first conception of a new idea to actually releasing that new idea in the marketplace in the form of innovative products and/or services available to customers. These costs can be divided by units produced (or serviced) in order to get a "unit cost of delivering the customer experience" that can be compared with competitors' costs, the average industry unit cost and so on.

But here the similarities end. I found at least four distinct mindsets at work when different people go about imagining their future choices strategically along the two obsessions that have just been described: value of the customer experience and unit cost of delivering it. Let us call these four distinct and restricted applications of mindset "strategic mindsets".

A trade-off way of thinking – the deep-seated belief that more of one thing automatically implies less of another thing (or vice versa) – naturally leads to imagining choices that play the value of the customer experience against the unit cost incurred in delivering it. Thus, trade-off-minded individuals and organizations imagine their strategic choices in terms of the following dilemma: either we create the highest possible value to customers even if this leaves us with unit costs that are well above those of our competitors, or we focus on having the lowest unit cost that can possibly be imagined even at the expense of reducing the value of our offerings to our customers. I call the former mental approach a "trade-off differentiation" strategic mindset, and the latter an "ordinary commodity" strategic mindset. Not surprisingly, both of these strategic mindsets are very similar to Porter's notions of generic strategies. The customer formulas that logically stem from these strategic mindsets are also clear examples of trade-off thinking and can be synthesized as: "We can either differentiate our products or services so much that our customers will be willing to pay a premium price for them (which will keep us in business in spite of our above average unit costs), or we can offer ordinary commodities but so inexpensively that the customer will still buy them (and we will manage to survive in spite of the low prices we charge because our unit costs are so far below average)."

Another way of thinking, that can be termed a "trade-down mindset", consists of imagining a strategic choice that will leave both you and your customer worse off: to offer a low-value customer experience while building up higher costs in your organization. I call this a monopolistic strategic mindset because it is quite obvious that only organizations enjoying a monopolistic – or quasi-monopolistic – position could actually survive with this way of thinking beyond the very short term.

However, there is another group of people out there that consistently applies a double-trade-on strategic mindset to imagine choices and customer formulas that simultaneously create highly valuable experiences to customers and lead to below-average unit costs of delivering them. As mentioned, these people and organizations systematically perform this amazing trick by imagining customer experiences with plenty of double-trade-ons built into them. Think of the innumerable and highly valuable customer trade-ons that easyJet pioneered – from the web-based easy-to-use travel agency and the super cheap prices for booking early, to the virtual ticket or the paid-for inflight menu – which also meant dramatically lower costs per seat and world-class occupancy rates for the organization. Think also of Cucinella's rechargeable house double-trade-ons, and those of Ikea as well. Not only that, consider all the extraordinary stories narrated in this book: the San Patrignano community with its No. 1 drug rehabilitation rates at half the cost; Medtronic's world-class lifelong medical solutions for some of the world's deadliest chronic illnesses alongside dramatically lowered healthcare costs; Zara's ability to bring new and inexpensive fashion items twice a week to thousands of sales points worldwide while generating superior margins and explosive revenue growth; and Grupo AJE's double-digit annual sales and profitability growth obtained by making high-quality drinks accessible to the masses in all sorts of low- and medium-income countries. They are all clear examples of double-trade-on strategic mindsets applied to imagining double-trade-ons built into radical customer experiences that help create entirely new futures for people.

The different strategic mindsets can also be seen quite clearly at play in the choices people imagine for their own individual futures, both personally and professionally. A classic example of the latter concerns people's individual strategic choices to invest in their own education and professional development throughout their adult lives, which will obviously shape their future options in the professional markets. On the one hand, there are individuals who tend to spend heavily in terms of time and money to enhance both their talents and their salaries with prospective employers. Conversely, we find a number of people offering underqualified skills at lower rates that may represent overall cost advantages for the employers hiring them. Very rarely, such as when an extreme scarcity of available workers gives unskilled labour unusually high bargaining power with employers, we can see the latter paying relatively high wages for underqualified skills. On the other hand, a double-trade-on strategic mindset applied to a person's own educational and professional choices encompasses at least two categories of knowledge workers that experienced significant growth during the first decade of the 21st century. One is the group of those who combine office hours with remote working from home, leading to an improved balance between personal life and work while still being able to maintain relatively high levels of productivity and salary. The other consists of highly talented professionals – such as star fashion designers, oenologists, performing artists, video game developers, R&D executives or sportspeople – who have built their professions around their true life-passions and whose exceptional levels of creativity and/or productivity performance are so outstanding that their employers will nearly always get an extraordinary return for their salaries – even if the latter are set at abnormally high levels.

Figure 3 schematically shows the interplay between the different strategic mindsets and the choices available to both individuals and organizations in order to imagine and build their own futures along the lines of value of the customer experience and unit cost of delivering it.

a mindset for creating higher futures

While much has been written about the individual as well as the organizational implications of both trade-off and monopolistic types of strategic mindsets, there has been relatively little attention devoted to the broader meaning of a *trade-on mindset* as it applies to the issue of strategically imagining the future. Here, I found a number of remarkable characteristics that are both typical and common to all the extraordinary stories of applied double-trade-on strategic mindsets I have come across. Once more, these examples aren't about illustrating one particular strategic mindset as inherently superior to another. They are about making us aware of the radically different natures of these strategic mindsets and their far-reaching implications whenever we imagine possible strategic choices for our own futures and those of our organizations.

Let us start by looking at the notion of a higher customer experience shown in Figure 3. A higher customer experience is the soaring level of empowerment that customers acquire in their lives as a result of consuming a specific product and/or service. Often this empowerment enables people to build their own radical new futures themselves. To understand whether a particular

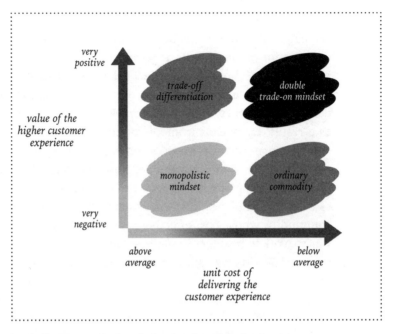

FIGURE 3 : Strategic mindsets to imagine the future

product or service leads to higher customer experiences, you have to observe those experiences within the broader context of the customers' unfolding lives. "No-frills" value-for-money air carriers like easyJet opened an unthought-of new world of possibilities for masses of people across Europe. Suddenly, sun-starved Northern Europeans could move to Mediterranean islands such as Mallorca, Corsica or Rhodes, from where they could then take a weekly commuting flight to work in Frankfurt, London or Brussels. Incredibly, this often meant faster commuting times with transport costs that were actually lower than their previous door-to-door car journeys between home and work. As a European resident back in the 1990s, I was amazed to realize that, at a certain point, the total number of scheduled daily flights to the Spanish island of Mallorca was higher from Germany than it was from Spain. In one village on Mallorca the number of German residents so outnumbered the locals that they elected a German mayor and launched a German-language newspaper. It is scarcely going too far to say that an entire generation of Europeans is growing up enjoying a quality of life and degree of cultural exposure that were unimaginable without the likes of easyJet. A massive availability of value-for-money flights together with a revolution in communications technology also meant that all of a sudden millions of people were able to live their dreams of becoming independent entrepreneurs, consultants or artists, and enjoy fuller lives as a result. Europeans from all countries intermingled, worked together in all sorts of ventures and even married one another as never before in their long and venerable histories. In a way, the real higher experiences happened to easyJet customers as soon as they left the planes. Likewise, members of the San Patrignano community, whose cost-effective approach to drug rehabilitation was to work in business initiatives that aimed at and consistently achieved world-class standards of excellence, simply got their lives back and projected themselves to new heights that no one – especially not themselves nor their original families – could have imagined before, even as a wild impossibility. Similarly, Grupo AJE's highly profitable offer of high-quality soft drinks that even lower income people could afford to buy encouraged the growth of countless value-for-money players across all sorts of consumer goods industries that, for the first time, began to embrace the vast masses of people in low and middle income countries as part of the market: a higher experience and a massive double-trade-on for these players, their customers and their countries as a whole.

Examples like easyJet, San Patrignano and Grupo AJE illustrate how a double-trade-on strategic mindset can drive higher customer experiences quite naturally. Instead – and almost by definition – customer formulas stemming from a trade-off differentiation strategic mindset can turn into higher experiences only for the exceedingly few super-rich, for whom an elite product or service so luxurious and expensive it defies the imagination nevertheless represents a negligible expense. This was the case with international air travel during the 1960s and 1970s, which only the rich and famous – the so-called "jet set" elite – could afford to use at will, while the rest of us were basically left out of the frequent flyers' market.

A double-trade-on strategic mindset can be just as pervasive as trade-off differentiation, though. It doesn't only apply to "no-frills" ideas, or cheap products, or services for the masses. It applies everywhere. Consider caviar, the sturgeon roe that has for centuries been consumed at the tables of European royalty and the few gourmet millionaires who could afford to buy the finest Beluga, Osetra and Sevruga varieties. During the 1980s, illegal overfishing, pollution and political instability in the Caspian Sea area – the traditional home of the world's highest quality colonies of sturgeon – drove the prices of Russian and Iranian caviar to even higher levels. This encouraged a number of entrepreneurs such as the Briton Alan Jones to imagine rebuilding the European sturgeon stocks in the warmer climate of southwest France, where the fish had all but disappeared during the nineteenth century. By chance, these fish-farmers discovered in 1993 that the Siberian freshwater sturgeon (*Acipenser baerii*) could successfully reproduce in captivity in their new location. This discovery led to a double-trade-on that revived the French caviar industry, which by 2005 was producing 17 tons of caviar a year (the largest output of any European country outside Russia), commanding prices of up to €2,000 a kilo. That same year, Claudia Boucher, an executive at French caviar producer Sturgeon, observed:

 A few years ago, the idea of caviar from [French] Aquitaine still had people chuckling. Then the [French consumer magazine] *60 millions de consommateurs* held a blind-tasting by experts in which the French caviar got the same score as Sevruga Russian caviar, which sells at double the price. That changed all the preconceptions.[17]

Better fishing methods, a closer proximity to the marketplace and more reliable logistics made French caviar a highly profitable business at half the price of its comparable Russian variety. However, even at such reduced price levels, by 2009 high-quality French caviar remained a delicacy for a few wealthy connoisseurs – though a much more accessible one than Caspian Sea caviar. So, if you thought about trade-on minded players exclusively as "no-frills" champions for the masses, think again. They may already be producing the top-rank caviar you will daringly treat yourself to one day as a once-in-a-lifetime experience.

Although the idea of "getting much more with a lot less" may at first seem nonsensical – or even suspicious – to some, a double-trade-on strategic mindset relies on its own robust logic and rationality. If psychologists like Carol Dweck are right in maintaining that our mindsets create our entire mental worlds, it follows that logical thinking and rational thoughts are a subset of mindset rather than the other way around. So, if a double-trade-on strategic mindset sounded a bit "illogical" to you when you first read about it earlier in this chapter – as it routinely does to many people I meet – this may just point at where you're coming from, or what you're used to, mindset-wise. Logical thoughts, ideas and outcomes driven by a double-trade-on strategic mindset are every bit as rational as those stemming from trade-off differentiation, as countless institutions and individuals have demonstrated over time. It is just a radically different – but equally powerful – logic compared with trade-off minded rationality.

As illustrated by organizations such as Zara, easyJet or Grupo AJE, a double-trade-on strategic mindset leads to imagining futures that actually create unprecedented customer experiences and whole new markets. Because these new customer experiences have lots of double-trade-ons built in, they often achieve explosive growth even in recessionary market conditions that affect their less customer-oriented and cost-efficient peers. As mentioned in the previous chapter, amazing growth is also the result of successful trade-on ideas of the future typically expanding laterally via economies of imagination; in other words through the transferring of radical images of the future, together with a purposeful mission and a powerful trade-on customer formula, into entirely different markets where such features are bound to flourish. Building upon easyJet's huge success, Stelios Haji-Ioannou applied the same dream ("building a brand that's popular with the masses"), the same purposeful mission ("making out of reach products and services accessible to all") and the same trade-on customer formula ("providing unmatched value for money to customers") to other industries with characteristics similar to those of European commercial air transport in the early 1990s, such as lack of transparency and customer orientation, overregulation, excessive complexity and low value-for-money offerings.

Although for key individuals within these extraordinary organizations it was emotional storming that let their imaginations loose in a trade-on direction, we invariably find real customers – or customer-like figures – in the eye of the storm. Whether it was personal tragedy, deadly terrorism in the Andean mountains, chance encounters with drug addicts in an Italian piazza or a passion for his profession that triggered strong waves of emotion in Stelios, the Añaños family, Vincenzo Muccioli or Amancio Ortega, it was the conjunction of these emotions with real customers that made them imagine easyJet, Kola Real, the San Patrignano community or Zara. In the following chapter we will describe how fateful and emotionally charged encounters such as these can spur radical dreams of the future that hold the power to profoundly transform the lives of everyone involved in them.

2

the second key:
customer obsession

....

Acting is the ability to live truthfully under imaginary circumstances.

Sandy Meisner (1905–97), American actor and acting coach

IT WAS SO EXHAUSTING, I didn't realize at first that I had finally reached it. Over the previous five days I had walked through deep rain forests and barely charted mountain trails, along breathtaking vertical cliffs overlooking thundering rivers far below. I was looking for Hatun Vilcabamba, the legendary capital of the sixteenth-century Inca kingdom in exile which, following the Spanish invasion, survived for another forty-odd years deep inside the inhospitable jungle that surrounds the Apurimac river, one of the main tributaries of the mighty Amazon. After its demise in 1572, Hatun Vilcabamba was forgotten for centuries, to the point where many early twentieth-century historians thought it no more than a myth. Now I was standing on top of a hardly accessible ridge, flanked on all sides by an awesome valley bounded by a majestic mountain chain entirely covered with vegetation. Behind me, there were the remains of two military towers superbly placed so that Vilcabamba's sentinels could spot anyone approaching from very far away. In front of me, an admirable Inca royal road descended all the way to the mysterious capital, which was hidden from view by giant trees. A tropical storm suddenly broke, and a sense of the past held me spellbound as I visited Hatun Vilcabamba's impressive stone buildings under the torrential rain. I imagined the last young and battle-weary Inca warriors looking at the same buildings, and perhaps murmuring the ancient prayers taught by the Hamawtha Wiraqocha in order to regain their strength and the inspiration to fight on.

Along the way to Vilcabamba, I had stayed at the homes of the hospitable villagers of Ututo, Vista Alegre, Urpipata and Concevidayoc. Because in 2006 the roads were still of poor quality, not helped by the frequent tropical rains, no vehicles ventured beyond the 3,500 metre-high Collpaqasa mountain pass, five days' walk from Hatun Vilcabamba. Locals traded their agricultural and textile products at the Pampaconas market, just beside Collpaqasa, and from there, they loaded their llamas and mules with food and other supplies and walked back to their villages. Their homes were exceedingly simple: just one room of about 40 square metres, where an entire family of up to five people cooked, ate, played and slept. They shared all they had with their visitors, looked happy and never complained. From Concevidayoc, it is a further two days' walk west through deep rain forest to reach the Apurimac river, which marks the border between the Peruvian departments of Cuzco and Ayacucho. If you cross the river and continue to walk west for another four days you will reach San Miguel Arcángel, the capital city of Ayacucho's La Mar province.

Back in the 1950s, when Eduardo Añaños grew up as the son of a well-off landlord in San Miguel, the town was not very different from the rural villages along the eastern banks of the Apurimac that I had visited in 2006. The absence of good roads and the inaccessibility of La Mar's territory, where the rugged Andean mountains meet the lush, impenetrable vegetation of the Amazonian rain forest, made San Miguel a charming but isolated place. As a result, wealthy landlords would live in their colonial haciendas with neither electricity nor telephones, and without the consumer goods enjoyed by the larger and better-connected Andean urban centres. The less well-off majority shared the same privations, with the crucial difference that their meagre rural incomes were insufficient to buy even the most basic consumer goods. The bucolic atmosphere offered a simple and quiet quality of life that nevertheless left everyone – the landlord and the peasant alike – craving for the variety of comforts and luxury articles that were available in the more sophisticated cities.

In 2006 most San Miguel adult residents still remembered quite clearly the first time that soft drinks showed up in the local stores. The memorable event happened during the mid 1970s, when many were still just kids. Peru's local leading brand, Inka Cola, had established its first bottling plant in Ayacucho to start distributing their products in the entire central Andean region. Coca-Cola and the other brands followed suit shortly after that. Since then, well-off La Mar citizens could afford a regular supply of soft drinks, but the rest could do so only once or twice a year, mostly to celebrate their birthdays and Christmas. About a decade after that, in 1988, childhood memories of provincial San Miguel probably came back to Eduardo Añaños's mind when two of his sons talked him into launching a new soft drink and taking the amazingly imaginative step of putting himself in the shoes of the vast majority of lower income rural Peruvians.

Adopting somebody else's perspective so skilfully that you can actually experience his or her feelings and thoughts is an astonishing human ability that started to attract the attention of psychologists during the early twentieth century, but it was practised by actors long before that. Both professions emphasize the central role that imagination, emotions and well-honed observation skills play in allowing individuals temporarily to mentally transform themselves into someone else. In fact, as already pointed out in the previous chapter, in all of the examples of great organizations cited so far in this book, we find their founders' imaginations being let loose to dream unthinkable futures as a result of their skilful and emotional empathy with either a customer or a customer-like figure.

✳ *the challenging art of perspective taking*

On the eve of the 21st century, psychological research distinguished between two different ways of "perspective taking" – in other words, perceiving someone else's situation. On the one hand, an "imagine-self perspective" occurs when you imagine how *you* would see a situation were you in the other's position and experience how you would feel as a result. On the other, an "imagine-other perspective" takes place when you imagine how another person sees and feels his or her situation.[1] Both forms of perspective taking are distinct from what psychologists call a "theory of mind"; that is, a series of perception-based beliefs which we use to represent the Self as distinct from others and to explain both other people's actions and our own. Instead, any form of perspective taking, in addition to a theory of mind, requires the performance of an act of imagination. You don't actually transform yourself into someone else nor literally see through another person's eyes when taking that person's perspective. Rather, through skilful observation – or based on information gathered in other ways – you just imagine how things look and feel from the perspective of someone else.

Experimental psychologists have found that people's perspective-taking abilities underpin many aspects that are central to human social understanding and interaction, from the capacity to evoke empathic concerns towards others and engage in cooperation, to the potential for behaving altruistically. Here, the distinction is significantly made between understanding and knowing objectively – that is, separate and impartial from what is being observed or considered – and the sensitive understanding and "responsively knowing" that stem from taking the perspective of another person's needs, feelings and desires. Conversely, psychologists associate the absence or serious impairment in the development of perspective-taking abilities with some of the most inhuman types of behaviour in existence.

An imagine-self perspective has been found to be psychologically different from an imagine-other perspective. The latter is not to be considered a simple projection or a mental simulation of the former. In fact, when enough information was made available to participants in laboratory experiments, psychologists found that these individuals could think about and feel for the other without first thinking about themselves. Moreover, an imagine-self perspective is not to be considered a stepping-stone to an imagine-other perspective; it is, at best, a slippery stone. The following situation illustrates this:

 Hearing that a friend was recently "dumped" by a romantic partner may remind you of your own experience last year when you suffered the same fate. You may be so caught up in reliving your own experience that you fail to appreciate your friend's pain. Especially if you found it easy to rebound, you may contrast your own experience with that of your friend, who is struggling. Rather than sensitive understanding and emphatic concern, you may respond with impatience and judgement.[2]

An imagine-other perspective also differs from an imagine-self perspective from a neurophysiological standpoint. In a classic 1969 experiment on empathy, the psychologist Ezra Stotland asked two groups of participants to observe a model (a young man undergoing a painful diathermy treatment, in which the heat of electricity is used to cut tissue or seal bleeding vessels), adopting, respectively, an imagine-other and an imagine-self perspective. While the first group showed more vasoconstriction, the second group experienced more palm sweat and reported feeling more tension and nervousness. Stotland interpreted these results as reflecting the imagine-other observers' concern for "the feelings they perceived the model as having at a given moment", whereas the imagine-self observers felt a personal kind of distress "not quite so tied to the experience of the model".[3] Neuroimaging studies have provided additional support for these types of findings. On the one hand, fMRI (functional magnetic resonance imaging) scans revealed that individuals undergoing imagine-self and imagine-other mental tasks activate brain cortical regions – such as the amygdala and temporal poles – that are involved in the experience of emotions. On the other, neuroimaging evidence also suggests consistent differences between the two forms of perspective taking. For example, individuals watching pictures of people in painful and non-painful everyday life situations from

an imagine-other and an imagine-self perspective revealed activation of brain areas involved in the affective experience of pain.
However, those individuals taking the imagine-self perspective
reported higher pain ratings and more extensive activation in the
posterior part of the insula, whereas the imagine-other participants activated the anterior part. In a different experiment, participants receiving painful electrical stimulation to the back of the
right hand showed increased activation of the right side of the
inferior parietal lobule, while participants who were signalled to
by their spouse or romantic partner – sitting beside them while
receiving painful electrical stimulation, with only their hands
visible – presented an increased activation of the left side. [4]

✳ *empathy*

As mentioned, most psychological research highlights empathy
as a crucial element to enacting an "imagine-other perspective".
In these studies, empathy is viewed as the ability to deliberately
put oneself into another person's position and share in his or
her emotions in order to better perceive and understand the
other's concerns, ideas, feelings, desires and reactions. In addition, psychologists use the term "empathic accuracy" to describe
how closely a person is able to infer a target individual's covert
thoughts and feelings. A commonplace assumption is to think
that the higher our degree of empathic accuracy, the better our
chances of social success. Another common presumption is that
two valuable factors that help increase the level of empathic accuracy are the degree of concern a person feels about the target
individual and the extent to which the target's actual behaviour
during an interaction is used as an important source of information. However, an experiment involving a large sample of newly
married couples studied during a three-year period found that
the level of empathic accuracy between the couples decreased
over time, while their accurate use of stereotypes – that is, the
partners' mental generalizations of how their thoughts and feelings differed from one another – increased during the same time
period.[5] These results suggested that over time people seem to
rely on mental constructions and imaginative simulations rather

than on the actual behaviour of the target person to infer what he or she might be thinking and feeling. In the case of the newly married couples in the study:

 It is as if [mentally] simulating how a messy kitchen would look to one's returning spouse or retrieving one's [mental] script for how the spouse would react to a surprise weekend getaway was as important – or more important – than monitoring the partner's actual reaction when couples tried to understand each other.[6]

Moreover, the same study also found that the degree of an individual's empathic accuracy is not necessarily a predictor of his or her social accomplishment – and, of course, this includes marital success:

 For example, while Kilpatrick et al. (2002) found that empathic accuracy had an initial boost on accommodative behavior and couple well-being among newlyweds, the effect of empathic accuracy lost strength after the first year of marriage. In other words, being more accurate (or inaccurate) about their spouse's thoughts and feelings did not seem to have long-term benefits for the status of the relationship (whereas other variables clearly do, such as simply being "nice" to each other, e.g., Gottman & Levenson, 1992). Sometimes, being "good enough" works just fine in real life.[7]

A number of studies have provided additional support to these findings, leading to the obvious question: if accuracy in discerning someone else's thoughts and feelings is not necessarily what gives us the advantage socially, then what is it about empathy that might increase our chances of social success? Psychologists have found that – with the possible exception of certain professions such as diplomacy or negotiating, where an extreme degree of empathic accuracy can make all the difference – what gives empathy its positive social effects are an individual's high level of motivation and verbal intelligence to create a coherent and consistent mental representation of the target person that is continuously modified and revised to incorporate new perceptions and novel interpretations.

The word motivation was first recorded in 1873. It came to

English from the Latin term *motionem*, through the old French word *motiver*, meaning "to move to action". The psychological sense of "inner or social stimulus for an action" dates from 1904.[8] Significantly, *motionem* is also the root of the English word emotion. If we take the etymological and the psychological interpretations of the word motivation and, as suggested, relate it to empathy, it reminds us that people tend to remain deeply appreciative of our heartfelt concerns and committed endeavours to better understand them, and often are fairly forgiving whenever they realize our inference about their thoughts and feelings is incorrect. Thus, paradoxically, rather than getting consistently high marks in empathic accuracy, what seems to make the difference when taking an imagine-other perspective is a strong drive and sharp, applied verbal skills to becoming just good enough at inferring the other's thoughts and feelings.

Nevertheless, there may be more to empathy than meets the eye. As imaginative individuals and organizations demonstrate every day, and everywhere in the world, empathically taking an imagine-other perspective often results in visualizing radically different alternatives to reality. Inhabiting someone else has the power to unleash powerful emotions. These feelings stir our imagination into visualizing things we never thought possible. Almost literally, our mind imagines new worlds that are seen through someone else's eyes. This was, in fact, the first step for individuals like Vincenzo Muccioli, Amancio Ortega, Stelios Haji-Ioannou or the Añaños family in creating new futures that at the time were simply inconceivable for most people.

However, experimental psychologists warn us about the crucial difference between people possessing the faculty to imagine themselves in another person's shoes, and their ability to adequately use this remarkable faculty. University of Chicago psychologists Nicholas Epley and Eugene M. Caruso succinctly illustrate this dilemma in the following way: "As anyone who has recently purchased a cell phone, computer, or almost any other technological gadget knows all too well, owning impressive technology and using it correctly are two entirely different things."[9] According to these psychologists, some of the main barriers restraining our perspective-taking abilities are: failing to "activate" this faculty in a timely way in the first place; remaining caught in egocentric tendencies that impede us from empathically reaching out beyond our own experiences and into those of the other person; and being unable to draw from a wealth of non-egocentric sources of information out there to create a "fleshed-out" mental representation of what the other person is thinking and feeling. Psychologists Michael W. Myers and Sara D. Hodges have speculated that the ability of literary writers – and, I should add, of performing artists as well – to convincingly create fictional characters parallels the types of skills that are required for us to remove these barriers and tap into our perspective-taking faculties effectively.[10]

❋ *an actor's key to inhabiting other people*

When British award-winning actor Daniel Day-Lewis was preparing for his role as a severely paralysed character in Jim Sheridan's film *My Left Foot* (based on the real-life story of Christy Brown), he broke two ribs as a result of sitting in a hunched-over position in a wheelchair continuously for several weeks. After his impressive portrayal of Christy Brown won him his first Oscar in 1989, Day-Lewis performed on stage as Hamlet at the Royal National Theatre in London. During the dramatic scene when the ghost of Hamlet's father first appears to his son, Day-Lewis broke down, crying convulsively, to the point where he had to be replaced by another actor. Although the incident was officially attributed to burnout, rumour had it that Day-Lewis had seen his own father's ghost on stage. Later on, in a TV interview with Michael Parkinson, Day-Lewis confirmed that those rumours were true. Over the following years, Day-Lewis underwent rigorous physical training and learned to live and hunt in the forest to research his character in *The Last of the Mohicans*; lost substantial weight (and spent time in a prison cell insisting that cold water be thrown at him) to prepare for the role of the wrongfully convicted Gerry Conlon; and trained for two years with former boxing world champion Barry McGuigan to play the leading character in the movie *The Boxer*.

Daniel Day-Lewis's career is a striking example of Method acting, a set of techniques relying on actors' own imaginations, emotions and memories to bring depth to a part and achieve realism in acting. Method acting is widely regarded as an American approach to performing, but although it was first taught in New York by Ryszard Boleslawski at the American Laboratory Theatre, which he founded in 1923, Boleslawski had been a student of the Russian theatre director and actor Konstantin Stanislavski, who pioneered Method acting in the late nineteenth century. Stanislavski's acting Method had been inspired in turn by the Russian theatrical school of psychological realism developed by Alexander Pushkin, Nikolai Gogol and Mikhail Shchepkin at Moscow's Maly Theatre. Among Boleslawski's students in New York were Lee Strasberg and Stella Adler who, together with Sandy Meisner, Cheryl Crawford, Harold Clurman and 28 other actors, formed the Group Theatre in 1931, the first American acting ensemble to follow Stanislavski's ideas. The Group Theatre disbanded after a few years, but Strasberg and Adler went on to develop their own independent teaching and acting careers that revolutionized American actor training, with many of their students becoming some of the best known Hollywood actors of all time, including Marlon Brando, Paul Newman, Robert de Niro, Al Pacino, Julie Harris, Geraldine Page, Ellen Burstyn, Warren Beatty, Martin Sheen and Benicio del Toro.

Strasberg and Adler had fierce debates over the interpretation of Stanislavski's acting Method that parallel the distinction experimental psychologists make between the imagine-self and imagine-other perspectives. On the one hand, Strasberg taught that actors must use their emotional memories – in other words, draw on their own experienced emotions of past events – in order to relate to a character and bring depth to a part. This is somewhat analogous to using an imagine-self perspective as a stepping stone to an imagine-other perspective. On the other hand, Adler famously retorted: "Don't use your conscious past. Use your creative imagination to create a past that belongs to your character."[11] In psychological terms, this is similar to our going straight to an imagine-other perspective without first thinking about ourselves.

In actual fact, the outstanding practitioners of Method acting seem to have followed a mixture of acting techniques over their careers. While Brando would draw on his personal psychoanalytical depths for his disturbing portrayal of an American widower in the sexually charged movie *Last Tango in Paris*, and Day-Lewis evoked his own family ghosts in his portrayal of Hamlet, the same actors would prepare for other memorable roles by immersing themselves in their characters' scripted lives and in the physical contexts they had experienced, even at the cost of enduring extreme psychological and physical hardship. Similar examples abound, suggesting that great Method actors open-mindedly use both their own emotional memories and a carefully drawn programme of actual physical and emotional experiences closely related to their roles in order to heighten their imaginations into empathically inhabiting their characters. As a result, these actors could deliver extraordinarily "fleshed out" interpretations that often went well beyond what the original scriptwriters or playwrights had in mind. In Tennessee Williams's play *A Streetcar Named Desire*, Stanley Kowalski is portrayed as a brute and a rapist. However, Brando's on-screen performance gave Kowalski a contradictory mix of physical – yet attractive – crudeness with a ruthless but charming intelligence that captivated audiences. Brando's interpretation evidences a deeply empathic psychological identification with his part that turned his on-screen version of Kowalski into a much more alluring and complex role than the disagreeable character as conceived by Williams. Similarly, in the movie *The Godfather*, see how Brando strokes a cat, buys groceries from street vendors, sniffs a rose and spontaneously performs a myriad other details that are not in novelist Mario Puzo's original portrayal of Godfather Vito Corleone, suggesting on-the-spot improvisations arising from a fertile imagination obsessively immersed in the character.

Throughout their careers, Method actors illustrate two qualities that are crucial in order to convincingly take on a character's perspective. First, they demonstrate an extremely high degree of open-minded and empathic motivation to research their characters – even disagreeable or repulsive ones. As mentioned, the etymological root of the word motivation suggests a heart-felt compulsion to take action, to move in a certain direction. Accordingly, a second characteristic of Method acting performers is to immerse themselves obsessively in their characters' psychology by going deep inside the texts and subtexts of the script as well as through real physical experiences that are the same as – or closely similar to – those lived by their fictional (or real-life) characters. As a result, they develop an empathic understanding of their characters' psychology and generate a wealth of external information that prompts their imagination into creating extraordinarily rich and colourful mental representations of their roles.

This obsessive external focus also helps Method actors avoid egocentric tendencies, an issue that parallels observations by experimental psychologists that taking an imagine-self perspective as a stepping stone to an imagine-other perspective in real life can actually inhibit our ability to empathically relate to what the other person is feeling and thinking. This issue, which Day-Lewis experienced when he broke down during *Hamlet*, was already raised by Stanislavski when he observed that actors using – and abusing – emotional memory were given to bouts of hysteria. Treading carefully with one's own past emotions is a classic piece of advice that experienced theatre directors give to both professional actors and beginners. I always remember, back in 1982, our university theatre director Carlos Gassols warning us – a bunch of teenage amateur actors – against an undisciplined use of our emotional memories leading to our bringing on-stage our own characters rather than the roles the audience expected us to incarnate.

✳ *customer obsession driving unthinkable futures*

Unlike performing artists, most individuals taking another's perspective in real life target actual people rather than fictional characters, and they do not need to possess the acting brilliance of a Marlon Brando to be hugely successful at it. However, I have observed that some individuals taking the perspective of certain people with the open mind, self-forgetting empathy and obsessive commitment of an experienced Method actor can as a result unleash their minds into imagining unthinkable futures for them. Back in the mid 1970s, Vincenzo Muccioli noticed drug-addicted youngsters living in the streets of his native Rimini and started to approach them. At first he was rejected or ignored, but he continued to visit them for a year, and slowly got to know them. He made it a tradition to invite a number of them to join his family for Christmas at his San Patrignano farmhouse. After one of these Christmas gatherings, he had a long discussion with his wife Antonietta, after which they both decided to invite a few young addicts to live at San Patrignano. The kids came to live and work on the premises together with their own children on two conditions: that they stopped taking drugs and that they agreed not to ask for one cent from the state or the local government.

Like Muccioli, many great Method actors preparing for the role of a young addict would have gone out on the streets for a year to empathically and open-mindedly intermingle with them. It was, of course, a completely different motivation – the lifelong commitment to help them – that made Muccioli's experience stand out. During the year he took to get to know these youngsters, he made two crucial discoveries. First, he realized that drug addicts were not intrinsically sick people, though their addiction was extremely taxing to their minds and bodies. Secondly, he became aware that most of these youngsters ended up in the streets because they did not have a supporting family. At the same time as making these discoveries, Muccioli and his wife started to get even closer to young addicts by celebrating Christmas with them. In turn, this experience led to the even more daring experiment of inviting a few of them to become an extended part of the family. It was in this organic and spontaneous way that the San Patrignano community was born.

The first thing one finds amazing in this whole story is the unusual degree of open-minded empathy and courageous motivation that, from the outset, Muccioli displayed towards the youngsters he saw in the streets of Rimini. Most people noticing the same youngsters simply chose to disapprove and pass on by. A few others – ranging from well-intentioned citizens to social workers – did approach them, but either got discouraged by a harsh initial reception, or left after giving some material help, a word of support or a severe reprimand. Only the Mucciolis demonstrated the courage and motivation to persevere with an open mind, seemingly unaffected by commonplace and self-serving prejudices against young drug addicts living on the streets. In doing this, the Mucciolis displayed a stunning degree of loving concern that allowed them to profoundly empathize with these youngsters and reveal the extraordinary qualities buried deep inside their emaciated bodies. If, as psychologists suggest, taking an imagine-other perspective is a diabolically difficult thing to do, Vincenzo and Antonietta showed that mastering this ability with an open mind could bring about heavenly transformations in even the most marginalized members of our society.

Correctly and lovingly taking the perspective of drug-addicted youngsters living on the streets made the Mucciolis see and feel things that the other citizens of Rimini had completely missed or chosen to ignore. As a result, the couple could experience at first hand these youngsters' sufferings and feel their yearning for inclusion and family love. A few years of living together with a group of them reaffirmed the Mucciolis' initial discovery that it was mainly the lack of a supportive family and the psychological effects of social marginalization that separated these youngsters from those members of society regarded as more normal people. There is no other way to explain why the Mucciolis would take the astonishing step, during the late 1970s, of inviting increasing numbers of addicted youngsters to leave the streets and join San Patrignano, not as sick or diminished people, but as fully fledged members of their own family who were expected to achieve world-class standards of excellence in everything they did. By that time, Vincenzo Muccioli could in his own words describe how he and his wife had come to imagine San Patrignano as a huge and supportive family and a community of sorts where members could re-awaken their passions and develop their own bright futures anew in hitherto unthinkable ways:

 I'm not here to free drug addicts. At the heart of the drama there is no hashish, cocaine, heroin or ecstasy, there are no withdrawal symptoms, but there is Man risking being swallowed up by his or her own fears and emptiness. That's why I don't like to say or to hear people say that we are a community for drug addicts. We are a Community of Life, where people start living again after years spent on the fringe of society. Well, if we really need to find a definition, San Patrignano is a community against exclusion.

For many years the Mucciolis shared in all but the drug addicts' most harmful habits in order to obsessively get inside their thoughts and feelings and, as a result, were able to understand and help them like no other. Similarly, Eduardo Añaños's dream of turning Peru's vast and historically marginalized lower income population into real customers undoubtedly stemmed from actually sharing in their privations as a child growing up in rural and isolated San Miguel. Likewise, Stelios Haji-Ioannou had been a frequent flier before imagining an airline that made A-to-B air travel unbelievably easy for all of us. These and many other similar stories strongly suggest that great creators of the future actually live first-hand the experiences of their potential customers and see the world through these customers' eyes well before they come to imagine their radical dreams. Invariably, the opportunity to unlock their minds into imagining such powerful dreams of the future came about because of fortuitous and emotionally fraught events.

Emotionally charged atmospheres beget the momentous scenarios in which creators of the future choose to inhabit their customers' lives with the same selfless empathy and obsessive motivation shown by consummate Method actors. The Mucciolis' lives changed radically as a result of Vincenzo's emotive encounters with drug addicts in the streets of Rimini. The Añaños family's imagination was intensely heightened into dreaming about an entirely new soft drink after Shining Path terrorists destroyed their San Miguel hacienda. And Stelios Haji-Ioannou imagined a dramatically different life after deep trauma stemming from the tragic loss of one of the family's ships. Similar to these stories, I could find a similar powerful emotional trigger behind every great creator of the future.

Once it elicits a radical dream of the future, taking the customer's perspective can develop into a long-lasting obsession for the people deciding to live that dream, permeating all they will do to turn it into reality, from building an enthralling corporate culture or experimenting with a breakthrough technological application, to launching an extraordinarily innovative array of products and services. Consider the story of Italian fashion star Renzo Rosso, whose stunning global success with his Diesel brand of jeans and clothing prompted a leading Italian commentator to write in 2003 that "to understand the significance of Renzo Rosso's achieve-ment with Diesel, [you have to] imagine an American company from small town America reinventing spaghetti as a product and going on to become the leading brand of spaghetti in Italy."[12] By 2003 Diesel had in fact overtaken Levi's as the leading brand of jeans in the US youth market, many of whom thought that Diesel was a home-grown brand. However, Rosso had founded the company in 1978 in Molvena, a rural northeastern Italian town with a population of just 2,000, that only a decade before had just one car and one telephone. Rosso's absorbing passion for jeans as something much more than a cheap commodity aimed at the mass market started at a very early age and made him both a forerunner and the embodiment of a whole new and rebellious generation of denim customers. Said Rosso:

 I started to produce, stitch and cut my own jeans when I was fifteen years old, and from then on I have only worn jeans every single day of my life. It's alive. It's like an old house and a new house. An old house is much more warm. And with jeans we're doing the same.

In 1996, when Rosso opened his first US store in New York, customers immediately noticed that Diesel jeans were different. Diesel's "hush jeans" featured five pockets positioned differently to those on the traditional Levi's 501s, with stretchy fabrics and a low-slung cut that appealed to youth culture. Even the Diesel label was in a different place from the usual jeans label. During the late 1990s, Diesel's idea of jeans as fashion items with a high-end focused price range was both courageous and ground-breaking, reflected in the company's slogan, "Only the brave". Retail outlets were carefully chosen and the company deliber-ately pursued a strategy of relentless innovation of cutting-edge jeans, generating close to 1,500 new designs every six months. The way in which Diesel imagined these new designs was also different. Renzo Rosso rejected hiring top talent or star designers from other fashion houses. Instead, he formed a multicultural team of about 30 designers averaging 25 years of age, and encouraged them to "design only for themselves" and to keep "being open to new things, listening to one's intutition and being honest with oneself". To facilitate this creative state of mind, Diesel made a habit of sending its young designers scouting around the globe twice a year for inspiration. They immersed themselves in the social realities of the different geographic areas they chose – ranging from Cuzco and Mombasa to New Delhi and Sydney – where they would mix with the local youth, collecting loads of vintage clothing, music, videos, books, accessories and many other cultural items. Back home in Molvena, Diesel's designers would weave their impressions into the next collection. In 2005, Wilbert Das, the company's creative director, observed:

 [At Diesel] we find inspiration all day long. It's a 24-hour process. I think when you are creative you are like a sponge and you absorb everything that you see in your life. And it comes out exactly when you need it. But a lot of times we have the luxury to travel around the world and go not only to fashion capitals but also to central Africa or Asia or wherever you feel like. And being a sponge you just [absorb] all [kinds of] impressions, take them back home and rinse out the sponge.

The same year, Antonella Viero, Diesel's head of communications, described Diesel's underlying culture of bold creativity and relentless innovation:

 I think there is a Diesel way of doing things. I like to describe it as a lens through which you look at every single aspect of reality. You may be looking at social situations, or habits or even just at the way reality looks, but you look at it from a Diesel perspective [of] doing things in a different way, do them before the others, do them in an unexpected and unpredictable way.

True to their way of bravely doing the unexpected, Diesel's advertising was, from its 1991 beginnings, nothing short of revolutionary. The ads were provocative, irreverent and humorous, making an ironic comment on modern norms of work, play, sexuality, the cult of youth and even the inequality of income distribution between the northern and southern hemispheres. These ad campaigns broke every rule of the advertising book, communicating no clear message and in some cases not mentioning the product or even the brand. Diesel's radical approach to communications prompted Nike's legendary founder Phil Knight to observe that:

 There are two eras in advertising: before Diesel and after Diesel.

Similar to its cutting-edge clothing design philosophy, Diesel's ads operated outside the mainstream of mass-market media, favouring more targeted channels such as MTV, selected international magazines and the Internet. As a result of all this hype and innovation, Diesel's revenue in 2001 grew by 40 per cent across more than 100 countries, and by 2003 sales had rocketed, reaching US$760 million worldwide, with the US as its main market. Just four years later, by 2007, Renzo Rosso's wholly owned "Only the brave" corporation – holding Diesel as well as a dozen other global fashion brands, including Staff International, Martin Margiela and Victor & Rolf – had nearly tripled sales to more than US$2 billion. Beyond business success, and starting in the late 1990s, Renzo Rosso and Diesel received a succession of international awards in recognition of their central contribution to shaping the global cultural attitudes and socioeconomic trends of the new millennium. In 1997, for example, Ernst & Young named Rosso Entrepreneur of the Year in acknowledgement of Diesel's achievement in the US, while the same year *Select* magazine picked him as one of the 100 most important people of the world, and in 2005 the German edition of *GQ* named him Man of the Year. It was a long way from Renzo Rosso's teenage obsession with stitching pairs of jeans that looked rebellious but felt like an old, warm house.

These examples vividly illustrate how customer obsession – that is, the mental ability to empathically, constantly and passionately adopt the perspective of actual or potential customers – can stimulate our imagination into dreaming unthinkable futures for them. These examples also show how customer obsession can become a way of life for certain people, both motivating them into taking positive action and permeating all they do in order to turn their dreams of the future into reality. Yet many individuals who are ostensibly skilful at taking the customer's perspective won't develop it into a life-changing obsession. We still need to ask ourselves: what makes individuals such as Vincenzo Muccioli, Stelios Haji-Ioannou, Eduardo Añaños or Renzo Rosso take the fateful step from envisioning a captivating dream of the future through their customers' eyes to devoting their lives to relentless pursuit of that dream? In the following chapter, we will describe how *purposeful missions* are the vessels that allow such individuals to successfully make these kinds of life-changing passages. Often these ships will go out into barely charted seas, their courageous captains merely cherishing mental images of promising lands lying across the ocean. And as well as examining their swift vessels, we will also explore some of the main character traits that give these captains the strength to successfully navigate against the tides and through the storms.

3

the third key:
purposeful mission

....

The story of your life is not your life; it is your story.

John Barth (1930–), American novelist and short-story writer

ONLY MOMENTS BEFORE a Catholic priest managed to deliver him from the firing squad, 17-year-old merchant Isaías Fermín Fitzgerald López must have reflected on the absurd irony of having survived being stabbed by bandit Benigno Izaguirre, only to be faced with death once again. Two close shaves in less than a year should have been enough to convince anyone to opt for a quiet life. But Isaías Fermín was a precocious young man of unusual resolve, imposing physique and inexhaustible energy. After surviving his fateful encounter with Benigno Izaguirre and following the death of his father William Fitzgerald, an American sailor, there was nothing else to keep him in San Luis de Huari, the remote village overlooking Peru's fabulous northern *cordillera blanca* (white range) where Isaías Fermín was born on 6 July 1862. He decided to seek his fortune in the faraway Oriente region, the name Peruvians give to the vast expanse of lush Amazonian forest that lies east from the country's agreeable coastal and Andean valleys.

In 1879, when Isaías Fermín had set his sights on the Oriente, most of this region remained unexplored and inaccessible to all but the hundreds of ethnic groups that, for thousands of years, had continued to live deep inside the mysterious jungle. Charting the huge Amazon area that represented two-thirds of Peru's territory had been a government priority during the latter part of the nineteenth century. But on 5 April 1879 Chile declared war on Peru. On his way to the Oriente, with maps of the Amazonian rivers, but no personal identification papers, Isaías Fermín was captured by a military patrol, accused of spying for the Chileans, and swiftly sentenced to death. After his dramatic reprieve, he changed his name to Carlos Fernando Fitzcarrald and went into hiding in the Amazonian forests. For nearly ten years no one saw him nor heard of him. It was as if the jungle had swallowed the man.

He was to re-emerge in 1888 as Peru's wealthiest rubber baron. He had established himself in Iquitos – then a backwater town along the Peruvian section of the Amazon – together with his wife Aurora Cardoso, the Peruvian stepdaughter of a wealthy Brazilian merchant, and their four children, whom they sent at an early age to study in France. But Carlos Fitzcarrald was not a man to settle down. From 1890 to 1893 he explored an unspoiled wilderness more than five times the size of Holland, ribboned by the Ucayali, Apurimac, Urubamba and Madre de Dios rivers, and varying in altitude from 500 to 4,000 metres above sea level. To penetrate this challenging terrain, he devised an innovative method of taking his ship apart and transporting it piece by piece over the mountain ranges. It was in this fashion that he discovered an overland passage between the Mishaua, a tributary of the Urubamba river, and the Manu, a tributary of the Madre de Dios. Through this passage, ever since named the Isthmus of Fitzcarrald, he entered a spectacular natural area that a century later would become the Manu Reserve Biosphere, a UNESCO World Heritage Site and one of the largest and most biodiverse national parks in the world, home to over 15,000 species of plants, 250 varieties of trees and 1,000 species of birds – more than the total number of bird species found in the US and Canada combined. Fitzcarrald's explorations opened the first fluvial route from the Bolivian city of Riberalta to Iquitos, across more than

2,000 km of thick jungle. From Iquitos, the route continued for thousands of kilometres along the Amazon and across northern Brazilian territory all the way to Manaos and the Atlantic port of Macapá. From there, all the major European ports could be reached within a couple of months by sea. The new route opened by Fitzcarrald was considerably faster and easier, and much more economical than the strenuous itinerary followed by nineteenth-century Bolivian and Brazilian merchants along the Beni and Madeira rivers to Manaos.

Following his four-year Amazonian exploration, Fitzcarrald returned to Iquitos and bought a ship, the *Contamana*. With it, he continued to explore at a furious pace, founding prosperous agricultural colonies along the Mishaua and Madre de Dios rivers. In 1896, the Peruvian government granted Fitzcarrald the exclusive navigation rights over the Madre de Dios and Ucayali rivers. In April 1897 he went back to Iquitos to formalize a business partnership with Antonio Vaca Díaz – an extremely wealthy Bolivian from Riberalta – to transport goods from Bolivia and Peru to London and vice versa through the route he had opened. Two months later, while sailing down the river Urubamba, the ship *Adolfito*, with Fitzcarrald and Vaca Díaz on board, was wrecked in a whirlpool. The two men drowned on 9 July 1897, just three days after Fitzcarrald's 35th birthday. Two weeks later, when a search party found the bodies, Fitzcarrald's arms were still clasped around Vaca Díaz's corpse. This created the legend that Carlos Fernando Fitzcarrald – an outstanding swimmer – had died in a vain attempt to rescue his friend. It was of such legends that the myth of Fitzcarrald was made up, transforming him into the epitome of nineteenth-century Amazonian adventurers and explorers.

Myths apart, Fitzcarrald emerges as a mixed personality capable of tactfully addressing the Amazonian people in their own tongues, providing them with much-needed medicines and supplies, and at the same time engaging in bloody confrontations with the Mashcos tribesmen who violently opposed his explorations. By the end of his life he could command a 10,000-strong private army made up of blindly loyal Ashanincas, Machiguengas, Piros and other local natives; yet he firmly dismissed proposals to head an independent Amazonian break-away republic, threatening to shoot anyone who opposed Peru's sovereignty over the Madre de Dios area. Also, throughout his life Fitzcarrald demonstrated an obsessive fascination with the primeval and untamed forces of nature, together with a real passion for the sophisticated trappings of European civilization.

It was perhaps the latter aspect of his complex personality that almost one hundred years after Fitzcarrald's death prompted the German filmmaker Werner Herzog to make a movie inspired by the Peruvian explorer. The 1982 film *Fitzcarraldo* instantly became a cult hit, starring Klaus Kinski as a nearly insane "Fitzcarraldo" and Claudia Cardinale as Molly, his admiring lover who devotes her money and energies to helping him realize his obsessive dream of building an opera house in the middle of the Amazonian jungle and having Caruso – the world's top tenor at the time – sing in it. As with Francis Ford Coppola's *Apocalypse Now* and Stanley Kubrick's *2001: A Space Odyssey* – two films to which Herzog's *Fitzcarraldo* is often compared – the making of the movie was as dramatic as the movie itself. From the outset, Herzog had to face unexpected troubles. A border war between Peru and Ecuador made the first location for the film unavailable, so Herzog had to move deeper inside the Amazonian jungle and spend many gruelling months there together with his film crew and actors. He was obsessed with shooting a scene in which Fitzcarraldo's boat *Molly Aida* – a 340-ton detailed replica of a nineteenth-century steamship – was to be dragged over a steep mountain with no special effects. But halfway into shooting, Jason Robards, the original actor Herzog had chosen to play Fitzcarraldo, fell seriously ill with dysentery, and Mick Jagger, who played the role of a sidekick, had to go on tour with the Rolling Stones. Filming had to start all over from scratch, so Herzog left the jungle to get more backing from investors. When they told him to give up the idea of getting the ship up the mountain and asked him whether it would be wiser to quit filming *Fitzcarraldo* altogether, Herzog replied:

> How can you ask this question? If I abandon this project I will be a man without dreams, and I don't want to live like that. I live my life or end my life with this project.[1]

In the end, Herzog managed to raise new money and went back to the jungle, where he continued to film under extreme conditions. Kinski replaced Robards and all the scenes featuring Jagger were cut. Not only was the 340-ton ship hauled over a mountain – one of the most extraordinary scenes in movie history – but also the footage of the boat crashing through the rapids was shot on board, injuring three members of the crew in the process. The continuous struggle took its toll on both Herzog and the emotionally erratic Kinski; the two bickered constantly and even exchanged death threats in front of the more composed Ashaninca extras. *Burden of Dreams*, a 1982 documentary by Les Blank and Maureen Gosling about the making of *Fitzcarraldo*, shows Herzog and his mutinous crew deeply scarred by the whole experience of making this film. In the fourth year of his Amazonian ordeal, an exhausted Herzog says, "I am running out of fantasy. I don't know what else can happen now. Even if I get that boat over the mountain, nobody on this earth will convince me to be happy about that, not until the end of my days." At another moment in the documentary, Herzog looks as close to insanity as his own fictional character Fitzcarraldo when he bitterly describes the jungle as "vile and base", adding that "it's a land which God, if he existed, has created in wrath". Yet, with a staunch determination that the real Carlos Fernando Fitzcarrald would have undoubtedly appreciated, Herzog somehow managed to conclude *Fitzcarraldo*.

Although nearly a century separates them, central aspects of Carlos Fernando Fitzcarrald's story overlap strongly with those of both Werner Herzog and the fictional persona of Fitzcarraldo. All three are stories of near-failure, dominated by imperfect characters who were nevertheless able to obsessively embrace their radical dreams of the future, against all odds and with the consuming passion of true visionaries. For the real Fitzcarrald, the dream was about exploring the depths of the mysterious Amazonian jungle and attaining immense wealth and recognition in the process. For both Herzog and the fictional Fitzcarraldo, the dream involved bringing their sophisticated European idea of art to the core of the Peruvian jungle. On the other hand, the uncompromising way in which all three men pursued their dreams, as well as the intrinsic nature of the dreams themselves, raises acute moral issues about whether the personal and economic price – and, in the case of both the real and the fictional Fitzcarraldo, one has to add the terrible social, ecological and cultural costs involved in the realization of these dreams – was finally worth it. Nevertheless, all three men demonstrated the ability to communicate their radical dreams so powerfully that other people could share in those dreams and follow them. Last, these stories and the life stories of the men behind them are inseparable: anyone reading about the late nineteenth-century explorations of Peru's Manu area or watching *Fitzcarraldo* is likely to get a real insight into the core values and mixed personalities of Carlos Fernando Fitzcarrald, Werner Herzog and the fictional Fitzcarraldo.

The overlapping characteristics of these three stories suitably convey the notion of a *purposeful mission*, in other words, a radical dream of the future that fits the dreamer's inner personality and emotional core so strongly and completely that it becomes an integral part of his or her own Self and a compelling source of motivation to take action in order to realize it. As the stories of Fitzcarrald, Herzog and Fitzcarraldo demonstrate, there isn't necessarily anything logical about a purposeful mission – though the original dreamers will often go to extreme lengths to involve other people in order to rationally and perseveringly devise and follow an action plan to accomplish it. Rather, a purposeful mission is all about a personal or a group-based heartfelt obsession to turn a courageous dream into reality, an undertaking that often brings everyone involved in it to the edge of their moral value systems and psychological endurance.

❋ *when wild imagination meets your deepest emotions*

A *purposeful mission* is brought forth when a radical image of a potential future finds its natural home in an individual's emotional core – their heart of hearts. It is the haphazard event of wild products of your own imagination meeting your deepest emotions that makes your eyes sparkle and brings out the inspiring missionary within you. In the opening lines of his 2009 autobiographical book *Conquest of the Useless*, Werner Herzog gives a powerful insight into this process by vividly describing – after more than 25 years – the original mental images that would lead to his obsession with filming *Fitzcarraldo:*

> A vision had seized hold of me, like the demented fury of a hound that has sunk its teeth into the leg of a deer carcass and is shaking and tugging at the downed game so frantically that the hunter gives up trying to calm him. It was the vision of a large steamship scaling a hill under its own steam, working its way up a steep slope in the jungle, while above this natural landscape, which shatters the weak and the strong with equal ferocity, soars the voice of Caruso, silencing all the pain and all the voices of the primeval forest and drowning out all birdsong. To be more precise: bird cries, for in this setting, left unfinished and abandoned by God in wrath, the birds do not sing; they shriek in pain, and confused trees tangle with one another like battling Titans, from horizon to horizon, in a steaming creation still being formed. Fog-panting and exhausted they stand in this unreal world, in unreal misery – and I, like a stanza in a poem written in an unknown foreign tongue, am shaken to the core.[2]

This is the harrowing language of a possessed man. Herzog's portrayal is so rich and powerful it invites the reader not only to see his arresting images of the jungle but also to hear with extraordinary clarity the amazing sounds evoked by his imagination. An excruciating atmosphere pervades his whole description, affecting and involving us. It is as if he wanted us to share in the foreboding anticipation he must have felt as he prepared for the gruelling ordeal of actually filming his haunting mental images deep inside the Amazonian jungle.

A mixed feeling of fascination and apprehension is often experienced on the threshold of a purposeful mission – especially one's own. We sense the allure of a radical dream of the future, as if we had secretly expected something like it all along. At the same time we fear the dream, because deep down we know it might completely change our lives and those of the people we love. And sometimes this represents a frightening prospect. So we doubt initially, and even try to forget about that fateful dream altogether – but often to no avail. It is when we realize that *not* living our dream might harm us more than actually pursuing it that we summon the courage to turn that dream into our purposeful mission. At other times, chance events – like young Fitzcarrald losing his father and surviving two close encounters with death, all in under a year – leave us with very little to lose and everything to gain in following our dreams, making it easier for us to embrace our purposeful mission. On other occasions, it is a deep-rooted sense of personal and social responsibility that drives some individuals to transform an extraordinary dream of the future into a purposeful mission and devote their lives to accomplish it. The latter is often the case with socially inspired missionaries like Vincenzo and Antonietta Muccioli, the founders of the San Patrignano drug rehabilitation community. Their son Andrea Muccioli, who headed the community after Vincenzo's unexpected death in September 1995, said:

 If my father had continued blaming society and the institutions for not doing what they should have been doing, and if he hadn't done something in person, this place would never have seen the light. You are alive and rich if you manage to share what you are with another person and build something with others. I think that this was part of the educational principles that [my father] learned in his family.

The Mucciolis' dream was extraordinary and blatantly positive: to create a huge extended family where even some of the most marginalized members of society – such as drug addicts – would be lovingly included and supported in such a way that they could get their lives back and develop their remarkable talents. In many other cases, though, one has to look carefully through a moral lens at the nature of the radical dreams of the future, their associated purposeful missions and ways to accomplish them. After all, it is to a large extent the combined result of such purposeful missions – carried out by passionate groups of people everywhere and across all fields of human activity – that is constantly shaping the future around us. And this concerns us all.

✳ *the moral fabric of purposeful missions*

Real purposeful missions create a better world from every perspective, especially from the moral and ethical viewpoints. When
this is not the case, we should be talking about deeply flawed
missions instead. A problem obviously arises when it becomes
difficult to tell one from the other. In fact, some of the most
frightening characters in history have been able to mass-hypno-
tize people into following them, largely as a result of their diabolical ability to imbue their missions with a misleading – but very
palpable – sense of moral righteousness. Historians have shown
that the early success of Hitler and of Stalin was based, to a significant extent, on their ability to dress their evil designs with
messianic and righteous overtones. When people realized they
had been massively deceived, it was often too late. This raises
the issue of putting one's own purposeful missions and those of
others to the moral and ethical test from the outset. Only when
those missions speak soundly to our heads and feel right in our
hearts should we move forward to accomplish them. Whenever
this isn't the case, healthy moral and ethical standards should
guide us either to remain deaf to false cries in the desert – no
matter how seductive – or to keep working hard at turning alluring but flawed missions into purposeful ones.

Ethics and morals provide essential guidance for practical behaviour in all societies; they also constitute the main subject of many
scholarly disciplines. However, rather than taking a mostly academic approach in this book, it should be highlighted that the
way in which purposeful missions relate to ethical and moral
issues in the real world fits the etymological roots of these words
quite well. The term "ethics" stems from the Greek term *ethos*,
meaning a person's natural character, predispositions and traditional habits. In turn, the English word "morals" comes from the
Latin expression *mores*, signifying a person's character (whether
good or bad) and temperament. Thus in the classical Mediterranean civilizations, *ethos* and *mores* were used to describe the
character behind a person's practical habits and conduct, rather
than the physical actions themselves. It was philosophers like
Aristotle who pioneered a Western tradition of codified "ethical"

principles leading to "good customs" that in turn would achieve the "highest good" for society. We can find older and closely similar notions in the spiritual traditions of many ancient civilizations – from China, India and the Middle East to Peru – making it obvious that the establishment of "good" moral and ethical codes of social conduct is a universal aspiration of all mankind that pre-dates Western civilization. This has made many historians wonder whether it is possible to find a universal set of "good" ethical and moral principles of practical conduct that is common to all major civilizations throughout history. In this area, they found both good and bad news.

The good news is the principle of positive reciprocity that simply states: Do unto others as you would wish them do unto you. Historians have called it the Golden Rule, because it has been found underlying all major world religions and spiritual philosophies, ranging from Confucianism, Daoism, Hinduism, Greek rationalist philosophy, Judaism and the great monotheistic religions, to Zoroastrianism and the most ancient Andean doctrines of the Pacha-Yacha taught by the legendary Hamawtha Wiraqocha. More recently, the Golden Rule constituted a pivotal principle underlying the United Nations 1948 Universal Declaration of Human Rights as well as its 1976 International Bill of Human Rights. Moreover, we witnessed on the eve of the 21st century how the global community's application of the Golden Rule has been increasingly broadened to include the right of the natural ecosystems to be well treated. This shows how the application of the universal and ancient principle of positive reciprocity is far from static. Like a diamond of supreme beauty whose different facets scintillate differently under the constantly changing daylight, correctly practising the Golden Rule incessantly presents new challenges to mankind as our cosmic history dynamically continues to evolve.

The bad news is the literal application of the ancient principle of retributive justice, famously encapsulated by the Talion Law's dictum: An eye for an eye, a tooth for a tooth. Widespread application of this principle has often led to a vengeful and retaliating use of the Law, leading to endless warfare or the social marginalization – or even annihilation – of certain groups of people by others. It is crucial to highlight that, historically, the principle of retributive justice has not been universally advocated by all major world religions or philosophical systems – though, unfortunately, the case can be easily made that it has been very widely and unwisely practised by most societies across all eras.

The main idea here is that, as capable dreamers emboldened with purposeful missions, creators of the future are chief agents of social evolution that will often face first-hand the practical challenges of applying the Golden Rule – and avoiding the excesses of the Talion Law – in largely unknown landscapes and virtually unexplored territories. As they shape their new milieu, it is almost inevitable that the lack of data and the dynamic emergence of unprecedented issues will conspire against these creators of the future, making a deep, solid and wise understanding of the Golden Rule not just a desirable attribute but an absolute necessity to successfully achieving a purposeful mission. Otherwise, there will be just too many chances for it to go wrong.

When carrying out a purposeful mission, observing an ethical conduct – by which we mean here putting into practice the universal principle of the Golden Rule – can be just as important as the mission itself. It is only when dreamers of the future correctly apply this precious principle in both their aspirations and their conduct that we can properly refer to their yearnings as purposeful missions. However, making this kind of moral assessment is not always straightforward in the real world, and as a result in this field most of us find ourselves in need of training. The story of Carlos Fernando Fitzcarrald provides a very good illustration of this. Was Fitzcarrald a respectful explorer and an inspiring leader who mobilized people of diverse cultural and ethnic groups towards achieving a better life in their own natural environment; or was he a greedy adventurer and an unscrupulous predator of the Amazonian jungle and its peoples? Ever since his death in 1897, the jury has been out, with supporters and detractors putting forward their own arguments.

On the one hand, Fitzcarrald's critics highlight his punitive expeditions to kill scores of Amazonian natives and eliminate competitors as well as the wild behaviour of the nineteenth-century rubber barons that left a trail of devastation in their wake. On the other hand, Fitzcarrald's supporters argue that the negative stories about him are just slanders promoted by a handful of envious competitors and interested government bureaucrats from Bolivia and Brazil, who created a black legend about him after his death. In reality, Fitzcarrald showed a genuine and very early obsession with exploring the Amazon, which – so different from the typical rubber barons of that era – continued throughout his entire life, even after he became wildly rich and a happy family man. His exceptional achievements as an explorer, opening a far superior route linking the vast Amazonian territories to the main European and North American ports, were widely praised around the globe while Fitzcarrald was still alive. The French Colonel La Combe, who explored the vast Isthmus of Fitzcarrald area a few years after his death, wrote in 1904 that "Only a giant of the stature of Fitzcarrald could have accomplished such a task in so short time."[3] Eyewitness reports offer reliable testimony of Fitzcarrald's policy of persuading the Amazonian peoples to participate in his exploratory and commercial undertakings, and of his use of violence only in the last resort to repel the attacks of the Mashcos people as well as the armed invasions of Brazilian rubber farmers in their attempts to turn a huge area of Peruvian jungle into Brazilian territory (which they actually managed to do immediately after Fitzcarrald's death). The mountain passage that Fitzcarrald built across the isthmus he discovered – avoiding the cutting of lowland trees and allowing two previously separated river systems to be connected by means of a comfortable 50-minute trek – certainly remains an admirable achievement even by 21st-century standards. By comparison, most of the rubber barons who came both before and after Fitzcarrald look like vulgar mercenaries of foreign commercial interests, with none of the Peruvian explorer's longer-term vision and more culturally sensitive treatment of the native peoples. Likewise, Fitzcarrald's handling of the Amazonian forests, which left their awesome biodiversity essentially intact, offers a sharp contrast with the unchecked 21st-century logging, mining and farming of the Amazon that has created a huge environmental challenge of planetary proportions.

As I researched the historical literature on Carlos Fitzcarrald in order to write this chapter, it dawned on me that his approach to the exploration and management of the rain forests was in many ways well ahead of his time and was sharply different from the much more brutal methods of others exploring South America's and Central Africa's uncharted tropics at that period. Therefore I found myself leaning towards regarding his eventful life and career as guided by a genuine purposeful mission to open the Peruvian Amazonian jungle to rational exploration and commercial use. It would be excessive – perhaps even unfair – to expect a nineteenth-century explorer to have upheld higher scientific standards of ecological sustainability at all times, and for this reason alone I am fully aware that these views are very unlikely to become the definitive assessment of such a controversial figure as Carlos Fernando Fitzcarrald. But this is the very reason why his story constitutes such an appropriate parable to illustrate some of the central issues we are considering. It powerfully exemplifies that the real issue isn't beautifully crafting a mission statement so that it reads like a purposeful mission. It is instead about the likes of you and me being aware that living our radical dreams of a new future will probably stretch our current understanding of what constitutes moral and ethical behaviour. This means that as creators of the future we ought to be prepared to take risks in order to soundly apply the most ancient Golden Rule as we enter new territory, setting new standards of moral leadership that others can follow.

Another important issue, also illustrated by Fitzcarrald's pursuits, is being able to steadily maintain a moral course of action in spite of testing events and the widespread criticism that great innovators almost invariably attract at certain points of their careers. In the case of powerful characters like Fitzcarrald, such criticism is unlikely ever to fade away. On the contrary; as time goes by, it provides more depth and an adventurous scent of reality to the historical figure of an exceptional nineteenth-century Amazonian explorer. However, in other cases, as illustrated by Vincenzo Muccioli's experiences in creating the San Patrignano community, criticism can unexpectedly turn into persecution.

The development of San Patrignano was not free from controversy. Vincenzo Muccioli became the target of a series of lawsuits. He had learned by experience how the crises of abstinence could alter even the most determined drug addicts and at times, upon their prior request, he restrained them. In 1980 the Rimini police, tipped off by one runaway guest, raided San Patrignano in the middle of the night, to find that Muccioli had chained up four guests. Muccioli was taken into custody, but later released. He stood trial in Rimini in 1985 and was convicted. The appeals court in Bologna acquitted him in 1987, and the Supreme Court confirmed the acquittal in 1990. The "chain trial", as it was dubbed by the press, was followed closely on television, and for many Italians it became synonymous with Vincenzo Muccioli.

This was not the only incident brought into the limelight. During the mid 1990s Muccioli once again stood trial, this time for not disclosing his knowledge of the suspected manslaughter of one guest, Roberto Maranzano, by another guest. One of his accusers was a third San Patrignano guest, who commented in the press:

> We addicts have constructed [San Patrignano]-like modern slaves of a father-like "padrone" who has never raised a finger [to work] and who always had repression ready for those who did not agree with his rules.

(This same person was eventually re-admitted by Vincenzo Muccioli when in the terminal stage of Aids.) Vincenzo Muccioli was once again freed, but the episode was still regarded as very negative for the community.

Throughout its existence, San Patrignano has inspired both admiration and strong criticism, which has led to very tight management of communication and public relations. According to Vincenzo Muccioli's writings, there was also a positive outcome from all this publicity:

> One of the effects of the [chain] process was the enormous growth in the interest and the publicity around our initiative, which provoked an increase in the applications to enter [San Patrignano]. And the community grew as you were watching.

In Italy, drug abusers who wanted to quit drugs were told to "go to Muccioli". Many Italian tribunals started sending condemned drug addicts to San Patrignano as an alternative to serving a jail sentence. This custom accelerated in the early 1990s, and by 1994 around 40 per cent of the new entrants were serving a sentence or facing trial. Throughout all of the difficult events it had to endure in the 1990s, it is quite remarkable how San Patrignano kept scrupulously applying its cardinal principle of opening its doors to all drug addicts who were determined to quit – irrespective of gender, age, race, creed, profession or previous life story.

Another pivotal issue, showcased by all the extraordinary stories of creators of the future that I examined, is their ability to instil in others their own powerful sense of *purposeful mission*. This is quite different from the relevant challenge of communicating a "mission statement" to others in a clear, logical and stimulating way. Rather, it is about recognizing how purposeful missionaries, through a myriad daily rituals and spontaneous actions, are able to constantly create a powerful emotional atmosphere around themselves and their missions that drives others into a state of heightened responsiveness. There is, in fact, a crucial distinction between rationally introducing a "mission statement" to others in a deliberately planned way, and spontaneously sharing your inner, passionate obsessions with others – and most people can tell the difference right away. It is the genuine and sound moral conviction underlying those obsessions that fires up a missionary zeal in people and transforms a great dream into a contagious purposeful mission. The latter gives its apostle an aura of self-confident enthusiasm that is both alluring and difficult to define.

Back in the early 1970s, in the Spanish city of A Coruña, the brothers Antonio and Amancio Ortega were convinced that democratizing fashion was the way forward in the clothing industry. But at the time this was considered to be an extreme idea that all but a few enthusiasts dismissed as crazy. This wasn't very auspicious for the Ortegas, as they came from a family of modest means and had no previous business experience. However, in 2001, an executive of the Spanish Pastor Bank, which supported Antonio and Amancio in 1975, was quoted as saying:

In [the banking] business one can readily distinguish someone who believes what he says from someone who has learned to recite a booklet. From the outset the bank trusted him [Amancio Ortega]. I don't want to suggest that, back then, we envisioned the magnitude that his business would reach, but we could see it becoming a prosperous business, and could see that their tenacity would help Antonio and Amancio make a name for themselves in business. From the beginning, Amancio Ortega's absolutely forward looking ideas were what caught my attention the most. Thirty years ago, when I heard him for the first time, he sounded like one of today's experts in economics. Back then [in 1971], he already had all those theories that today seem so modern [...]. On top of this, it was obvious he had deep knowledge of the market he wanted to enter. His ability to enthuse and convince his interlocutor that his project, besides being perfectly viable, was also highly profitable turned out to be an infallible weapon in his hands.[4]

Why do purposeful missions possess some people with such force, and leave others relatively unaffected? I have found that one way to answer this question stems from the life stories of the possessed individuals, which show a number of common patterns that can help others unlock the missionary within themselves.

Let us start by reminding ourselves of one striking characteristic that is common to all stories of purposeful missionaries narrated in this book. Because in each of these stories a purposeful mission completely absorbed these missionaries' imagination, emotions, moral convictions and time, the story of these missions is inseparable from the life story of these individuals. As a result, an attentive historical look at how any particular purposeful mission actually unfolded over time is often sufficient for us to grasp essential insights into its main apostles' moral characteristics – and vice versa. I call this attribute self-referential, in the sense that a deep familiarity with the story of a purposeful mission automatically gives us a clear insight into the moral characteristics of the missionaries behind it – and the other way around. In the case of artistic creators of the future such as Werner Herzog, even the story of the making of a movie like *Fitzcarraldo* can offer us an insight into both the movie itself and the moral character of the man behind it. This is akin to a higher self-referential quality, where the story of making a fictional story gives us essential clues to understanding the moral character of the man behind the story as well as the fictional story itself. But the self-referential attribute of purposeful missions is not only useful for us in gaining valuable insights into the character of its missionaries via clever deductive thinking. It also suggests that the degree of an individual's Self-knowledge may be the key factor separating the would-be apostles of purposeful missions from those who are constantly struggling to find the genuine missionary inside themselves.

✳ *the key to unlocking the missionary within*

Throughout human history, "Know thyself" has always been a central dictum encapsulating real wisdom. More pointedly, all apostles of purposeful missions portrayed in this book – ranging from the socially inspired Mucciolis and the more mundane Ortegas, through to the adventurous Fitzcarraldo – strike us as endowed with a very special kind of Self-knowledge. From an early age these characters always appeared to be more or less consciously in touch with what writer Rhonda Byrne has called "the most magnificent version of You".[5] Throughout their lives, awareness of this potential became a source of vital energy for these people, waiting to crystallize. Sometimes this energy was only partially – or even mistakenly – channelled until the chance opportunity arose that directed it towards a purposeful mission to create new futures for real people. A natural acquaintance with their most magnificent Self gave these would-be missionaries the courage and the self-confidence to passionately turn their cherished dreams into the purposeful mission of their lives. The latter was the key for these people to live a self-referential life, by which I mean an individual surrendering to a purposeful mission so naturally, joyfully and completely that the account of achieving it becomes synonymous with the story of his or her life.

People feel instinctively drawn towards the exceptional courage displayed by heroic purposeful missionaries such as Mother Teresa, Nelson Mandela or Mahatma Gandhi, and feel curious to find out how these individuals came to abandon the aspirations of a "normal life" in order to surrender so completely to their missions. Although throughout their lives these missionaries attempted in vain to focus people's attention away from themselves and onto the purposeful missions they upheld, we are always finding inspiration in their biographies and in the near-miraculous ways in which they always seemed to enact – even through trying experiences that most of us would find utterly unbearable – the most magnificent version of Them.

How do some people manage to keep in touch with their most magnificent Self at all times, while others seem to lose sight of it completely? Let us start by addressing the latter issue. I have found that by far the main reason why we forget about our most magnificent Selves is that, over a long period of time, we won't allot time for Self-reflection in our daily routines. Nearly always the most important reason for this is the way in which we end up immersing ourselves in our worldly affairs. We often devote a large chunk of our time to work. We may also make time for our families and even find time for others. But we leave no time for our own Selves. As a result, we gradually forget about the bright childhood visions we held, and let darker experiences and fears about our Self-worth creep in.

Sometimes we even mislead ourselves into believing that what we currently do constitutes our genuine purposeful mission. We get a good job, a fair salary and even a happy family situation. But our eyes won't sparkle when talking about our jobs and eventually an uncomfortable sense of unrealized potential secretly starts to grow within us. This is what my Peruvian friend Nerit Olaya calls "holding the devil inside a bottle". According to an old Peruvian tale, the devil enters and exits a room through different openings. This is why, if it enters a bottle, you have to break the bottle in order to get rid of the devil inside. Nerit knew what he was talking about. He was born to act, and was by far the best actor in our college acting group in Lima during the early 1980s. Anybody could tell right away that his most magnificent Self existed on-stage. In 1983 he courageously left college to study drama in Peru's best acting school. But the terrible economic crisis that swept Latin America during the 1980s forced him to find work as editor of a series of economic publications – his second life-passion. It paid well and gave him a good professional standing. But Nerit's eyes wouldn't sparkle when talking about his work to his friends. And in early 2009 his body started to tell him he had been off-stage for too long. An inexplicable muscular rigidity would get him, sometimes in the neck, at other times in the shoulder or even in the joints. At the same time, he suddenly found himself becoming uncharacteristically irritable and mentally exhausted at work. During a visit to his home city of Sullana, in northern Peru's tropical coastal region, he suddenly realized that if he kept his artistic demons imprisoned in a bottle any longer his physical and psychological sufferings would start to seriously affect him. So, as soon as he found himself back in Lima, Nerit immediately began to work on a stage adaptation of Nietzsche's *Thus Spoke Zarathustra*. His eyes shone with moving intensity as he joyfully announced to me that his devilish bottle had finally been shattered.

Like Nerit, most people largely leave to sheer chance the task of getting back in touch with their most magnificent Selves. On the other hand, many individuals diligently apply strategies for Self-reflection throughout their lives, in order never to lose sight of it. The latter always require you to allot regular time to finding yourself in solitude. Interestingly, in most cases the practice of Self-reflection doesn't need a lot of time, but it does require a disciplined approach to profit from whatever time you manage to assign to it in your daily schedule. In particular, I will mention three common strategies for Self-reflection that help individuals lead a purposeful life and – eventually – find the missionary within. I have observed that some people practise just one of them constantly throughout their lives while others, like myself, engage in at least two of them, either simultaneously or sequentially. However, one should keep in mind that what makes the difference in the long run is the ability to develop a serious and regular habit of Self-reflection, more than the specific technique one chooses.

Meditation is one of the oldest approaches to the practice of contemplative Self-reflection. Because of this, there is a variety of meditation methods one can choose from, and sensible people often try a few of them before deciding which one works best for them as individuals. For most people I know, the best meditation method is the one that feels right to them intuitively and spiritually. In my own case, it was the simplest approach that helped me to find the inner responses I was looking for. It is called Vipassana Meditation. I stumbled into it at 40 years of age when I found myself out of a job and with the opportunity to reinvent myself around more meaningful aspirations. I realized that over the previous decade and a half I had worked in a series of very successful jobs that gave me the illusion of living a purposeful life. Deep down, I remained doubtful that this was the case, but unable to tell exactly why. A ten-day Vipassana Meditation experience in peaceful seclusion at the sunny Swiss mountain village of St Imier helped me clear my mind of a lifetime of existential debris. It was a profoundly energizing experience that made me see much more clearly than ever before the most magnificent version of myself. The unforgettable experience of St Imier ushered in one of the most creative periods in my life, instilling in me a new and growing sense of purpose. You won't be surprised to learn that meditation has been a regular habit in my life ever since.

Building your support team is another strategy for Self-reflection, and is advocated by Bill George, one of the creators of the future portrayed in this book. Over the 1990s, as CEO of Medtronic, George gave the company a renewed sense of purposeful mission that transformed it into a global leader in medical technology. In an inspiring 2007 article, George described how a lifelong habit of building a support team helped both him and the members of his team gain the Self-awareness that allowed them to lead more integrated lives and develop the authentic, purposeful leaders within them:

 In 1974 [I] joined a men's group that formed after a weekend retreat. More than 30 years later, the group is still meeting every Wednesday morning. After an opening period of catching up on each other's lives and dealing with any particular difficulty someone may be facing, one of the group's eight members leads a discussion on a topic he has selected. These discussions are open, probing, and often profound. The key to their success is that people say what they really believe without fear of judgment, criticism or reprisal. All the members consider the group to be one of the most important aspects of their lives, enabling them to clarify their beliefs, values, and understanding of vital issues, as well as serving as a source of honest feedback when they need it most.[6]

In a similar way to Vipassana Meditation, George's approach to building a support team is seemingly simple and far from new. At heart, this approach echoes – almost step by step – the old traditions of enlightened dialogues that philosophers like Socrates and Plato made so popular in ancient Greece around the fourth century BC. However, what individuals like Bill George and his teammates once more demonstrate is that a disciplined, consistent and committed approach to Self-reflection is what makes the difference in the long run.

The practice of solitary pastimes is another useful approach to Self-reflection. This strategy somewhat overlaps with the idea of practising a hobby, with the difference that a solitary pastime involves spending time with yourself only, in combination with the practice of a physical, artistic or intellectual activity that invites quiet contemplation. Again, this approach to Self-reflection has very old roots. It was given the Latin name of *otium* in ancient Rome, which is the origin of the English word otioseness. It must be observed that the ancient term *otium* didn't have the connotation of apathy that otioseness has in modern English. *Otium* was, however, used as antonym to *negotium*, a Latin term literally meaning "denial of *otium*", from which both the English word negotiation and the Italian term *negozio* (meaning business) derive. Thus, rather than leading into apathy, the practice of *otium* was regarded by ancient philosophers such as Seneca – and even twentieth-century ones like Bertrand Russell – as a desirable discipline for individuals wishing to detach themselves from worldly affairs in order to develop a moral and balanced strength of purpose in their daily lives.

It was, in fact, while engaged in one of my favourite solitary pastimes, that of trekking in the central Andean ranges, that I made the startling discovery that is described in the next chapter. It is well known that missionaries of all eras have invariably started their work by forming a core team of individuals who passionately share both their radical dreams of the future and their purposeful missions. Moreover, I had found that these initial core teams of apostles always displayed five leadership qualities, irrespective of cultural, geographic or organizational differences. I knew this could not be a coincidence, as these findings stemmed from examining a highly diverse sample of organizations across several countries. This extensive study could not prepare me, however, for the amazing discovery I made as I learned the enthralling ancient legends of Wiraqocha during my trekking holiday. According to these legends, in 15,000 BC a mythical Andean teacher by the name of Hamawtha Wiraqocha had already recognized these same five leadership qualities and taught them to the people by walking from village to village over a vast territory that today forms part of the three South American nations of Peru, Bolivia and Ecuador.

As we shall see in the next chapter, the fascinating story of how this wise Andean sage of remote antiquity first identified and taught these precious leadership qualities can be as inspiring as the actual findings themselves.

4

the fourth key:
Wiraqocha leaders

Coniraya viracocha
runa camac
pacha camac
yma aycayuc
canmi campam
chacraiqui campac
runayqui ñispa.

(Cuniraya Wiraqocha
organizer of mankind
and the world
you have all things possible
yours are the country fields
yours is Man: Me.)

Excerpt from the *Huarochirí manuscripts*, a relation of ancient Peruvian myths collected by Francisco de Ávila around 1598

IT WAS WHILE TREKKING across the Urubamba – the sacred valley of the Incas – and along the mighty Willka Mayu river, which the ancient Peruvians likened to the Milky Way, that it hit me. I suddenly realized that the key findings of a study I had wrapped up just before my trip had been well understood thousands of years ago. In 15,000 BC,[1] the Wiraqocha, the *Hamawtha* or Wise Man of this ancient Andean land, first unveiled the subtle individual forces that still allow organizations today to unlock their power to create their own successful futures. Based on a highly diverse sample of multinational corporations as well as social organizations I had examined over the previous three years (see Table 1 on page 141), I discovered that organizations with a group of leaders cohesively tied to a purposeful mission were capable of continuously delivering new and extraordinarily positive futures for all of their stakeholders. At the heart of these organizations I invariably found a diverse leadership team passionately embracing a common purposeful mission to deliver in the real world a shared dream of the future that was simultaneously radical, very positive and extremely alluring. In addition, the key members of these outstanding organizations very clearly demonstrated through their daily actions five qualities defined as:

1. *Wholeness* – this quality relates to a person's aptitude for transcending dilemmas or seemingly conflicting views by carrying out wholesome actions, i.e. actions that integrate differences harmoniously, as if they were parts of a coherent totality, rather than either "balancing" or holding those differences apart.

2. *Tolerance* – this quality relates to a person's aptitude for identifying and continuously testing his/her own mental models about others in order to interact and empathize with very different people without preconceptions or prejudices.

3. *Walk-the-talk* – this quality relates to the importance a person places on being coherent in thoughts, values, words and actions, and on developing the habit of demonstrating this coherence in real life with his or her own behaviour.

4. *Generosity* – this quality relates to the degree to which a person demonstrates his or her support and empathy towards others by giving his or her own time to face-to-face mentoring, coaching, supporting and helping develop others – regardless of their status or formal position.

5. *Patience* – this quality relates to the importance a person gives to the process of building a common language with other people who speak different technical and/or native languages, and the level of perseverance and endurance that he or she demonstrates throughout this process.

These findings would not have been at all surprising to Hamawtha Wiraqocha. According to ancient Andean legends, he walked the highlands of Peru thousands of years ago, tracing the trail of what later became the Qhapaq Ñan – the magnificent Inca royal road

Organization	Main activities	Headquarters
San Patrignano	Life-rehabilitation	Italy
Zara	Fashion & logistics	Spain
Grupo AJE	Beverages	Peru & Spain
Medtronic	Medical equipment	US
Diesel	Fashion apparel	Italy
easyJet	Commercial airline	UK
Novartis	Life sciences	Switzerland
Renault–Nissan	Automotive	France & Japan
Delancey Street	Life-rehabilitation	US
IDEO	Industrial design	US

TABLE 1 : Some of the imaginative organizations I have examined

stretching across the forbidding Andean terrain for thousands of miles, from 20° south all the way to the equator. That is why local inhabitants still refer to this engineering masterpiece as Wiraqochaq Ñannin, or the Path of Wiraqocha, a name that in the Andean world also serves as a metaphor for the spiritual journey of self-awakening that Hamawtha Wiraqocha taught to the people as he walked the land. Several thousand years later, I found that this metaphor has the power to describe why some organizations are able to unlock their power to imagine and create new futures – and why others aren't.

✳ *the path of Wiraqocha*

The sixteenth-century chroniclers who accompanied the first Spanish invaders of the Tawantinsuyu – the so-called Inca empire – recorded the earliest European versions of the life and deeds of Apu Qon Teqsi Tunapa Wiraqocha Wajinqira, a name later shortened to Wiraqocha. According to their writings, many thousands of years ago, following a Pachakuti – a great cataclysm that abruptly changed the entire face of the planet and returned humankind to a primeval, savage state – Wiraqocha had emerged from an island on the Titiqaqa lake – the vast expanse of navigable water at 3,810 metres above sea level which straddles the border of Peru and Bolivia. This is where Wiraqocha began his mythical journey.

He walked towards the northwest, carrying a staff in his right hand, and with a bag containing a few possessions strapped to his back. He was a tall, thin man with a severe face who spoke with a deep, grave voice and wore a four-pointed crown on his head. A few miles into his journey, Wiraqocha met his assistant, who accompanied him faithfully on his travels. Their journey took them to Qosqo (today the city of Cuzco), from where they descended into the sacred Urubamba Valley, along the Willka Mayu river. It was in this valley that Wiraqocha mystically received the divine inspiration that transformed him into a Hamawtha, a wise man who knows the ways of the stars and the movements of the heavens above. Wiraqocha spoke in the ancient language of the Qheshwa highlands, recounting what he had learned to men and women. He said that our material reality on earth reflected the cosmic harmony of the heavens above, and that a proper understanding of the principles governing the cosmos was therefore the key to unleashing our full potential as human beings. This is what was known since antiquity as the Pacha-Yacha: the art of enacting earthly actions that are in harmony with the cosmic principles governing the heavens. Because divine inspiration and boundless love underlay all his words and actions, Tunapa Wajinqira was named the divine and giving Lord: Apu Qon Teqsi. He was also named the Wiraqocha because he taught that the harmonious fusion of the male and female energies is the central governing principle that makes the cosmos evolve and grow. Wiraqocha explained that, in the beginning of time, this fusion had created the living foam that floats over the oceans, which in turn generates all the living forms that populate our planet Earth.

Thus Wiraqocha taught men and women about the movement of the stars, the constellations and the dark clouds, and how to measure and record time and the flow of the seasons. He also named the animals and birds, and taught agriculture. And it is due to Wiraqocha's wisdom that the Andean communities – called *ayllus* – have from time immemorial known how to irrigate the land with marvellous engineering works that made even

FIGURE 4 : One of the oldest images of Wiraqocha, at the Kalasasaya temple, near Lake Titiqaqa. *Photo: Piero Morosini*

the highest mountainsides abundant with agricultural produce. Was it in the highland ayllus or in the lush mountain valleys that Wiraqocha fell in love? Only the stars that guided his steps know the answer to this question. But the woman whom Wiraqocha loved made him pause in his travels and bore him two sons: Ymaimama and Tocapo. From an early age, Ymaimama's eyesight was able to perceive the smallest flowers and insects from a great distance, while Tocapo's vision could recognize every heavenly star in the heavens and its earthly shadows.

And when his sons were strong enough in body and mind, Wiraqocha ordered them to walk the land. He told Ymaimama to journey into the hot eastern jungle that teemed with verdant life, in order to give names to all the trees, flowers and fruits he would find along the way and to teach the people who dwelled in the forests which plants could cure and which ones could kill. And he told Tocapo to travel into the temperate western coastal lowlands and build a large house overlooking the ocean, there to teach the peasants how to measure the full path of the Sun across the sky. After sending his sons away to fulfil their missions, Wiraqocha felt ready to continue his northwest march.

As he continued his journey, Wiraqocha taught the people how to behave in accordance with the principles of the Pacha-Yacha in order to unleash the potential of the ayllus. Paramount amongst these principles was Wiraqocha, or the art of attaining with each daily action a harmonious fusion of the male and female energies that lie within each human being. He taught that no matter how different its individual members are, every organized community has a Qosqo: a sacred centre to house all of these differences. It is by passionately embracing their Qosqo that communities – big or small, rich or poor, simple or sophisticated – find the inspiration and drive to fully unleash their growth potential. Wiraqocha taught that in every encounter between human beings – no matter how great their differences – our mindset must be like Tinku, a word meaning a meeting point between equals, like the point at which two streams of equal size meet to create a larger, more powerful river. Wiraqocha taught Ayni – the art of giving first in order to receive – as the key principle that makes the energy of a group of people multiply well beyond the sum of its individual members. Another of his teachings was Jupa, or the art of using language to include third parties in a dialogue, in such a way that three people end up thinking like a pair. Finally, Wiraqocha reminded people that Pacha-Yacha meant acting rather than contemplating. In other words, individuals must demonstrate through their concrete, daily actions how behaving in accordance with such principles as Qosqo, Wiraqocha, Tinku, Ayni and Jupa unleashes the potential of an individual or human community to its fullest extent and in harmony with the cosmos.

In all the places he visited, the people met Wiraqocha with the greatest respect and eagerness, as the fame of the Hamawtha's words and actions spread faster than an Andean windstorm. However, in the ayllu of Calca, which can be reached after a day's march north from Cuzco, the local inhabitants gave Wiraqocha a most violent reception. These villagers angrily rejected his message and expelled the Hamawtha, shouting harsh words and throwing stones that nearly killed him. In response, Wiraqocha brandished his staff and let forth a raging fire that reduced the entire village to ashes. Today, outside the Calca ayllu, a large, dark mountain stands, blackened with the ashes that Wiraqocha's fire inflicted on the disgraced inhabitants who in those ancient times had dared to reject the sacred wisdom of the Pacha-Yacha.

Wiraqocha continued his journey northwest, making his way across vertiginous cliffs, towering mountains, dense forests, mighty rivers and deep canyons. The Hamawtha continued to teach people in every village he encountered along the way. Some of these villages became major cities, such as Cajamarca, Chimor or Tumipampa. And it was from Tumipampa – today known as Cuenca, in southern Ecuador – that Wiraqocha descended towards the ocean and rested on a most beautiful, pristine beach called Manta. There, as the sunset turned the heavens red, Wiraqocha bade the people farewell and entered the sea – some say in an impressive sailing boat made of light wood and hard straw, some say just walking over the foam of the oceans – and headed west, never to be seen again.

✳ *Wiraqocha leaders*

More than 170 centuries after Wiraqocha carried out his memorable trek across the Andes, I found that, similar to the Hamawtha's journey, organizations embarking on the missionary task of creating a radically new and positive future must also pursue an unexplored path that is often fraught with testing obstacles requiring great resolve and wisdom to overcome. Meeting this challenge requires individuals who are capable of demonstrating throughout the journey a passionate commitment to a purposeful mission and behaviour that is in accordance with what the ancient Hamawtha Wiraqocha taught thousands of years ago. This is why I call these individuals *Wiraqocha leaders*. They are dreamers committed to the mission of delivering radically new futures, who always start their journeys by encouraging similar individuals to join in.

The first distinctive characteristic of Wiraqocha leaders is that they understand and passionately embrace their organization's Qosqo at all times. This is usually clearly spelled out in the institution's purposeful mission. When attracting other members to join them in their journey, Wiraqocha leaders ensure that the new recruits have a genuine emotional connection with the organization's Qosqo. Consider the husband-and-wife team of Vincenzo and Antonietta Muccioli, who built the San Patrignano community into the most effective drug rehabilitation institution in the world, around the amazing purposeful mission of training marginalized people and helping them to achieve extraordinary things. For over thirty years the main therapeutic approach for achieving this mission involved not the conventional medical use of drug substitutes like methadone, but the practice of communal work with world-class standards of excellence and within a supporting family environment. Awareness of this remarkable place spread and slowly grew. However, in the midst of this growth, Vincenzo Muccioli, as head of the community, started a tradition of having a long chat with each newcomer at least once before they entered. This was an opportunity to test their personal determination and to check if they were committed to giving up drugs, but it was also to lay down the rules. For Muccioli, determination to quit drugs and follow San Patrignano's few but non-negotiable rules was proof that the newcomer really was wholeheartedly committed to achieving the community's purposeful mission. Still, Muccioli did not close the door on those who had left and later wished to return. At any given time, in fact, as many as a third of San Patrignano's members have been admitted more than once.

Similarly, Bill George, the former CEO of Medtronic who during the 1990s helped transform the company into one of the world's leading medical technology multinationals, explains how sharing a genuine and passionate commitment to achieving a common purposeful mission became a central selection criterion for the organization's key leaders:

 [In 1990 when I arrived at Medtronic] we promoted several [functional managers] who were in their 40s to general management jobs. And in addition to that we went out and recruited a number of general managers from other companies. Now, one of the key criteria was whether they saw the [Medtronic] mission [of "restoring people to full health"] as something they would really buy into, whether they were really interested in that. And I know I told a couple of them: Look, if [our company mission] does not turn you on, don't come here.

The second characteristic of Wiraqocha leaders concerns the qualities showcased by their individual practical behaviour as each of them walks the path towards achieving the common purposeful mission. In this area, I discovered that the key behavioural principles that Wiraqocha taught such a long time ago were, in essence, the same qualities I found at play within the leadership cadres of those organizations that excelled at creating new and positive futures for all of their stakeholders (see Table 1). In other words, through the quality of their individual actions, the Wiraqocha leaders of these remarkable organizations very clearly demonstrated the qualities of wholeness, tolerance, generosity, walk-the-talk and patience.

Wholeness is reminiscent of ancient Peru's myth of Wiraqocha. As vividly portrayed in this myth, wholeness stands for the harmonious blending of an individual's male and female traits in his or her leadership behaviour and actions. This is encapsulated in Novartis CEO Daniel Vasella's description of the characteristics that he looked for in selecting the company's initial group of leaders. Against the historical background of an extremely high failure rate of mergers, acquisitions and alliances, these leaders had to realize in practice the unprecedented dream of creating a new global pharmaceutical champion from the 1996 merger of Ciba-Geigy and

Sandoz – two Swiss companies that, in the past, had been middle-rank players at best. Not surprisingly, a competitor sarcastically greeted the Novartis merger with the comment "If you put two crows together, you do not get an eagle." In May 2006, however, the Swiss business publication *Bilanz* hailed Novartis as one of the most important milestones in Swiss economic history. In ten years, Vasella and his team had managed to create an innovative pharmaceutical leader with groundbreaking drugs and an impressive financial record. In the process, Vasella had been listed by *Time* magazine in 2004 as one of the world's 100 most influential people, and in the same year he was named "the most influential European business leader of the last 25 years" in a poll of *Financial Times* readers. By that time, it was very clear to all that Novartis had been thoroughly successful in achieving the seemingly impossible dream of creating an eagle out of two crows. One of the first steps Vasella had taken to accomplish this was selecting leaders capable of displaying the quality of wholeness in their behaviour:

 [In March 1996] we nominated [Novartis's top 300 managers] based on our knowledge of the people and clear criteria: we wanted performance, we wanted integrity, we wanted people with a certain experience. For us it was important to identify people who were willing to "make cuts", even if they hurt. So, on the one hand, these were people who needed to be very cool headed and very cool blooded. On the other hand, these people also needed to be compassionate and have empathy, and react to what others were experiencing, and support and help them.

Another important aspect of Wiraqocha leaders is tolerance, a quality similar to the ancient Peruvian notion of Tinku. In other words, it stands for the type of mindset a person must have in order to engage with other people (no matter how different they may be) as equals, without pre-existing mental models, cultural prejudices or preconceptions. This quality is crucially important, and especially so when achieving a great dream of the future requires working across different national, professional and organizational cultures, as in the 1999 alliance between the French carmaker Renault and Japanese carmaker Nissan. From the start of his appointment in June 1999 as the chief operating officer (COO) of the Renault–Nissan alliance, Carlos Ghosn, a South

American of Lebanese descent and French education, undoubtedly realized that reviving a nearly bankrupt Nissan within the
framework of a French–Japanese cultural combine was a radical
dream that no one had ever attempted before on such a scale. In
fact, after the Renault–Nissan alliance was announced, it inspired
such widespread scorn from observers and competitors alike that
the eagle jibe about Novartis seemed mild by comparison. When
General Motors vice-chairman Bob Lutz learned that Renault had
spent US$5.4 billion to buy a 36.6 per cent stake in Nissan, his
comment to a journalist made instant news:

 Renault would be better off buying US$5 billion of gold bars,
putting them on a ship and dumping them in the middle of the
Pacific.

Bob Lutz was not the only one who viewed a merger between
two companies from such culturally different nations with an
enormous degree of scepticism. The international financial press,
company executives, management academics and consultants all
over the world concurred. Pessimism prevailed, as this selection
of comments shows:

 Much has been made of the culture clash between Daimler and
Chrysler but it will be nothing compared to Nissan and Renault.
At their core, they are both nationalistic and patriotic, and each
believes its way is the right way to do things. We will have quite
a teething period for the first year or two as they feel each other
out.

Two mules don't make a racehorse.

I would have preferred Renault to take 51 per cent even if it
meant having to assume Nissan's debt on its balance sheet.
That way Renault could have become the real boss and set some
firm direction, rather than having to negotiate.

French taxpayers may be left footing the bill for Renault, whose
top managers were perhaps blinded by the brilliance of their
own vision.

Even the most optimistic observers reckon that the payoff
horizon – assuming that the alliance can overcome its enormous
business and cultural hurdles – will be long-term, not short.

As we have seen, mainstream managerial theories and empirical evidence dictate that a large percentage of mergers and alliances are destined to fail. And Renault and Nissan themselves weren't exactly stars in the automotive industry. Admittedly, Renault had just been taken off the losers' league of carmakers after a remarkable comeback that was turning losses of US$680 million in 1996 into combined profits of US$1.65 billion in 1998 and 1999, but at the same time the company was still recovering from a highly publicized failure to merge with Volvo in 1995. A distinctively French and European carmaker, Renault had never run a global operation: in 1998 the company sold no cars in the US and only 2,476 units in Japan, the world's two largest car markets.

Meanwhile Nissan was nearly bankrupt in 1999. Since 1991 it had been losing money and market share continuously, and car production had dropped by 600,000 units, with the result that Nissan's factories were running at a disastrous 53 per cent of capacity. The company's product portfolio was aging, and it had ten times as many suppliers as Ford and four times as many manufacturing platforms as Volkswagen. Its US$20 billion debt mountain was more like that of a medium-sized developing country than that of a large carmaker.

The two companies were however complementary in geographic scope and skills. Renault had a flair for marketing and design, and was strong in Europe and Latin America. Nissan was an engineering powerhouse with a strong market presence in Japan, North America and Asia. Against that, the two had no history of working together. To complicate matters, in March 1999 the French state had a 44 per cent controlling stake in Renault, and Nissan, as Japan's second largest carmaker, was a highly emblematic symbol of the country's industrial strength. Not surprisingly, after its alliance with Nissan was publicly announced, Renault's share price fell, and three separate rating agencies issued negative reviews of the company's debt.

On a sunny afternoon in Paris in mid March 2004, almost five years to the day after the Renault–Nissan alliance had been so universally condemned, Renault's president Louis Schweitzer

was preparing to retire. Seated comfortably behind his office desk
at Renault's headquarters, he told a journalist:

> The future is rosy. Clearly we have the pieces in place that
> are required for growth [...]. Renault–Nissan has been an
> incredible, and in many ways unexpected, success [...].
> Someday, maybe – I hope so – Nissan may help [Renault's
> re-entry into] the US [market].

Renault's original US$5.4 billion investment in Nissan was
worth US$18.4 billion in March 2004. This made Renault's 36.6
per cent stake in Nissan (which Renault increased to 44.4 per
cent in 2003), worth more than the total market value of the
French carmaker itself. In 2004, Nissan's head of Europe (and
former Renault executive) Patrick Pelata called it "the biggest
return on investment in the history of the automotive industry".
Amazingly, the major Japanese company that in March 1999 had
been virtually bankrupt was just five years later posting profits
of US$7.6 billion, and its 11 per cent operating margins were
the highest in the industry. Not surprisingly, ever since 2004,
competitors, practitioners and academics around the world have
unanimously regarded the alliance as a successful model.

Its unlikely success also catapulted one of its main architects,
Carlos Ghosn, to stardom levels in the international business
media. The incredible story of how he and his leadership team
had managed to revitalize Nissan became a series of textbook
cases eagerly studied in international business schools. These
cases showed that Ghosn had started the turnaround of Nissan
by providing an example of tolerance at work. Although he did
not speak Japanese at the time, he addressed the people in Japan
directly, without pre-existing mental models, cultural prejudices
or preconceptions. Said Ghosn:

> I am not going [to Japan] with any preconceived ideas.

Ghosn encouraged the few Westerners he brought with him to
Japan to do the same thing:

> [In July 1999] I handpicked seventeen [French executives]
> from Renault and brought them to Nissan. I chose people
> who were around 40 years old, experts in their field, very

open minded and coaches, not people who wanted to play it
solo [...]. [Before coming to Japan I told them:] we are not
missionaries. We are not going there to teach the Japanese
[about] the role of women in Japanese business. We are there to
help fix Nissan, that's all. Any issue that does not contribute to
that is of no concern to us.

Amongst the seventeen Renault expatriates whom Ghosn brought
to Japan were Patrick Pelata and Thierry Moulonguet, who, as
heads of Nissan product development and finance respectively,
would play a critical role in the company's revival. Once in Japan,
Ghosn oversaw the reduction of Nissan's board of directors from
37 members to ten. When Nissan's President Yoshikazu Hanawa
asked Ghosn who he wanted as Japanese members on the executive committee board, he replied:

> I don't know. You choose. You know me, so please, you pick
> them – knowing what you know of me.

Immediately after this, Ghosn formed Nissan's leadership team:

> I requested that 1,500 profiles of Nissan employees be posted
> in headquarters to select about 200 people for nine cross-
> functional teams. I was looking for young mavericks who would
> be the backbone of the next Nissan leadership generation.
> Multicultural experience was not considered an absolute
> requirement for success, but it was a value-added. I think
> that the basic personal qualities of an individual can always
> overcome any lack of experience. It is important how you
> handle small frustrations. And when you have taken time to
> understand and accept that people don't think or act the same
> way in France or in Japan, then the cultural differences can
> become seeds for innovation as opposed to seeds for dissent.

In early 2000, Nissan's new leadership cadre was in place. It was a
reduced group of 200 executives, not permanently housed at the
company's Tokyo headquarters, as had been the case until then,
but spending time there on a project-by-project basis. Together
with this new leadership team, Carlos Ghosn presided over one
of the fastest, most successful corporate turnarounds ever.

The leadership qualities sought by both Vasella and Ghosn in
order to realize their unprecedented corporate dreams reveal a

bias not only for high-performance results and for being able to make difficult decisions, but also for coaching others and spending time supporting them when they are undergoing difficult challenges. For this quality of empathy and willingness to support and nurture others I use the term "generosity", a trait reminiscent of the ancient Peruvian notion of Ayni – in other words, the collective principle of giving first in order to receive.

The French–Japanese leadership team that was put in place at Nissan in 1999 also provided a very good example of integrity, which most of the Wiraqocha leaders I have spoken to summarize as "walk-the-talk", or leading by example. In 1999, Ghosn defined walk-the-talk behaviour to Nissan employees in a way that echoes Wiraqocha's ancient notion of the Pacha-Yacha:

> What we think, what we say, and what we do must be the same. We have to be impeccable in ensuring that our words correspond to our actions. If there are discrepancies between what we profess and how we behave, that will spell disaster.

Finally, patience in crafting a common language and a mutual understanding that helps include and align an organization's key members are important leadership qualities reminiscent of Jupa. Ghosn vividly explains how patience was essential for the members of the Renault–Nissan alliance in creating a common language and building real understanding across cultural boundaries:

> [In 1999] I told the old guard [of first-generation Nissan managers]: You will speak English. Learn it immediately if you must, or you're out. But some key words were not understood in the same way by different Japanese people or even different French people. So I asked a mixed Renault–Nissan team to establish a dictionary of essential terms. The 100 or so entries included clear definitions for terms like "commitment", "authority", "objectives", "transparency" and "targets".

✳ *Wiraqocha leadership: a journey for all*

Nearly thirty years after it started in 1971, Mimi Silbert's eyes still shine with genuine excitement and determination when she describes the Delancey Street Foundation to me. Dr Silbert was full of optimism when leaving Berkeley University after completing her PhD degree in criminal psychology and criminology in the late 1960s. She was confident that she had built up a store of knowledge that would allow her to help the people least equipped to face life in society. This small (five-foot), energetic woman started working in the State of California's toughest prisons, applying all the techniques and approaches she had learned at university. However, she soon realized that she was not making much progress. As Dr Silbert explains:

 During my doctoral degree I had studied several fields that, in essence, tell a criminal that: "You have something wrong with you inside. Let me work with you and get you okay. And then you'll stop committing crime." I was even happily teaching criminology at Berkeley. But luckily I worked in a prison, and it took me a very short time to find out that all those theories were of course not true. Because crime is interactive, something that happens between a person and their society. What needs to be fixed is this interaction.[2]

What followed was a startling development for someone fully trained in advanced scientific research methods. Dr Silbert had realized that the roots behind criminal behaviour were to be found neither in society nor within the criminals themselves, but in the interaction between them. However, rather than trying to apply conventional scientific approaches in order to build a new theory of crime based on her important discovery, she simply looked at her own past to work out the next step. This wasn't a criminal past, though – far from it:

 For me it was a matter of looking at what had worked for me all my life. I grew up in a very poor neighborhood of immigrants in Boston. My parents were from Eastern Europe, and during my first twelve years my grandparents, aunts, and uncles also lived with us. It was a typical American immigrant family. Everybody lived together in our little flat, and everybody helped each other. And the idea was that the children were going to have the American dream. I realized as a therapist, as a person, that everything that had worked in my life could work for others as well. I was doing a lot of therapy and people were saying "thank you", and "what a good person". But I realized that what makes any human being successful and happy is not really therapy or punishment, but just to be enabled to achieve things.

Mimi Silbert decided to try her own way of helping people who had hit the bottom of society. She met John Maher, a one-time alcoholic and drug addict and a former member of Synanon, an alternative drug rehabilitation community that used a therapeutic method based on self-examination through group truth-telling sessions. John also had a burning desire to help the so-called underclass of society achieve success, so he and Mimi teamed up. Mimi found an exclusive mansion in the Pacific Heights neighbourhood of San Francisco that had previously housed the Russian consulate. It was an exquisite site, on the very top of the hill, and just across the street from some of the city's most aristocratic families, going back several generations. The two obtained a mortgage and bought the house in 1971. Mimi explains:

 As the saying goes: "You can't cure an alcoholic in a bar." We are trying to teach desperados to climb up, so the surroundings are important in order to walk-the-talk and build confidence in these people. But also, the fascinating point is that it was actually cheaper to buy a big home than it was to buy apartments. You just have to be willing to live with the family instead of each person having their own separate life.

Mimi and John moved in with a handful of hard-core drug addicts with a history of crime, gangs and prison sentences, who were nevertheless determined to positively change their lives. Together, they immediately started their first moneymaking venture, because they did not want to receive any government money. Instead, their idea was to learn everything they needed to know to become successful in society. Mimi had started to think about possible jobs that these people could do to get them into a positive cycle of achievement and break their vicious cycle of crime, drugs, prison, broken-up families and homelessness. But the first real venture came about by chance. When they had moved in, as she describes it, "the neighborhood went absolutely crazy about having a house full of drug addicts and criminals in the vicinity." So Mimi and the residents went around to their neighbours, trying to be nice and volunteer their services, in order to win them over. Mimi describes what happened next:

> At one large, luxurious mansion, the owners asked us to clear everything out because they were having a ballet that same evening. One of our guys picked up a piano and said: "What do you want me to do with this?" And a lightbulb went on immediately over my head: "Moving: that's what we could do!" Our people typically are all in prison for years, doing nothing but lifting weights. They all have those big arms. So, when we went home we wrote an ad saying "Moving? We'll do it for less," and we put it on everybody's car windshields in the neighborhood. When the first person called and described what they wanted to move, we phoned the largest American moving company and then quoted a much lower price. We rented a truck and uniforms and everybody showed up. People were thrilled. We did our first move really well and our client recommended us to other people. Slowly we started to get more jobs.

The business gradually grew by word of mouth and operated for almost a year until a government official knocked on the door to remind them that removals was a licensed and regulated business. Mimi paid the fine and sent off a few of their people to school to get a mover's licence. Observed Mimi:

> That's how our trial and error policy was started at Delancey Street. We're going to make a lot of mistakes. The only thing you do is say, "I'm sorry, we'll fix it." If you don't take risks, you will never get anywhere.

Eventually, the removals company resumed its operations and became very successful. Numerous other ventures followed suit, amongst them a print and copy shop, a car wash, a trendy bookstore café in San Francisco Bay, and a gourmet restaurant with a different menu every day. Sitting at a table in her waterfront restaurant on the elegant San Francisco Embarcadero, just across from Pier 34, Mimi explains:

> I want to prove a point, which is that ordinary people – or like in our case less-than-ordinary people – can do extraordinary things. It does not take what everyone thinks it takes. It takes structure, willingness to teach each other, mutual support. [...]

Let's start with the moving company. We don't have "just" drug
addicts working there; we have serious criminals, who have
stolen all through their lives. These people, some of whom are
pretty new, go into people's homes, packing their valuables,
their jewelry. Everything that in the past they wanted to break
in to steal. But they do not put a dollar in their pockets, they
simply move it. Our moving company has become the largest
on the US West Coast because it offers the best service and has
the lowest record of theft and complaints in the industry. More
importantly, it has taught our people integrity and character.

✳ the key to forming a Wiraqocha leadership group

Individuals like Mimi Silbert, John Maher, the Mucciolis, Daniel
Vasella, Bill George or Carlos Ghosn highlight the real key to
forming a group of Wiraqocha leaders. For any individual person,
this key is to address the challenge of him or herself becoming
a true Wiraqocha leader. It is as a result of this inner transformation that any individual naturally gets to attract other like-
minded people capable of turning a radical dream of the future
into reality. As we have seen, from ancient times onwards,
becoming a real Wiraqocha leader has essentially meant practising the sacred art of the Pacha-Yacha. In other words, passionately embracing a purposeful mission that genuinely makes your
eyes shine, and walking towards achieving it while observing in
words and actions the qualities of wholeness, tolerance, generosity, walk-the-talk and patience.

Of course, across the many industries and organizations around
the globe there is a myriad specific technological skills and functional knowledge – as well as a series of salary and other incentive
mechanisms – that need to be in place for any leadership group to
perform properly. However, what the Delancey Street Foundation,
the San Patrignano community and all the other extraordinary
organizations portrayed in this book demonstrate so powerfully
is that, from a leadership perspective, it is the determined, passionate commitment to a purposeful mission, together with the
five behavioural qualities described above, which in the long run

makes the real difference between the successful creators of the future and all the rest.

For most individuals embarking on their own personal journeys to becoming Wiraqocha leaders, the main challenges usually are recognizing what truly makes their eyes sparkle as individuals, and avoiding common pitfalls when learning the art of behaving according to the principles of wholeness, tolerance, generosity, walk-the-talk and patience. Awareness of what really makes your eyes shine helps you discern whether or not any given purposeful mission will truly turn you on. Once you have found it, it doesn't need to become the purposeful mission of your life, but it will certainly set you on the path to eventually discovering a great dream of the future that you might choose to devote your life to. In all the remarkable organizations we have looked at, there is always a core team of a few individuals who keep a life-long commitment to sharing the mission and a common dream of the future. Others move on to continue their existential quests elsewhere until they eventually find the purposeful missions of their lives. Gradually, these journeys allow them to develop their ability to behave according to the qualities of wholeness, tolerance, generosity, walk-the-talk and patience.

Regarding the challenge of recognizing what it is that truly makes your eyes sparkle, the good news is that you already know about it. For some of us, however, the bad news is that our conscious minds may have temporarily forgotten about it after a lifetime of doing things that are different – sometimes extremely different – from what truly excites us. There is a variety of reasons for this oblivion, often involving deeply emotional experiences in the past. Sometimes, it may be an absence of support early on in our family and school environments, or insufficient determination to pursue our life passions, or even traumatic past experiences that prevented us from doing so. Thus, recognizing what really excites us is more about bringing it out than figuring it out. There are several ways other than by pure chance of doing that. One approach that I have seen work very effectively consists of group sessions run by an experienced coach using a video camera. This is a simple yet powerful technique, even with extremely difficult

FIGURE 5 : A masterly abstract representation of the portrait of
Wiraqocha (seen in Figure 4) woven as an *unku* (shirt) in
Peru around 1000 AD. *Photo: Piero Morosini*

personalities, such as a German graphic designer whom we will
call Hans (not his real name).

Young, extremely formal and quiet, Hans was by far the most
challenging participant in a group of fifteen men and women of
various nationalities who had gathered for a three-day programme
on "reinventing our lives". When, on the first day, it was Hans's
turn to sit down in front of the group (and the video camera), he
looked at us with a deeply sceptical expression. The coach asked
him to keep repeating the names of people who really meant a lot
to him until, eventually, Hans's eyes glittered with barely with-
held tears when naming his mother and his sister. Then the coach

asked him about what really turned him on. His answer had to do with graphic design. The coach asked the group, "Are Hans's eyes shining when he talks about graphic design?" Many voices yelled the same reply: "No!" When Hans challenged the group's response, the coach invited him to see for himself on the video playback the indisputable evidence of his own unexcited eyes. So Hans talked about other things, ranging from his favourite hobbies to his dream travel destinations, but to no avail. His eyes never really came alive.

On the last day of the programme, Hans asked to do a session again. By that time, all the other participants had successfully brought out their inner passions in sometimes deeply emotional group sessions, and were excitedly working at various ways to reinvent their own future lives. But we were all really curious to watch Hans once more. He stared at us silently with a dark expression that made some participants visibly uncomfortable. After a few tense minutes he suddenly closed his eyes, and his mouth twisted in a rictus of anguish before he said, in a strangely grave voice, "I love to destroy people's reputations." When he opened his eyes again, they were glowing with a diabolical yet magnetic intensity that none of us had thought him capable of possessing. His pale face had turned red and sweaty with excitement, and his smile was one of profound relief. It was as if a ton of bricks had been lifted off his shoulders.

Over the next half hour, Hans told how his conservative family and religious schooling had buried his natural rebellious streak under a thick layer of guilt. Neither the coach nor the other participants said anything judgemental. Everyone was just amazed and fascinated to hear Hans talking at uncharacteristic speed. During the rest of the day, Hans joined a few people in the group to work at reinventing his future around his inner passion. When his turn came to debrief his work, it was easily the best presentation of the entire class. He announced to us that he would launch a new tabloid magazine in the small German village where he lived that would focus on exposing the double lives of local politicians. As a next step, he would create a talk show on the local radio station, where local people could put those duplicitous politicians on trial. According to Hans, this would be a shocking but much needed revolution in the conformist and hypocritical environment of his home town. "Exposing our bad leaders is a great service to our democracy: I don't have to feel guilty about destroying those people's reputations," he enthusiastically told us, with a more than mischievous twinkle in his eyes.

The story of Hans is typical of many people I meet who cannot convincingly answer the simple question: what is it that *really* makes your eyes light up? On the one hand, it shows how sometimes the simplest things are the most difficult for us to accomplish. On the other hand, it highlights how a supportive group and the capable and caring figure of a real coach can help us transcend those difficulties. Without exception, all the organizations portrayed in this book have institutionalized these supporting and coaching roles under a variety of names, ranging from "buddies" and "mentors" to "partners". But it is perhaps San Patrignano's "guardian angels" that provide one of the most beautiful and insightful illustrations of this crucial role.

❋ *fallen angels become guardian angels*

It was my mother who, when I was very young, first told me about guardian angels. She said to me that every person had a guardian angel, though many of us ignored it. The angel was always there to lovingly protect us from any evil, give us strength whenever we felt weary, and get us back to the roots of our own goodness during troubled times. My mother even taught me how to pray to my guardian angel. It was a beautiful prayer in Spanish, every word of which I still remember. What my dear mother could not tell me then was the name of my guardian angel. This was probably why, many years later, as an adult, when I came across a French book entitled *Our Guardian Angel Does Exist* (*Notre ange gardien existe*), I immediately bought it.[3] In the opening pages of that book I saw, neatly arranged in a Cabalistic image of the "Tree of Life", the names of nine principal archangels, each leading a chorus of eight guardian angels. In total, there were 72 guardian angels, each of which corresponded to five days of the year, or five zodiacal degrees. I noticed that all of the guardian angels' names ended in either -el or -ah. And this is how I learned that my guardian angel's name was Rehael, while my son's guardian angel was Pahaliah. This fascinating book, however, could not prepare me for my first physical meeting with actual guardian angels. This took place in 1999 at the San Patrignano community, where I expected to find nothing more than fallen angels.

The San Patrignano community has never had either therapists or guards. Newly arrived drug abusers – called "guests" – are confronted with a smaller group of people who remain the nucleus of their relationships in the community. Living quarters and working places are shared by five to ten people. Among these, one or two longer-established guests become the newcomer's guardian angels, meaning that they have a special responsibility to look after him or her. A female San Patrignano guest has described why the role of a guardian angel is so important in helping even the most marginalized members of society to turn their lives around to accomplish extraordinary things:

 When you arrive at San Patrignano, they put you next to some people, one or two of whom always are by your side. These people have also experienced the same thing in the past. In other words, they are former drug addicts who are feeling better and therefore are able to help out and support the newcomers through their problems, their ups and downs, their feelings of withdrawal. They always follow you, they are with you all day long, teaching you the rules, the "to dos", how we live with others in this community. More than this, they really care for you. They give you warmth because that is what you need the most when you have just arrived here. The newcomers' relationship with these people is never easy at the beginning, because they have to tell you the rules. But, in my experience, the people who followed me when I had just arrived at San Patrignano are the ones whom I love, trust and admire the most. And now that I'm feeling better, I myself have the opportunity to give them something back, and also – at least I hope so – to help and support other newcomers.

Another female guest further describes the loving and supporting role of San Patrignano's guardian angels in helping others get through their critical moments:

When one of my friends decides to go away, I try to be as close as I can to her, because I think that's maybe a critical period for her and she needs more affection, someone to talk to in order to discuss and address her problems.

In addition, at San Patrignano there was always one guest responsible for each dormitory; this guest ensured that newcomers were properly integrated. Said one former guest:

 The first two months are difficult. You have to renew your commitment each day. You are constantly reminded that "It is you who have chosen to come here – we didn't come looking for you." It is only when you wake up in the morning and do not ask yourself any more why you are here that you are on the right track. This can take up to two years. Once human relations are re-established, it quickly develops. So you pass from a phase of antagonism towards life and human relations to an active phase. The rediscovery of passions.

At this point, guests can focus on rebuilding themselves, and take on even more responsibility by helping one of the new entrants and becoming their guardian angel. For new guests, on the other hand, the guardian angel is the proof that this is a contest they can win. As Vincenzo Muccioli's son Andrea puts it:

 You start from a situation in which you are absolutely not responsible for yourself, not the slightest. At the end you become responsible not only for yourself, but also for other human beings. This you achieve in so many different time frames.

As illustrated by San Patrignano's guardian angels, when it comes to rediscovering and developing one's inner passions, being coached is as important as providing coaching to others. It is through giving and receiving emotional support and examples of behaviour that individuals gradually learn to develop the qualities of wholeness, tolerance, generosity, walk-the-talk and patience. No less importantly, caring coaching also helps individuals avoid the common pitfalls that most people encounter when gradually learning how to practise those qualities.

✳ *transcending common pitfalls*

One common pitfall – especially for analytically minded people – is to confuse the intellectual understanding of a personal quality with an individual's capacity to actually demonstrate it. The quality of wholeness, for example, is about transcending opposites in our actions, not in our minds. When Daniel Vasella set out in March 1996 to implement the seemingly impossible dream of merging Ciba-Geigy and Sandoz to form Novartis, he and his leadership team realized that thousands of people would lose their jobs as a result. In order to transform this traumatic exercise into a more positive experience, Novartis went out of its way to create several mechanisms for those employees who were laid off, ranging from generous exit packages to launching relocation programmes and even creating a large fund to financially support those who wanted to start up new ventures. For the Novartis leaders, wholeness wasn't about engaging in a philosophical debate as to whether or not it is possible to simultaneously lay people off and make them happy. Rather, it was about enacting a decent exit process as well as creating a generous and effective safety net for those who had to go.

Similarly, another common pitfall is to assume that tolerance means studying cultural differences rather than developing the ability to suspend judgement when actually meeting people who are different from us. I like to describe our cultural prejudgements and stereotypes as subconscious creatures inside our minds who – similar to the little monsters in Steven Spielberg's 1984 film *Gremlins* – nearly always manage to stay hidden and spawn other small and destructive beasts. Tolerance is about the difficult task of finding the cultural gremlins that hide inside our heads, and placing them in a sealed box where they cannot escape or multiply. Instead, many people who are imperfectly aware of their deep-rooted cultural stereotypes nevertheless immerse themselves in learning about cultural differences through academic courses or short visits abroad. Sometimes they identify their inner cultural gremlins as a result. More often, however, these experiences paradoxically reinforce these people's cultural prejudices and multiply their internal cultural gremlins. It was to avoid this pitfall from the outset that Carlos Ghosn demanded that all the French managers he brought from Renault to Nissan's Tokyo headquarters should empty their minds of any cultural preconceptions about Japan or Japanese culture, and instead focus externally on boldly implementing the incredible dream of turning the depressed Japanese carmaker around and transforming it into a global champion in less than three years.

Another common pitfall is to believe that generosity is about giving resources or sending e-mails with general advice to other people, rather than giving our own time to others in order to genuinely empathize with them, listen to what they are going through and caringly support them. It is this kind of personal support that builds cohesiveness inside a Wiraqocha leadership group, giving it the inner strength to fulfil its daunting mission of creating unimaginable futures for the rest of us. Like San Patrignano's guardian angels, the most successful coaches I have met are always there when their people really need them. They speak very little, but listen a lot. In a way, they become our spiritual mirrors, reflecting what they see in front of us without judgement. Occasionally, they ask deep, tough questions, but they expect no answers. These outstanding coaches know that sometimes silence is the best response. This is why we feel understood by them even when they are not talking at all.

When it comes to walking-the-talk, a typical pitfall for many people is to believe that practising it is about wearing a composed mask at all times and being extremely conservative in making promises – for fear of not being able to deliver on them. But on the contrary, walking-the-talk is really about behaving with authenticity rather than acting out a character. Daniel Vasella says:

 I think walking-the-talk comes from integrity and self-discipline. So, I think you should not normally try to say "I'm walking-the-talk," because then you are acting. And you should not "act" in the sense of playing theatre. You should "be". So you have to be authentic in what you do, otherwise you will not be able to sustain it. Secondly, walking-the-talk also means respecting and getting respect. And maybe not looking for being liked. Because you may have to do things which are not likable at all.

Instead of shying away from making daring promises, all the extraordinary creators of the future portrayed in this book mainly demonstrated walk-the-talk behaviour by timely delivery of ambitious commitments that to most people seemed unthinkable in the first place. As I describe in more detail in Chapter 6, it is this consistency that generates trust and respect around Wiraqocha leaders who, through constantly walking-the-talk, inspire others to follow them and together build new and extraordinary futures around us. Observes Vasella:

 [During the implementation of the 1996 Novartis merger] we put very clear deadlines and milestones [in place, establishing] what we wanted to achieve by [a very specific] date. It became an iron rule: you had to [achieve your goal] and finish it by the agreed deadline. It had to be achieved with no excuses.

Regarding patience in building a common language, the most frequent pitfall I have observed – especially within international teams – is thinking that this quality is about ensuring that all members of a Wiraqocha leadership group are able to communicate in the same national language. Instead, patience to build a common language refers to the characteristics of perseverance and endurance that are required throughout the process of bringing about a mutual understanding amongst a group of highly diverse people. It is only when its members develop a strong level of mutual understanding that a Wiraqocha leadership group can be successful at sharing a common dream of the future, and working effectively towards its realization. However, building mutual understanding and speaking the same national language are quite different things – and the latter does not necessarily lead to the former. This is what the great Irish playwright George Bernard Shaw (1856–1950) certainly had in mind when he famously maintained that "America and Britain are two nations divided by a common language." I still remember the fifteen-strong leadership group of the logistics function in one of Europe's leading carmakers who, when asked to write down the definition of the word "logistics", produced fifteen very different descriptions ranging from "integrated supply chain" to "global transportation systems"! These people came from six different countries (including Britain and the US) and were all fluent in English, and twelve of them had worked together in the same logistics group for the previous three years, while others went back even further. This is far from being an isolated example. It highlights the fact that – beyond sharing the same linguistic base – any group of people really only becomes capable of building mutual understanding after its members have taken explicit steps to develop shared meanings around key words. This is often the result of a long, deliberate and patient process involving the development of certain tools such as a dictionary of key terms. Once more, the experience of together developing such tools is as important to the group as the tools themselves, because it represents concrete steps towards shaping a common culture of mutual understanding.

Patience in developing a common language is not to be confused with the general character trait of patience either. In fact, I found that all of the extraordinary organizations portrayed in this book were both extremely impatient to achieve their own ambitious commitments, and remarkably persevering in building mutual understanding within their Wiraqocha leadership groups. In the case of the Renault–Nissan alliance, for example, Carlos Ghosn started out his COO tenure in Japan by asking a mixed team of French and Japanese managers to create a dictionary of about 100 key English words. To many observers around the globe, this looked like an ominous waste of time that would set the tone for a predictable corporate disaster of catastrophic proportions. However, for Carlos Ghosn and his Wiraqocha leaders, developing a mutual understanding from the outset was crucial not only to share their astonishing dream and common mission of turning Nissan around in less than three years, but also to achieve this aspiration well *ahead* of the deadline.

To sum it up, the greater an organization's ability to attract, inspire, coach and retain Wiraqocha leaders, the stronger their ability to create new and extraordinarily positive futures. Furthermore, as the first Hamawtha showed us, the ultimate mark of true Wiraqocha leaders is their passionate vocation to discover new paths by tirelessly walking unknown trails and by immersing themselves in journeys every bit as fascinating as the one taken by Wiraqocha in the majestic Andean landscape. Like the legendary Hamawtha's trek, these travellers' journeys invariably start with a revelation. Just a few miles into their courageous trips, Wiraqocha leaders pause as if suddenly assailed by the urge to gather additional strength to fulfil their missions. They look around, and almost by magic find multiple responses that will help them continue their trip with renewed energy and determination. And this is the story that will unfold in the following chapter.

5

the fifth key:
tinkunacuy

....

Lejano, lejano,	*(Far away, far away,*
río amado,	*beloved river,*
llévame	*carry me*
con mi joven amante,	*with my young lover,*
por en medio de las rocas,	*through the stones,*
entre las nubes de lluvia.	*between the rainy clouds.)*

Ancient *huayno* (traditional Andean rural folk music) lyrics from Calca, Peru, recorded in 1946 by Peruvian novelist José María Arguedas (1911–69)[1]

SWIMMING WITH A YOUTHFUL VIGOUR that belied his advanced age, Emilio Huamán Huillca left the rough river and, reaching a large nearby stone, sat down in quiet contemplation, seemingly unconcerned by the fabulous jungle that surrounded us. I felt that the old sage was about to tell me another story of ancient Peru. After a few minutes of silence, he smiled and, looking at me with benevolent eyes, started to speak in his soothing tones. Huamán Huillca said that, many thousands of years before Columbus reached the South American mainland in 1498, ancient Peruvians had coined two words that defined their romantic relationships. When loving sparks scintillated between a man and a woman, then *suanacuy* followed. The enraptured couple robbed each other (*sua* means to steal in the Qheshwa language) so that, all of a sudden, a young girl disappeared from her *ayllu* (an Andean community). If they realized that a young boy was also nowhere to be found, their parents would just murmur "suanacuy" to each other with an understanding smile. This meant that there was nothing to worry about. The couple had departed to a secret place, just the two of them. Maybe to the ruins of some abandoned temple down the valley, or maybe to some enchanted forest, or a captivating mountainside next to a blue lake. After a few days, the young couple would return to the community. If their eyes were shining, everybody in the ayllu knew they would enter into *tinkunacuy*. The word *tinku* signifies encounter, and in the context of a romantic relationship it meant that the two of them would start living together like a married couple. They would share their dreams together, and if after a few months their tinkunacuy turned out to be all they had imagined, they would formally join their lives together before their community. Otherwise, they would simply leave each other and get ready for suanacuy with another person.

The widespread practice of tinkunacuy in ancient Andean society suggests a degree of egalitarian treatment for women that had no real equivalent in Western societies until the second half of the twentieth century. It also reveals that in ancient Peru women were as free as men when it came to exercising their sexuality. The priests who accompanied the Spanish invaders of the Inca realms in the first half of the sixteenth century were scandalized by tinkunacuy. It puzzled them that ancient Peruvians could, at the same time as practising tinkunacy, also be monogamous, and that adultery could bring strict punishment for both parties. Thus, observing sixteenth-century Andean society at first hand, one baffled Spanish chronicler wrote that:

There were true marriages amongst our Indians; however, they did not know the name for it and these days they use our name. [...] Each man has only one wife, with whom they share their entire lives. [...] In the same way, women can marry only one man and a man could not repudiate his wife. [...] Even if single men and women are far more licentious than us, and fornication is allowed, they punish adultery a lot more severely than we [the Spaniards] do. These barbarians despise virginity

– which amongst any other men is looked upon with esteem and honour – as a vile and insulting thing [...] and therefore single women enter into sexual relationships quite freely with any man they fancy. Men do not get upset if their brides do not arrive virgins to the wedding – quite the contrary, it disappoints them to discover that their wives are still virgins because they think it means that nobody loved them. From this error derives the abominable abuse that nobody takes a wife without having met her in advance and tried her for many days and months and – it is shameful to say it – only good concubines become good wives.[2]

Because of these kinds of perceptions, the Spanish conquistadors decided during the second half of the sixteenth century to teach these "barbarians" their own brand of civilization. Across the Andean communities, they transformed the practice of tinkunacuy into "servinacuy" (from the Spanish word *servir*, meaning to serve). This was much more than a change of name, though. From then on, the relationship was no longer to be an equal one. Servinacuy was about one partner – and you can easily guess which – serving the other. And, while the dominant partner kept extensive privileges, the other was left with comparatively few rights. Fortunately, tinkunacuy survived in enough remote Andean communities to make a comeback within the more liberal context of 21st-century Western culture. (In an ironic twist, in 2006 one of my Spanish friends was visiting Peru. With no prior knowledge of tinkunacuy, but after having discovered it in his travels, he expressed to me his impression that "the Andeans are finally learning to apply our modern egalitarian treatment of women" in their ancient communities.)

There is more to tinkunacuy than meets the eye. The partners expect – and are expected by the community – to marry, and so they prepare mentally and emotionally as individuals beforehand. Then both partners give the best of each other openly, truthfully and respectfully, to experience life together and nurture shared dreams of a new future as a married couple. However, at the same time, the community also knows that the test may not succeed and makes it clear to the couple that this will be just fine. As a result, the two of them feel free to try out a new life together unburdened by expectations of a long-term commitment. Tinkunacuy thus resolves for the Andean people the timeless paradox of building solid conjugal relationships. On the one hand, a couple does get the chance to build its shared dreams of the future together. On the other, they get to know each other, take risks and experience first-hand the practicalities and uncertainties of cooperating with each other as a couple before entering a lifelong commitment.

Successful creators of the future operate in ways that closely parallel the dynamics of tinkunacuy. They start out by forming a group of Wiraqocha leaders; in other words, individuals who share a radical dream of a new future as well as a purposeful mission to realize it, and who demonstrate the qualities of wholeness, tolerance, generosity, walk-the-talk and patience in their behaviour. As a next step, these Wiraqocha leaders undergo a period of social initiation and experimentation that usually lasts a few months and resembles tinkunacuy in three essential aspects. First, these Wiraqocha leaders put their group chemistry to the test by developing mutual trust, support and cooperative relationships amongst them. Next, they go about nurturing a creative environment to try innovative ways of realizing in practice their shared dream of a new future. This process is not abstract. On the contrary, it typically leads to a concrete prototype of the new future that can be rolled out on a larger scale. Third, the Wiraqocha leaders test their prototype of a new future, ensuring that it involves a fresh set of multicomplementors. The latter are players whose products, services or technologies reduce the costs of building the new prototype of the future and increase its attractiveness to people. Multicomplementors have an almost magical effect on the prototype that is being built, making even the most radical and unthinkable ideas of a new future possible.

In contrast, many groups and organizations that fail to create new futures start by instilling a strong sense of hierarchy within their teams without first going through their social initiation and experimentation stages. In other words, they basically forget about tinkunacuy and instead go straight into a sort of servinacuy. As a result, they typically struggle to nurture an open and trusting environment that stimulates real creativity. Accordingly, their prototypes of a new future tend to represent small changes to the status quo and involve few or no new additions of multi-complementors. When rolled out in the real world, these proto-types, rather than powerfully shaping a new future, will introduce barely noticeable variations to the current situation.

❊ *multicomplementors*

As mentioned, when it comes to creating the future, the practice of engaging in an initial period of socialization and experimenta-tion – so-called tinkunacuy – ought to result in the design of a concrete prototype underpinned by an innovative use of multi-complementors. The latter notion evolved from the idea of "com-plementors" developed during the late 1990s within the fields of game-theory and management strategy. In 1997, the American game-theorists Barry J. Nalebuff and Adam M. Brandenburger posited that in addition to buyers, suppliers, substitutes, new entrants and competitors there exists a sixth market force, which they called "complementors". Complementors were defined as players whose products or services created an extra profit for any given company either by increasing demand for its products and services or by reducing its costs. More specifically, Nalebuff and Brandenburger maintained that:

 A player is your complementor if customers value your product more when they have the other player's product than when they have your product alone.[3]

[...]

A player is your complementor if it's more attractive for a supplier to provide resources to you when it's also supplying the other player than when it's supplying you alone. A player is your competitor if it's less attractive for a supplier to provide resources to you when it's also supplying the other player than when it's supplying you alone.[4]

[...]

Customers and suppliers play symmetric roles. Competitors and complementors play mirror-image roles.[5]

This is a two-fold definition of complementors, from a customer (demand-side) and a supplier (cost-side) perspective respectively. Examples of complementors from the customer side are organizations offering sausages and mustard, or Scotch whisky and ice. Many customers will appreciate their sausages more when seasoned with mustard, or would rather have whisky on the rocks than drink it straight. Similarly, a business whose use of another company's supplier allows the latter to cut prices across the board is an example of a complementor on the supplier side. Nalebuff and Brandenburger gave the following illustration of the fact that many companies are *both* competitors and complementors with respect to their main suppliers:

American and Delta [airlines] compete for landing slots and gates. But although they are competitors for airport facilities, they are complementors with respect to Boeing, a key supplier. When American and Delta decide to commission the next generation airplane, it's much cheaper for Boeing to design a new plane for both airlines together than to design a new plane for each of them separately. Most of the development costs can be shared, and the greater demand helps Boeing move down the learning curve faster, too.[6]

Significantly, Nalebuff and Brandenburger noted that the same logic of complementors also applies to specific activities taking place under the roof of a single organization. They give the example of the US government defence programmes, where cutting the funds of some development projects, such as fighter planes, increased the costs of other defence programmes that share common development activity in the areas of avionics and navigation. Similarly, within any sizable company, a specific division can share common suppliers, logistical operations and the like, with other divisions of the same company. Killing off one of these supply-side complementors may sharply increase the company's costs across the board.

Although Nalebuff and Brandenburger did not explicitly point this out, some players can be complementors from both the customer and the supplier side. These are what I call multicomplementors. A multicomplementor is any player that simultaneously makes a customer value your product or service more *and* makes it more attractive for multiple suppliers to provide resources to you. It may sound magical and decidedly odd to many, but very visible examples of both complementors and multicomplementors are all around us, only they are sometimes called different things. For example, when you read in the business media about two major automotive players having just entered into a "strategic alliance" to collaborate in product development and procurement, this could also have been described as an agreement to turn two large companies into each others' multicomplementors. This will especially be the case if, as a result of the alliance, one partner's superior product design helps the other launch more alluring products for its customers, and if the two players' main suppliers will see it as considerably more attractive to provide resources to both partners together instead of each of them separately. Likewise, when you read in the press that a value airline has just opened a new route that involves utilizing a previously under-used airport near a major city, this often provides another example of multicomplementors. In 1995, for instance, when easyJet started its first international route, it initially decided to use Luton airport – at that time little used – instead of the major London airports such as Heathrow or Gatwick. This represented considerably lower airport costs for the company (which both Luton airport and its suppliers were happy to provide, as this allowed renovation of the facilities and significant expansion of the business), and happy customers, as, in 1995, Luton airport was uncrowded and within easy reach of central London.

However, in spite of reading about them almost daily in the media, many people fail to recognize multicomplementors. Nalebuff and Brandenburger give us an insight into why this might be the case:

 People are so accustomed to viewing the business world in warlike terms that even when other players are both competitors and complementors, they tend to see them as only competitors and fight against them. They focus on the evil Mr Hyde and overlook the good Dr Jekyll.[7]

Invariably, the radical new futures created by the extraordinary organizations that are portrayed in this book are based upon an innovative use of multicomplementors. When creating a new future, the discovery of novel multicomplementors is in fact a crucial aspect of the social initiation and experimentation phase that we metaphorically call tinkunacuy. In the case of the 1999 strategic alliance between Renault and Nissan, engaging in a very deliberate tinkunacuy period created a platform to turn two massive players – which most conventional financial analysts would have only described as potential "competitors" – into very active multicomplementors. This wasn't an obvious or straightforward challenge at all. As we have seen, most observers had actually dismissed the idea of a successful French–Japanese automotive alliance as unrealistic, calling it a disaster in the making even before Renault and Nissan had the opportunity to fully unveil their plans. However, the way in which the alliance was originally formed provides a powerful illustration of how the initial socialization and experimentation period can become a decisive element in turning an unlikely dream of the future into reality, against all the odds.

❊ *the social initiation of a French–Japanese marriage*

The Renault–Nissan alliance in March 1999 required the realization of a radical dream of a new future that most rational individuals at the time saw as nearly impossible to accomplish in the real world. It is easy to understand why. Not only was this the first time in the history of capitalism that a sizable Western company had joined with a giant Asian multinational. It was also the fact that Nissan was essentially bankrupt and Renault had – at best – a rather mixed performance track record. But it was the psychological and historical barriers that were the most formidable. Here was Japan's second largest carmaker, historically a proud symbol of the country's industrial might, not only in financial dire straits, but about to be headed and fixed by a team of foreigners from a Western company. Across vast sectors of Japanese society, this was simply inconceivable. But this was not all. In order to fix Nissan, the company's new leadership would have to resort to "Western style" measures – such as massive lay-offs, plant closures and the elimination of huge numbers of suppliers – that were so far from the Japanese historical approach to management that financial analysts at the time unanimously considered them to be unviable in Japan.

Renault–Nissan was much more than just a radical business initiative. If successful, it would completely change Japanese business culture and have an irreversible impact on the whole of Japanese society. Similarly, the way in which Western countries looked at Japan – as an admirable yet culturally distant nation where the Western way of doing things would never work – would change beyond recognition if the alliance succeeded. Centuries-old prejudices held by both cultures stood to be fundamentally challenged.

Which is exactly what happened. By 2004, Renault–Nissan had easily become the most successful international alliance of its size in the history of modern capitalism. When it was first announced, it was called "a marriage of desperation for both parties". It would have been more accurate to have called it a tinkunacuy period that would become a long-term marriage.

In June 1998, Renault's president, Louis Schweitzer, disregarded advice from investment bankers against a direct approach and wrote to Nissan's president, Yoshikazu Hanawa, proposing broad strategic cooperation. He sent a similar letter to the president of Mitsubishi Motor Cars (MMC). Hanawa's answer, unlike MMC's, was quick and enthusiastic. In July 1998, an internal support team sketched a framework for cooperation. Schweitzer and Hanawa met a dozen times over the ensuing months to learn to trust each other and imagine a future alliance between their companies.

Hanawa gave an insight into the atmosphere the two leaders created during these initial stages:

 With many people around, it is difficult to tell each other the truth, and that is why I decided to negotiate alone. [...] I believe the process leading up to an alliance is all about telling the truth; dishonesty only makes the process longer. [...] I was impressed with Mr Schweitzer's courageous decision to embrace a new business opportunity.

After their initial meetings, from July to December 1998 Schweitzer and Hanawa picked 100 engineers and managers from both companies to work together in joint study teams without any formal objective. Instead, they went through a six-month living experiment of free exchanges with the aim of forging a formal alliance between the two companies. What the companies did during this period of social initiation explains much of the subsequent success of their alliance.

As a first step, the 100 engineers and managers were encouraged to drop their mental stereotypes about France and Japan and concentrate on hard business fact-finding. Free from cultural stereotypes and from following pre-conceived goals, the teams set a voyage of discovery in motion. Some of those involved recall the prevailing feelings:

 The kind of information that we were sharing with each other prior to the alliance agreement was a very rare case ... since both sides had strong individual needs to make themselves stronger, the joint study took place sincerely.

It was extraordinary in terms of synergies. We really believed in it. [...] Quite frankly, we were so complementary in terms of geography, products, and personality ... so we had great confidence.

By working together with neither prejudices nor pre-established goals, the teams found a common ground as well as concrete opportunities for collaboration between the two companies. They created an initial prototype of how the alliance could work, fully backed up with the most relevant data. Armed with this hard business information, in October 1998 Schweitzer prepared a two-page mock press release entitled "Nissan and Renault join forces".

Schweitzer explained:

 We had to move closer strategically, but it could not be a simple acquisition or a merger, because a Franco-Japanese merger is no easy matter... I suggested to him [Hanawa] that three people from Renault should become members of the Nissan board of directors: the COO, the vice-president of product planning and the deputy chief financial officer. I only asked for those three.

Hanawa observed:

 I did not agree with it [the mock press release] from the start, of course. But I was not surprised. Through our discussions, I felt that Mr Schweitzer always had a more comprehensive view of the partnership than I did.

On 10 November, Schweitzer, Ghosn (who would become COO and later CEO of Nissan) and Douin made a presentation to the Nissan board of directors describing the benefits of a large-scale collaboration between the two companies. The presentation drew heavily on the findings of the joint study teams. No formal commitment was yet in sight, but it was decided that the work of the joint study teams would continue until December 1998.

Both Renault's Schweitzer and Nissan's Hanawa had clear ideas of what they wanted from a strategic alliance. But they were unfamiliar to each other and had no history of working together. As in tinkunacuy, they set a living process of social initiation in motion to test their companies' ability to work cooperatively and deliver on the promise of a shared future. The process itself had useful outcomes: to allow for joint discoveries, to develop an initial prototype of the alliance, to test their ability to share knowledge trustingly and openly, and to create new social capital in the form of valuable social networks between the two companies. The six-month social initiation process also gave Renault an advantage over competitive suitors such as Ford or DaimlerChrysler, as it then was. The latter companies resorted to a more conventional due diligence process. In other words, they carried out static analytical evaluations rather than an actual experiment of social collaboration, and focused on finding synergies based on past and current strengths, rather than on jointly imagining a shared future. It is in fact revealing to compare Renault–Nissan's approach to social initiation, and what this led to during the subsequent negotiation stages of their alliance, with what happened to some of their competitors who took a more conventional approach to initiating their own strategic alliances.

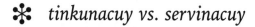 *tinkunacuy vs. servinacuy*

March 1999 saw two archetypal approaches to alliance negotiation and closure at play in the international car industry. On the one hand, Juergen Schrempp, at the time CEO of DaimlerChrysler (formed in May 1998 after the "merger of equals" between German Daimler Benz and American Chrysler), had a two-month due diligence carried out to assess the prospect of an alliance with Nissan. Then, on 9 March, he met at length with his management board in a hotel on the shores of Lake Geneva. A "green team" of company managers focused on the likely benefits of an alliance with Nissan. A "red team" focused on the drawbacks. After listening to both sides, Schrempp and his management team made a decision. The next day, Schrempp flew to Tokyo and met for three hours with Nissan's Hanawa.

DaimlerChrysler broke off alliance talks with Nissan after that meeting. Soon after, following a similar process, DaimlerChrysler entered into an equity alliance with the ailing Japanese carmaker MMC, wherein the former acquired a 34 per cent stake in the latter for US$2.1 billion. When signing that deal, Schrempp remarked:

 They [MMC] are the ideal partners for us.

Renault's approach to negotiating an alliance with Nissan was different. In their case, both the substance and the style of their alliance negotiations were an organic result of what the two companies achieved during their social initiation stages. In other words, these negotiations were not just about signing an alliance deal following a sound due diligence assessment. Rather, the prospective allies enacted a process of social commitment that codified the mutual pledges stemming from their earlier experiment of working together. This is made evident by examining the negotiations of the Renault–Nissan alliance in greater detail.

In August 1998 Schweitzer had already proposed to Hanawa:

 We have a firm and trusting relationship. To make our relationship stronger, why not think about holding each other's shares?

To which Hanawa replied:

 Nissan, frankly, has no money to spend on buying Renault stock.

The Frenchman responded:

 We can talk about this again in the future. From Renault's point of view, there is no future for us if we cannot work together with Nissan.

The proposal soon became that Renault would buy a stake in Nissan. Hanawa outlined four conditions any foreign buyer had to meet: to keep the Nissan name, protect jobs, promote restructuring under the lead of Nissan and pick a CEO from inside Nissan. Schweitzer did not object. At the same time, Hanawa told Schweitzer Nissan would need to raise US$6 billion in cash. This was well above Schweitzer's US$3 billion limit. In November 1998, Hanawa visited DaimlerChrysler's headquarters and was greeted with a proposal to invest in Nissan. He flew to Paris the next day to inform Schweitzer that he planned to continue negotiations with the German-American carmaker. A disappointed Schweitzer remarked:

 We cannot provide the amount of cash Nissan needs. If Renault cannot tie up with Nissan we will eventually be driven out of the market.

However, on 10 March 1999, DaimlerChrysler's Schrempp abruptly called off alliance talks with Nissan. Hanawa considered his options. He decided to approach Ford's CEO Jacques Nasser, with whom he'd had earlier contact.

Before he could do so, Hanawa received a confidential note from Schweitzer saying that there was hope that Renault could make a much larger investment in Nissan than he had proposed earlier. But Schweitzer requested that, no later than 13 March, Hanawa sign a "freeze" agreement preventing Nissan from approaching other carmakers until talks with Renault were completed or called off. Hanawa flew to Paris. After inspecting the "freeze" agreement, he still could not pin down the exact amount of Renault's investment in Nissan. "Please trust me," said Schweitzer.

Hanawa signed the "freeze" agreement. On 16 March 1999, the Renault board approved a US$5.4 billion investment to purchase a 36.6 per cent stake in Nissan. The following day, Renault and Nissan announced a signed alliance agreement that closely resembled the two-page mock press release that had been written back in October 1998 during the social initiation process of the alliance. Said Schweitzer:

 The decision we made during the final negotiations was not to change our position. It was an important choice on our part to say: "It's not because DaimlerChrysler is not around that we are changing our proposal." I decided not to [change the proposal] because I felt it would destroy the relationship of trust, which was indispensable for us to work together.

Hanawa added:

 The fact that we agreed on the terms of equal position was important for me, as dominance destroys motivation.

Over the next three months, a new leadership team was set in place at Nissan, made up of 18 French managers from Renault plus 200 Japanese managers selected by the new COO, Carlos Ghosn. Some of these had actively participated in their companies' tinkunacuy experiences over the July–December 1998 period. In July 1999 – exactly one year after Renault and Nissan had initiated their successful corporate tinkunacuy – this large group divided itself into nine sub-teams and set to work. They picked up the initial prototype of the alliance fashioned during their tinkunacuy experiences, and decided to scale it up and roll it out under the name Nissan Revival Plan (NRP). As described in detail later, in Chapter 6, the NRP was essentially built on the predicament of achieving seemingly impossible commitments in a very short time. For example, in October 1999 Nissan publicly announced that it would launch 22 new car models in just three years, a feat that only Toyota had been able to attempt in the past and that contrasted sharply with Nissan's previous track record of under half a dozen new car models over the previous three years. In addition, Ghosn promised that Nissan would return to profitability in just one year, something that seemed inconceivable to most people – including many Nissan employees – based on the company's continuous losses over the 1990s.

Beyond these examples of exceedingly ambitious commitments, the NRP was, at heart, about transforming Renault and Nissan into each other's massive multicomplementors. From then on, Nissan's new models would acquire some of Renault's trademark design flair and marketing sophistication, to help make them popular with customers once more and reverse a decade-long negative value trend of the Nissan brand. At the same time, working together helped both Renault and Nissan generate massive cost reductions, a crucial part of which came from both companies' key suppliers, who saw it as much more attractive to work with the new alliance than to deal with either party separately. Creating a platform to work effectively as multicomplementors was crucial for Renault–Nissan to become recognized as one of the world's most successful alliances by March 2004.

By way of contrast, in April 2004 DaimlerChrysler announced that it would pull out from MMC, ending their alliance in failure. These companies experienced no tinkunacuy period during 1998; instead, during the early months of 1999 they moved hastily to conclude their alliance after a two-month analytical due diligence. During the latter, DaimlerChrysler and MMC did not go through anything that even remotely resembled Renault and Nissan's imaginative exchanges and joint discovery trips. The DaimlerChrysler–MMC alliance therefore had nothing comparable to the audacious prototype of a radical new alliance that Renault and Nissan had dreamed and built together with the participation of so many people from both organizations. As a result, their goals seemingly aimed at gradually fixing long-standing MMC problems rather than creating a radical new future for both partners. Rolf Eckrodt – the DaimlerChrysler executive heading the turnaround of MMC – did not have Carlos Ghosn's radical commitments for the launch of new models, and some of his organizational changes – such as reducing the average age of executives from 58.4 to 54.4 years – looked rather modest by comparison. The lack of an open and truthful social initiation period was also to prove disastrous for the DaimlerChrysler–MMC alliance, as Eckrodt failed to fully grasp the significance of a decade-old defects problem that MMC had played down for decades. When the company publicly acknowledged these problems in 2000, it never quite recovered from the loss of reputation and the associated product recalls, especially in the critical US market.

Interestingly, the US$38 billion merger between Daimler Benz and Chrysler also ended in failure, in May 2008 – exactly ten years after it was initiated and dubbed "a marriage made in heaven" by its former CEO Juergen Schrempp. In a similar way to the 1999 alliance with MMC, the DaimlerChrysler merger underwent model due diligence, but no real tinkunacuy period. Accordingly, the joining companies made two firm commitments publicly: to obtain US$1.4 billion in savings during the first year of the merger (equivalent to just over one per cent of the combined companies' annual turnover), and to complete the integration process within three years. In a way, DaimlerChrysler's approach to merger integration was opposite to the exceedingly audacious commitments and the powerful platform for multi-complementor work that Renault and Nissan would set out to build so quickly in mid 1999. When, after achieving their early post-merger savings, it became apparent in late 1999 that the former Daimler Benz and Chrysler would be managed as separate entities in order to maintain the integrity of their brands and their distinct pre-merger corporate cultures, the joint company's share price experienced a sustained period of decline. Sadly, when it finally moved to reverse this situation, DaimlerChrysler would eventually discover it was a case of too little, too late for both customers and investors.

In November 2000, one prominent shareholder, Kirk Kerkorian, actually sued DaimlerChrysler for US$9 billion, claiming that investors were fraudulently induced to support the German company's 1998 purchase of Chrysler, and that the German executives then running the company never intended to live up to their promise that the combination of Daimler Benz and Chrysler would be a "merger of equals".[8] As a result of all this, in spite of a few strong years, by 2005 Chrysler started to be increasingly looked upon by their German partner as a financial drag that threatened to engulf the entire company. Thus the May 1998 marriage between Daimler Benz and Chrysler ended in an unceremonious split in May 2008. By contrast, in 2008 Renault–Nissan – the so-called "marriage of desperation" born of a successful tinkunacuy – was in its eighth consecutive year of posting record financial results, and represented a benchmark model for successful cross-cultural alliances all around the globe.

✳ *many roads to tinkunacuy*

Creators of the future do not always need to engage in spectacular mergers, acquisitions or alliances to unleash the seemingly magical power of both tinkunacuy and multicomplementors. Often this happens organically. The corporate tinkunacuy period that Amancio Ortega organized in early 1975 – twelve years after leaving his job at the Spanish department store La Maja – included his own wife at the time, Rosalía, his elder brother Antonio, and Antonio's wife Primitiva. In 1963 they had together created Goa Confecciones in the Spanish city of A Coruña, manufacturing dressing gowns with La Maja as their main customer. But by 1975 their dream was not only to manufacture apparel, but also to distribute and retail it. The fact that none of the members of the original Goa Confecciones group apparently remember who had the initial idea of Zara, or who came up with that name in the first place, testifies to the strong atmosphere of team-based creativity that pervaded this experimentation phase. The group actually decided to experiment with two prototypes showcasing two very different approaches to retailing clothes. The first prototype was a conventional store called Sprint that sold Goa lingerie and other well-known brands, mostly from Spain. The second prototype, called Zara, opened on 15 May 1975. This wasn't a conventional store. In Zara, Amancio Ortega and his team tried two novel ideas, born of their own direct experiences with customers. Cecilia Monllor, author of *Zarápolis*, describes how this new idea was articulated in the minds of Ortega's team members:

 People, especially women, are interested in fashion, new things, they are attracted by forward-looking design, but most people cannot afford the prices in the boutiques. We [Amancio

> Ortega's team] cannot afford to accumulate unsold stock either, nor we can live ignoring the trends. Let us manufacture inexpensive clothes that look very much like those that are sold in the exclusive boutiques, and let us do it at the same rhythm of the changing tastes of society.[9]

This idea would become mainstream in the textile industry by the end of the twentieth century, but in 1975 it was absolutely revolutionary. It implied creating three novel things. First, a just-in-time approach to manufacturing that at that time was being pioneered by Toyota in the automotive industry, but was unheard of in the textile sector. Second, it needed a state-of-the-art logistics operation, capable of quickly and constantly replenishing Zara's shelves with new designs as the old models were sold. And third, it required a cutting-edge information system that smoothly connected and monitored the entire Zara process, from the design shop all the way to the retail store.

The Sprint prototype coexisted with Zara, but after four years it was closed down. The Zara prototype did work, however. In fact, over the next decade and a half the Zara model exploded in Spain and became ready to conquer the international markets, which is what happened in 1989, with the opening of a Zara store in Portugal and an emblematic store in L'Opéra, Paris. The next decade witnessed an unprecedented escalation that saw Zara stores multiply on a global scale. Growth continued unabated over the ensuing decade, turning the early prototype into the world's largest clothing retailer by June 2009.

By then, Zara's pioneering just-in-time operations – inspired by Toyota's manufacturing approach – had become the wonder of the textile world. All production, regardless of its origin, was received in two distribution centres in Spain: A Coruña, serving the Iberian, American and Asian markets; and Zaragoza, serving the European market. Distribution to the European market was by truck; the rest of the world was replenished by air, even if that entailed additional costs to the final product. Deliveries were not held back until an economic order quantity was achieved; instead, they followed strict periodic delivery schedules (twice weekly), even if that meant sending a half-empty truck across Europe.

Ortega involved himself in every detail of the business, and even in the logistics. He decided that no existing retail warehouse system would suit Zara's requirements, and so in 1984 he set out to invent his own. As the business expanded rapidly around the world, he looked at the operations of DHL, the courier company, to see how they organized themselves in order to send parcels to so many different destinations. Once again, he adapted, as in many other areas of the business, a solution from another industry that best suited his vision for success.

Because formal pre-season forecasting and planning existed only for basic items – and no forecast at all was used for fashion items – replenishment of the stores was completely demand-driven. To accommodate this practice, store managers made their own demand estimations, deciding what and how much to order, placing two orders per week for each section of the store – kids, men and women. Twice a week, store managers downloaded electronically the current product catalogue, placing their order within 24 hours. Ordering deadlines were stringent – if a store failed to meet them, the distribution centre simply repeated their previous order by default. This deadline-orientation was required to synchronize the stores with the delivery schedule. Added to this were sales incentives, which served to keep store managers aligned with the best interests of the company.

One logistics manager at Zara commented:

 My biggest challenge was keeping the system effective in the context of the chain's 20 to 30 per cent annual growth.

Zara's early tinkunacuy experimentation phase had built an unprecedented and exciting customer experience for both women and men. Customers kept coming back because they could always find a plethora of new items at very affordable prices, and they knew that the store did not replace any designs that were sold out. It was now or never. So they chose to buy. Though invisible to them, this customer experience was made possible by literally hundreds of multicomplementors that allowed Zara to perform the seemingly magical operation of delivering new cheap-chic fashion items to thousands of stores all over the world twice a week while keeping costs – and prices – well below the industry norm.

In fact, unlike retailers such as H&M and Gap, Zara manufactured half of all the clothes it sold, which tended to be the trendier items that required faster delivery times. Moreover, and uniquely in the clothing industry, Zara did not outsource its logistical and delivery operations to third parties, but ran them itself. This gave Zara a multicomplementors base unmatched by any other fashion player. For example, H&M and Zara are multicomplementors because it is more attractive for shopping centres to offer many top apparel stores that together bring in more high-quality customers than either of them can do alone. In addition, the shopping centres' desire to have both H&M and Zara stores can result in better deals for each of the companies. However, besides these types of multicomplementors that are available to any top apparel retailer, Zara uniquely benefits from multicomplementors in the logistics industry as well. In other words, although they are normally regarded as different industries, over the second half of the 1980s Zara was the first fashion company that made multicomplementors out of leading logistics players such as DHL and even outstanding just-in-time manufacturers such as Toyota. Because of the revolutionary way in which it was built during those years, Zara's entire approach to apparel manufacturing and retailing casts a much wider net of potential multicomplementors than players like H&M or Gap can muster, giving the company additional ways of simultaneously making its customers happier and reducing costs.

Vincenzo Muccioli, founder of the San Patrignano community, is another example of a successful tinkunacuy leading to a revolutionary prototype of social work that incorporated novel multicomplementors. Over the first half of the 1970s, Muccioli had made a habit of befriending, listening to and helping drug-addicted youngsters living on the streets of Rimini. In the process, he had become convinced that these young people were not inherently sick but simply lacked the support of a family. In 1975, after a long conversation with his wife Antonietta, the two of them decided to engage in a daring experiment. They invited a few of these youngsters to live with them at their San Patrignano farmhouse near Rimini. These young people quickly became part of their family, sharing in all aspects of farm work. After three years, the Mucciolis discovered that their new family members had completely recovered from their addictions without the help of any drug substitute.

Thus, almost by accident, by the late 1970s the Mucciolis had created a powerful prototype that within less than twenty years would see San Patrignano become the world's largest and most effective drug rehabilitation community. This prototype added two new clusters of multicomplementors to the activity of drug recovery. On the one hand, any type of professional activity started up by San Patrignano – from high-quality wine production to artistic carpentry and premium artisan work – involved turning key players in each of those sectors of activity into multicomplementors of drug rehabilitation. For example, as mentioned in this book's Prelude, early on the community inexpensively acquired critical intellectual capital in the form of retired *maestri* (master artisans) in each of their designated professional activities. These *maestri* gladly donated their time to teach their unique skills to San Patrignano's youngsters. This was a most unusual set of multicomplementors to be associated with the therapeutic activity of drug rehabilitation. However, they resulted in the development of outstanding professional activities that not only helped self-finance the community through the sale of products and services to outside customers, but also constituted a central therapeutic element for drug recovery. On the other hand, both the Italian government and the Rimini local authorities soon discovered that the San Patrignano community was a very effective multicomplementor of public spending. For example, every year since it was founded in 1979, San Patrignano has saved the Italian state hundreds of years' worth of incarceration, equivalent to millions of euros. Moreover, the Rimini local authorities saw a revival of artisan activities that gave new work to the old *maestri* and helped get drug-addicted youngsters off the streets. As a result of all this, communities like San Patrignano have now helped the Italian government to spend taxpayers' money more efficiently, and to offer the country a steady supply of former drug addicts, completely rehabilitated and well trained, ready to join the nation's workforce.

✳ *the key to a successful tinkunacuy*

As the above examples suggest, tinkunacuy is a necessary step of social initiation and experimentation for all people embarking on a journey to build radically new and positive futures. It applies to all kinds of discovery journeys, involving large organizations, small companies or just start-ups; international groups of people or more culturally homogeneous ones; profitable ventures or socially minded initiatives. It can also take many forms, depending on the varied contexts in which it is applied. However, in all cases, tinkunacuy is a very natural initial step for any group that sets out to live their shared dreams of the future. And as DaimlerChrysler undoubtedly found out, skipping it can be very risky.

This raises the question of what it takes to make a successful tinkunacuy. The stories narrated in this chapter suggest three crucial factors. First, by far the best stage at which to engage in tinkunacuy is at the start of a journey. The initial mixed teams of employees from Renault and Nissan, the Amancio Ortega team that created Zara, and the Mucciolis all built a radical prototype of the future and set a tone of open exchanges, mutual trust, creative mindset and courageous experimentation that were to become decisive for their subsequent spectacular success. Groups that won't start out by carrying out tinkunacuy either realize it is much more difficult to do it further down the road, or simply find out the hard way what a great opportunity they missed at the start of their journeys.

Second, successful tinkunacuy requires a special kind of group mindset that drives great conversations about a prototype of the future. One aspect of this mindset has already been described in Chapter 1. It has been called a *trade-on mindset* – in other words the pervasive, deep-rooted predisposition to perceive and interpret reality with the mental eyes of being, doing and gaining much more with a lot less. As explained in detail in Chapter 1, a trade-on mindset is necessary for any group embarking on the building of a new future, because it imbues it with an optimistic and almost magical mental attitude that renders possible the seemingly impossible. Another aspect of the group mentality that is required for successful tinkunacuy is the multicomplementor mindset. It means looking at *any* players through the lens of cooperation. Not only is this crucial for creating a positive atmosphere for group work; it also helps the team identify the potential multicomplementors that will render their new prototype of the future both attractive to customers and cost effective. However, as previously mentioned, adopting a multicomplementor mindset is often rendered difficult because people sometimes make a mental habit of looking for "competitors" everywhere. This often leads to imagining a journey towards a new future predominantly in warlike terms. And this is not useful for successful tinkunacuy, nor does it facilitate the creative task of identifying potential multicomplementors. Instead, a more cooperative mindset tends to conceive a pool of mutually supportive players, where the new idea of the future can grow vigorously.

To help teams adopt a multicomplementor mindset, I invite them to participate in "multicomplementor simulations". I fashioned these group exercises after the "competitive simulations" that are sometimes used to train corporate executives, with the crucial difference that the emphasis is on creating great customer experiences underpinned by an innovative use of multicomplementors, rather than on fighting competitors. In multicomplementor simulations, typically a larger group is divided into sub-teams and given the challenge of radically reinventing a specific customer experience involving a certain product or service. In order to do this imaginatively, the team members go out to observe as many customers as possible engaging in their experience. Often the team members act as customers and go through those experiences themselves. In this way, almost naturally, they get to identify a number of multicomplementors that customers actually suggest to them, or that they imagine while going through the customer experiences themselves. Back in the meeting room, the teams engage in brainstorming sessions and positive discussions, trying to articulate a new customer experience that builds on the best aspects that they have both observed and tried. The process is repeated iteratively a number of times, until a concrete, visual prototype of the new experience is built. The prototype is tested with actual customers whose comments and feedback help refine it. The last step is to share, compare and contrast the various prototypes that have been built by the sub-teams. Multicomplementor simulations can be designed in various ways, involving just a few hours or an entire week. The key to their success is not the actual quality of the prototypes themselves, but the effect that this working process has in developing a multicomplementor mindset and in strengthening an attitude of cooperation within the team.

As a trade-on and multicomplementor mindset develops within the team, the ability to nurture an atmosphere that favours great conversations for creative exchanges and imaginative group prototyping work becomes a third key factor for a successful social initiation and experimentation process. A number of very creative organizations such as Diesel or IDEO have embedded this nurturing ability into their mainstream processes for new product development. Over the 1990s, Diesel's "nurturing process" helped it become one of the world's leading fashion powerhouses. This process encapsulated the company's culture of encouraging its people to be brave and courageous about expressing themselves freely without fear of being shamed. This means that Diesel employees, sometimes without formal design training, can create new collections or realize creative ideas within the company. Diesel's nurturing process was key for the company to set one of the world's most creative fashion teams in place without recourse to design stars. The company product and sales managers constantly travelled abroad to experience new things and gather novel ideas from the grassroots. Diesel's nurturing process then ensured that all these ideas and experiences were transformed into exciting prototypes of new fashion collections. The final choices were very much based on intuition. A Diesel executive said in 2004:

 The Diesel process is about rejecting control and limitations. It's about trying to reinvent continuously, about getting away from what you just did. Diesel is not a company that really built itself by grabbing the top talent from other clothing brands or graphic studios. It's nurtured them here. When you do any kind of creative work, you need to be brave. Because it is like exposing yourself. It is like being naked in a way. You really open yourself up to other people's approval, or their appreciation, or their ridicule.

Likewise, since it was founded in 1991, the influential industrial design firm IDEO in Palo Alto, California, applied a process and a context for nurturing great conversations leading to a myriad radical new prototypes – ranging from high-tech medical equipment to the first computer mouse for Apple – which have contributed to creating new futures around us. In July 1999, the ABC *Nightline* programme in the US aired a special report on IDEO's distinctive process. In it, news reporters challenged an IDEO team to completely reinvent a new and better shopping cart in just five days, and then filmed what happened as the team went about designing the new cart. The report was a classic for *Nightline*, becoming one of their most requested video/DVD products ever. In the report, we hear David Kelley, one of IDEO's co-founders, explaining some of the key factors behind IDEO's success:

 The point is that we are not actually experts at any given area. We are experts in the process of how you design stuff. So we don't care if you give us a toothbrush, a toothpaste tube, a tractor, a space shuttle or a chair. It's all the same to us. We want to figure out how to innovate by using our process, applying it.

[…]

It is one thing to be able to make a [new] product once in a while. But if you can build a culture and a process where you can routinely come up with new ideas: that's what companies really want.[10]

Watching the *Nightline* report on the company gives a unique insight into how IDEO teams so effectively nurture an environment and a process that stimulate creative exchanges and great conversations for group prototyping work. Underlying a cacophonous working context that looked as lively and colourful as a kindergarten playground, there was a hidden harmony and a rigorous process at work. The IDEO team itself was very diverse in gender, age span and professional backgrounds. They started out by choosing a facilitator and by defining their challenge very clearly: they would totally redesign a shopping cart so it would be safer, offer a better shopping and check-out experience, be less vulnerable to theft and cost no more to build and maintain than the current cart. This was a trade-on plan: getting a lot more for the same (or lower) cost. Next, they went out to observe and learn everything they could from people who built, used and repaired shopping carts. Back in IDEO, they shared all they had learned by taping photographs and pictures of what they had observed on to a big whiteboard. Amazingly, at IDEO's meeting room – at the very heart of Silicon Valley – there was neither a computer screen nor PowerPoint slides to be seen: only the big whiteboard. The team then went into a "deep dive": in other words, a brainstorming of sorts that follows clear rules ensuring that great conversations take place. These rules were posted on the walls so everyone could read them: "defer judgement", "build on the ideas of others", "encourage wild ideas", "go for quantity", "be visual", "stay focused on the topic" and "one conversation at a time". Over the next hour or so, hundreds of ideas flowed and ended up on the whiteboard. Afterwards, the team chose the best ideas by voting with Post-it notes. At this point they split the group into four sub-teams to build four different prototypes, each of them around a different need area: safety, lower theft, better shopping and improved checkout. The *Nightline* report ended with the four prototypes being integrated into one and shown around to a couple of supermarket employees, who provided feedback on it.

The above examples suggest that every journey for creating the future has to start by articulating the following elements: a group of Wiraqocha leaders bearing a collective mindset that favours trade-on thinking and cooperation; a playful context that stimulates creativity and self-expression; and a process to nurture an atmosphere of creative exchanges and great conversations for group prototyping work. The harmonious interplay of these three elements is key to a successful period of social initiation and experimentation that we have referred to in this chapter as tinkunacuy. When inspired by a radical dream of the future and the purposeful mission to realize it, these simple elements can articulate a concrete prototype that renders even the most implausible aspects of a shared dream both possible and visible. In spite of this – and however exciting – this prototype is just an initial step towards the creation of a new future. In the following chapter, you will discover what are the next steps towards making these radical prototypes become part of the future lives of people like you and me.

6

the sixth key:
gentlemen's promises

··

The irony of commitment is that it's deeply liberating – in work,
in play, in love. [...] To commit is to remove your head as the
barrier to your life.

From "The Way I See It" (cup no. 76, Starbucks), by Anne Morriss

ALL OF MARCUS TULLIUS CICERO'S rhetorical genius
was not enough to save his own life during a most dangerous age
in the history of ancient Rome. He openly took sides with Brutus
after that nobleman, together with other aristocrats, had Rome's
most powerful politician, Julius Caesar, killed in the Senate on 15
March 44 BC. A year after this fateful event, in a letter dated June
43 BC, Cicero confidently assured Brutus (who had by then taken
military control of northern Greece) that he could persuade Caius
Caesar Octavian (Julius Caesar's adopted son and designated
heir) to give up his political ambitions. Meanwhile, Cicero delivered a ferocious verbal onslaught against Antony, one of Julius
Caesar's trusted generals and probable successors, prompting the
Senate to declare Antony an outlaw. However, when Octavian
and Antony crafted an uneasy political alliance in September 43
BC, it was the beginning of the end for Cicero. The two auto-
crats agreed on a proscription, which was a brutal Roman way
of eliminating political enemies by summarily executing them.

Some historians maintain that Octavian – a former student of Cicero – strenuously tried to keep his former teacher's name off the proscription list. But Antony was unmoved. His henchmen caught up with the old man as he was trying to make his way out of Rome in order to join Brutus in northern Greece. He looked unkempt and weary after weeks of fleeing persecution, yet he drew aside the curtain of his litter and stretched out his neck, saying, "Here, veteran, if you think it right, strike." It is said that a few days after Cicero's execution, Fulvia, a former wife of one of Cicero's political enemies, took the dead man's head just before it was nailed on to the Speaker's Platform in the Roman Forum, opened its mouth and pierced its tongue with hairpins. These were violent times indeed.

In spite of his cruel death, historians remember Marcus Tullius Cicero as one of ancient Rome's greatest statesmen and a patriot who throughout his life fought to defend the Republic's ancient liberties against the monarchical tendencies of men like Caesar and Octavian. He is also hailed as one of the foremost speakers, linguists and literary authors in classical Latin. From the seventeenth to the nineteenth century, the formation period of most modern Western nation states, Cicero's life, speeches and writings inspired central aspects of the political constitutions of countries such as France, Great Britain and the US. In addition, Cicero's writings – covering a broad range of subjects that included moral duties, old age, friendship and piety – as well as his voluminous correspondence, much of it addressed to his friend Atticus, rank amongst the most influential works in Western culture. This is in part due to their quality and accessibility, which made them an important part of the teaching curricula of European schools up to the first half of the twentieth century. In particular, his refined letters became the source of countless aphorisms that were still popular in many European countries at the dawn of the 21st century.

It was in Italy – Cicero's home country – that I often heard one such aphorism, attributed to the great statesman, that asserts *Promissio boni viri est obligatio*, which can be translated as "A gentleman's promise is his duty". This old Latin proverb is frequently quoted in Italian transactional contexts in order to highlight the value of a person's honesty that both underpins and transcends any written agreement. However, in addition to this, I found that Cicero's classical adage encapsulates a key approach for certain individuals and organizations towards creating radically new and positive futures. From social institutions such as the San Patrignano drug rehabilitation community to fashion leader Zara, medical equipment giant Medtronic or the unlikely French–Japanese alliance between Renault and Nissan, consistent and timely delivery on clear gentlemen's commitments lies at the very heart of these organizations' uncanny ability to turn innovative small-scale prototypes into new futures for all of us. In order to grasp this seemingly magical capability, it is quite useful to go back in time to the venerable Roman Republic to properly understand how Cicero and his contemporary Roman citizens viewed a gentleman's promise.

❋ *a Roman gentleman's promise*

Let us start by acknowledging that Cicero clearly equates the value of a promise to the inherent qualities of the individuals making it. The phrase he uses to describe those qualities – *boni viri* – literally means good men, and has been only approximately translated to the word gentlemen, which carries a modern definition of certain characteristics associated with being good individuals. Interestingly, though, Cicero actually coined his own Latin term, *humanitas*, to define the attributes of "good men" or "gentlemen" in ancient Rome. This word is the root of many important English terms such as human, humankind, humanity, humane and humanism. As these English words suggest, *humanitas* encompasses the basic notions of what makes any individual human being human. For Cicero and his Roman contemporaries, the term *humanitas* carried two additional meanings. On the one hand, it denoted the essential attributes of civilized individuals that – in their view – made them collectively superior to the barbarian tribes living outside the boundaries of the Roman Republic. On the other, it included the character traits that made every civilized individual a unique *persona* – an individual person – distinct from any other human being.

Cicero's notion of *humanitas* carried strong practical connotations
that shed important light on the intrinsic nature of a gentleman's
promise, Roman-style. *Humanitas* in fact comprised several prag-
matic rules of conduct that embodied the very essence of what
commendable civilized behaviour meant for ancient Roman citizens. On the one hand, precepts such as *benevolentia* (goodwill),
mansuetudo (gentleness), *facilitas* (affability) and *severitas* (aus-
terity) characterized the manner in which all gentlemen ought
to conduct themselves within a civilized society. On the other
hand, precepts like *dignitas* (dignity, merit or reputation), *gravitas* (authority) and *observantia* (respect) represented the kind of
behaviour that defined every Roman citizen as a distinct individual person. How an individual citizen behaved according to
these practical precepts of *humanitas* determined the levels of
social credit accorded to him or her. This direct relationship
between an individual citizen's personal *humanitas* and his or her
corresponding level of social credibility was called in Latin *honoris*
– a central attribute of *humanitas*, from which the English word
honour comes.

Significantly, for ancient Roman citizens *honoris* and *dignitas* were
not exactly understood as intrinsic attributes of every human
being (which is the modern sense of these words, encapsulated,
for example, in the United Nations Bills of Human Rights), but
rather as the level of social esteem and credibility accorded to
every individual citizen as a result of the moral value and respect-
ability of his or her personal actions. Honour and dignity were,
for ancient Romans, personal attributes of *humanitas* that had to
be gained through individual actions, and were necessary in order
for every civilized person to perform subsequent acts with the
benefit of social credibility, recognition and respect. Not surprisingly, ancient Roman law was the first in history to protect its
individual citizens quite comprehensively from attacks against
their personal honour and dignity. Since these were not understood in abstract terms, but could be identified and weighed for
every individual citizen, damages to a person's honour and dignity
could be quantitatively assessed – and so could the reparations.

It follows that, in the ancient Roman Republic, an individual's personal degree of *humanitas* defined him or her in relation to their fellow citizens. A person's demeanour in addressing others, together with his or her acquired *honoris*, described them as properly as their own names. It is in this context that the Latin adage *Promissio boni viri est obligatio* ought to be understood. For the likes of Cicero, both the content and the consequences of a "gentleman's promise" were primarily referred to the specific degree of *humanitas* of the individual person making that promise in the first place, and only secondarily to the context within which that promise was made. In other words, a person's *dignitas* – and therefore his or her *honoris* – were at stake every time that person made a promise. This is why – within the moral context of *humanitas* – a gentleman's promise automatically became his or her personal duty. There was an increase in a person's *humanitas* every time he or she delivered on a promise, and this was good news for that person, because that meant a correspondingly higher social esteem and appreciation for him or her.

Unfortunately for Cicero, the opposite was also true. In the ancient Roman Republic, not delivering on a promise carried not only a loss of *honoris* for the procrastinator but also the personal obligation to face the full consequences of his or her failure. Cicero certainly knew this when, in January 43 BC, he proposed to the Senate that Octavian – who at the time was only twenty years old – be given Propraetor status. According to Roman law, this would make the ambitious young man eligible for military command. Many senators feared that, once he enjoyed that status, Octavian would use it to transform the Republic into a sort of monarchy, which had been the overt design of his adoptive father, Caesar. To allay these fears, Cicero, an outstanding politician who enjoyed the highest *gravitas* of any member of the Roman Senate, made a severe promise to his fellow senators:

 Members of the Senate, I promise, I undertake, I solemnly swear, that Caius Caesar [Octavian] will always be such a citizen as he is today and as we should especially wish and pray he should be.[1]

Sadly, this was not to be. As soon as he had Roman legions under his command, Octavian revealed himself as an extraordinarily

precocious politician and general, capable of coldly outman-
oeuvring far more experienced rivals to rapidly build himself a
strong power base as leader of the Caesarean party. He then used
his power to muster increasingly serious opposition to the Roman
Senate. At this point, Cicero realized that his only hope of saving
the Roman Republic from Octavian's monarchical designs was to
persuade Brutus to bring his troops to Rome in order to protect
the Senate. On 25 July, Cicero requested in the firmest way that
Brutus should "lend support to our tottering and almost collaps-
ing commonwealth at the earliest possible moment".[2] However,
in his last surviving letter, dated 27 July 43 BC, Cicero admitted
to Brutus that:

 As I write, I am in great distress because it hardly looks as
though I can make good my promises in respect to the young
man, boy almost, [Octavian], for whom I stood bail to the
Republic.[3]

Brutus was unimpressed by Cicero's requests, so Cicero desperately tried to address the Roman Senate. But they all remembered
his fateful promise made in January. Cicero had evidently lost a
lot of his *honoris* in front of those whose support he most needed.
So when Octavian marched on Rome at the head of eight legions
in August 43 BC, all that was left for Cicero was to organize his
own undignified escape from Italy. Deep down, though, he must
have known that it would all be to little avail and that the end
was near. When, on his way out of Rome, he reached his country
villa for the very last time, he ominously predicted, "I will die in
the country I have so often saved."[4] He did.

Cicero's last pledge to the Senate reminds us of two additional
characteristics of a gentleman's promise, Roman-style. On the
one hand, these promises required a strong degree of personal
courage by the individuals making them, as they involved very
serious risks to these individuals' *honoris* whenever they failed to
deliver. Partly as a result of this, gentlemen's promises were, for
the likes of Cicero, strongly emotional commitments. Not only
did they put their reputations at stake, but the ability to deliver
on one's promises was also inextricably linked – via *humanitas* – to
any civilized individual's essential sense of personal identity. It

is therefore apparent that in the ancient Roman Republic, a person's identity, word and personal dignity were, in fact, different facets of the same diamond.

On the other hand, gentlemen's promises were based on a strong sense of personal awareness and confidence in one's own capabilities rather than on the likelihood of these promises matching any predictable course of events. In other words, these promises denoted personal commitments to act and achieve a certain outcome rather than to adequately react to a foreseeable future scenario as it started to unfold. Cicero gave a dramatic example of this when he promised the Senate that Octavian would remain "such a citizen as he is today" should the young politician become legally eligible for military command. In 43 BC, not only was Octavian's likely defection from the Republican cause obvious to any intelligent observer such as Cicero, but also authoritarian generals such as Sulla, Marius and Octavian's own adoptive father, Julius Caesar, had in the past very seriously compromised the Roman Republic's ancient liberties. Therefore, when Cicero made his last, fateful promise to the Senate, he was being supremely confident of his own capacity to persuade the young politician to stay loyal to the Republic, rather than trusting Octavian's perfectly foreseeable political designs. Had Cicero made exclusively calculating promises rather than gentlemen's promises, he would have bided his time and reacted to Octavian's actions once they started to unfold more clearly. Only then would he have made promises that were aligned with the political tides.

❋ *strategic objectives aren't gentlemen's promises*

Something similar to this latter approach – attempting to predict a future scenario with a significant degree of accuracy and then react to it by making calculating promises that match the foreseen events – was articulated during the mid 1960s into a sort of scientific method to plan for the future within organizations. Denominated "strategic planning", over the 1970s and 1980s certain academics and corporate leaders embraced this method as a way to devise and implement strategies that would enhance the competitiveness of every business unit within an organization. It involved separating an organization's *thinking* functions (carried out by "strategic planners" whose main task was to devise business strategies) from the *implementation* activities (performed by managers who had to achieve specific objectives). The strategic planners created the planning horizon of an organization by constructing forecasts for the future. Depending on the type of environment an organization moved in, its planning horizon could range from just a few years to around ten years – or even more in exceptional cases. An organization's planning horizon typically included analytical forecasts for every central aspect of competitiveness, such as macroeconomic data, competitors' expected moves, customer trends and so on. Based on these forecasts, the strategic planners devised strategies for every single business unit of an organization. These strategies were then translated into strategic objectives for the managers of the organization, specifying the results that had to be achieved and the time available to obtain them.

Already in 1994 leading academics like Henry Mintzberg were highlighting some of the crucial differences between the "strategic planning" approach to detachedly calculating objectives for the future, and the "gentlemen's promises" way of personally committing to a future result:

 The problem is that [strategic] planning represents a calculating style of management, not a committing style. Managers with a committing style engage people in a journey. They lead in such a way that everyone on the journey helps shape its course. As a result, enthusiasm inevitably builds along the way. Those with a calculating style fix on a destination and calculate what the group must do to get there, with no concern for the members' preferences. But calculated strategies have no value in and of themselves; to paraphrase the words of sociologist Philip Selznick, strategies take on value only as committed people infuse them with energy. [5]

A committing style of management requires looking inward to one's own courage and capabilities in order to make honourable gentlemen's promises that can emotionally involve and motivate others. In this way, everyone in the group becomes subjectively convinced that the promised results can be achieved – even against the odds – and turns the commitment to achieving those results into their duty, at both individual and group level. Instead, the strategic planning approach to calculating objectives stems from an outward-looking attitude, underpinned by the assumption that the future can be accurately and objectively forecast. Mintzberg's criticism of this latter belief still applies many years after it was originally made:

> In 1965, Igor Ansoff wrote in his influential book *Corporate Strategy*, "We shall refer to the period for which the firm is able to construct forecasts with an accuracy of, say, plus or minus 20 per cent as the *planning horizon* of the firm." What an extraordinary statement! How in the world can any company know the period for which it can forecast with a given accuracy?

> The evidence, in fact, points to the contrary. While certain repetitive patterns, such as seasons, may be predictable, the forecasting of discontinuities, such as a technological innovation or a price increase, is virtually impossible. Of course, some people sometimes "see" such things coming. That is why we call them "visionaries". But they create their strategies in much more personalized and intuitive ways.[6]

Gentlemen's promises are not reactively made for a future that has been analytically forecast in advance. They are the subjective vehicles for certain individuals in creating a new future. They are neither detached nor analytically drawn but based upon an individual's inner awareness and self-confidence of what *can* be achieved. This inward confidence rests on a personal mixture of rational knowledge, intuition and experience that are actively projected into the future. If strategic planners' goals – established at the end of an impersonal and highly analytical process – are typically called strategic objectives, then the future results that a gentleman's promise aims at could be appropriately termed *subjectives*.

One of the main consequences of the subjectivity of gentlemen's promises is that their underlying ideas of the future often look radically different from what detached "experts" or even people at large consensually expect. This is because gentlemen's promises tend to rest on both the subjective imagination of the individuals making them as well as on their personal conviction that what has been imagined can in fact be achieved. By contrast, strategic planning objectives inevitably reflect the underlying assumptions of the forecasting methods utilized, which typically tend to favour linear projections of the past into the future. As a result, these objectives conceive futures that seldom represent radical discontinuities from the near past, but rather constitute gradual variations of the status quo. The underlying assumption of future states unfolding both linearly and gradually often makes objectives-minded experts overlook the sudden upheavals that are constantly and naturally shaping the future around us. Thus, when an individual's gentleman's promise to deliver a radically new future meets with certain people's scepticism, this isn't necessarily telling us anything factual about the likelihood of such a future becoming a reality. The difference is mainly in the eye of the beholder.

The subjective nature of gentlemen's promises can also be understood in another way, which perhaps constitutes the most important difference between it and scientific approaches to management, such as strategic planning. Gentlemen's promises put the gentlemen's personal honour and reputation at stake, and this has a deeply emotional effect both on the individuals making those promises and on the people around them. As a result, all people affected by a gentleman's personal commitment – customers, employees, suppliers – are motivated to take action and deliver on those promises. Instead, the attainment of any specific set of strategic planning objectives does not necessarily rest on personal commitments. Rather, it is typically made dependent on market forecasts, as well as on a specific allocation of internal resources within the organization. If any of these fails to materialize in the forecast fashion, then these objectives are revised further down the road. In this way, responsibility for the adjusted objectives is diluted amongst strategic planners, managers and those in charge of resource allocation within the organization, as part of a routine monitoring process. Moreover, if market forecasts stray wildly from the predicted course – say, as a result of an "unforeseeable" economic crisis – then the objectives are revised accordingly (downwards, in this case) owing to "external events" or "exogenous factors", for which neither an organization's strategic planners nor its managers take direct responsibility.

By contrast, rather than attempting to forecast the future or adapt to unforeseen events, imaginative individuals and organizations use gentlemen's promises to emotionally engage and mobilize people in a journey towards creating radically new futures – even against the odds. They do this as part of a rational process, though. First, they put themselves in their customers' shoes in order to imagine unprecedented experiences for them. Next, they passionately embrace the mission of making those radically new experiences a reality, and recruit other people who share in the same passion. Together with them, as a following step they engage in a social experiment to work creatively and build a concrete, small-scale prototype of the new future that has been imagined. It is at this point that the imaginative team makes gentlemen's promises that mobilize an entire organization to scale up the prototype and implement it on a much larger fashion. This represents the moment of truth that commits a bunch of individuals, armed with the relative certainty of an innovative prototype, to creating a new future. For many people unfamiliar with the new dream or its associated prototype, these gentlemen's promises will inevitably sound impossible to attain in the real world. As the unexpected success of the March 1999 alliance between Renault and Nissan demonstrated, gentlemen's promises can in fact motivate certain people to abandon a courageous journey that – from a detached, analytical perspective – appears way too radical. However, for those individuals who remain committed to the journey, a gentleman's promise exerts such a powerful motivating effect that it encourages them to obtain results that, to most outsiders, seem almost magical.

✳ *the key to delivering on gentlemen's promises*

In 1999, there was a global economic crisis. Stemming from the twin recessionary forces of a bursting dot-com financial bubble in the US and the monetary collapse of important Latin American, Asian and European emerging economies, the crisis made every economic prediction for the millennium year of 2000 look decidedly bleak. (And the predictions were justified: 2000 turned out to be another year of global economic crisis.)

This made the Nissan Revival Plan (NRP) – unveiled by the company's Brazilian COO Carlos Ghosn at the Tokyo Motor Show on 18 October 1999 – sound distinctly baffling, not only to the world's automotive analysts, but also to the general public. In October 1999, everybody knew that the car industry was amongst the most vulnerable to any economic crisis of global proportions, and was usually the first to be hit. However, against this dismal background, Ghosn, speaking in front of hundreds of people and TV cameras from all five continents (including simultaneous video-conferencing to thousands of Nissan's executives and employees all over the world) was confidently presenting an ambitious set of aspirations for Nissan that was unprecedented in the entire history of the industry. The fact that, even as Ghosn addressed the Tokyo Motor Show crowds, Nissan was on the brink of complete financial and market collapse – it had posted major losses during seven consecutive years prior to 1999 – made the whole experience feel unreal to many. Some industry experts in the audience must have shaken their heads in disbelief at the dim chances of success of any large-scale international alliance – let alone French-Japanese ones like Renault–Nissan. But, to anyone able to hear him in October 1999, there was no doubt of what Carlos Ghosn was actually saying:

 What are our commitments? There are three main commitments. First one: return to profitability for fiscal year 2000. Second: an operating profit superior to 4.5 per cent of sales for fiscal year 2002. Third: 50 per cent decrease of the current [US$12.6 billion] net debt level for fiscal year 2003. This decrease will be done at the same time that we will increase investments from the very low level reached in 1998, which represented 3.7 per cent of our net sales, to more normal levels of 5 per cent of net sales. I know and I measure how much effort, how much sacrifice and how much pain we will have to endure for the success of the NRP. But believe me, we don't have a choice and it will be worth it. We all share a dream; a dream of a reconstructed and revived company, a dream of a thoughtful and bold Nissan on track to perform profitable growth in a balanced alliance with Renault to create a major global player in the world car industry. This dream today becomes a vision with the NRP. This vision will become a reality as long as every single Nissan employee will share it with us. [7]

No wonder, when Ghosn unveiled the plan, that few people actually shared in his dreams or believed that Nissan would achieve its ambitious commitments. The company's stock, already at record lows at the time of the October 1999 Tokyo Motor Show, fell a further 5 per cent in less than two weeks after the NRP announcement. A Japanese analyst captured the prevailing mood:

 It is impossible for Japanese managers to carry out such a drastic restructuring programme.

This analyst wasn't only reacting to the inherent difficulties of reviving a virtually bankrupt carmaking giant in the midst of a major global recession. He was also being historically minded. In or prior to 1999, no large organization in Japan had ever made massive layoffs, closed plants or got rid of suppliers in order to save purchasing costs. Not one. On top of this, Ghosn's bold aspiration of launching 22 new car models in three years required Nissan to make staggering leaps in product development capabilities that no carmaker had ever managed to accomplish before. However, against this historical background, in October 1999 it suddenly transpired that Nissan – Japan's second largest carmaker – had to achieve all these unprecedented results *right away* if it was to live up to the public commitments made by its leader. It is hardly an exaggeration to presume that everyone hearing Carlos Ghosn speak at the Tokyo Motor Show in 1999 must have thought he was naively attempting the unthinkable.

Ghosn, a veteran executive of the car industry, certainly knew all this. But rather than back down, he stuck to his ambitious commitments 100 per cent, even though they were regarded as unrealistic by most competitors, industry experts, international media and qualified observers. Said Ghosn:

 The big risk is that if you announce ambitious [commitments], people will not believe you. They'll say, "He said 100 per cent, but if he gets 50 per cent he'll be happy"... Well, we want 100, and we're going to get 100. If we don't get it next year [2000], that's it. We will resign.

This real story showcases the first reason behind the ability to successfully deliver on gentlemen's promises – no matter how wild these may seem to other people. It is the sheer courage to put one's personal honour and reputation at stake when committing to a promise. In my experience, everyone immediately recognizes personal courage when it is really there. Its magnetic power easily crosses linguistic, cultural and geographic boundaries, inspiring some people and deterring others, but effortlessly communicating to all. Had he been able to travel to the future from the first century BC, Cicero would certainly have appreciated Carlos Ghosn's performance at the 1999 Tokyo Motor Show. Here was the Brazilian expatriate leader of a French multinational, giving honourable commitments in Tokyo that made thousands of people around the world gasp. In a nutshell, this illustrates the very essence of gentlemen's promises. They are courageously and honourably made, with no conditions, no strings attached, no ifs, buts or ands. Instead of hedging his bets behind company history or market forecasts (both of which were, at the time, exceptionally gloomy for Nissan), Ghosn made exceedingly ambitious commitments based on the conviction that his dream about a powerfully revived Nissan could be quickly achieved. Most intelligent observers dismissed those commitments as unrealistic, but Ghosn and his leadership team dramatically put their personal reputations and dignity 100 per cent behind them: "If we don't get it next year [2000], that's it. We will resign."

Contrary to every expectation, Nissan fulfilled – and in most cases exceeded – all of the NRP's stated commitments. This is shown in Table 2 on the following page, where the "Promised" column gives a second clue to understanding how Nissan's leadership team managed to deliver on their amazing gentlemen's promises: these promises were stated in such a simple and clear way that everyone could understand them. To this effect, Nissan's leadership team in fact defined their gentleman's promises as a number and a deadline, which they honourably and totally committed to achieve by the agreed date or else face the consequences. That was it. Simple. Clear.

One of the results of establishing honourable commitments with this particular kind of simplicity and clarity is what happens on the receiving end. Speaking in 2003 about Carlos Ghosn's communications, Nissan senior vice president Toshiyuki Shiga said:

 His speech is really amazing. His speech is very simple and very understandable. And clearly pointed out what points Nissan should improve. He really shows just five points. And after listening to his speech everybody understands what we are able to do.[8]

Mr Shiga's statement has become my personal benchmark for simple and clear communications across boundaries. My thinking goes: if you were a Brazilian of Lebanese origin working for a French organization, and you managed to get a Japanese executive from a Japanese company to describe your speech in English – a language foreign to both of you – as "very simple and very understandable", then, as they say, "you made it" as a world-class communicator. There is, around the world, an almost magical power in gentlemen's promises that are simply and clearly stated as a number and a deadline.

When asked "How did Nissan manage to pull off these astonishing results?", Ghosn often responded that "cross-functional teams" had been a key ingredient for success. He was referring to Nissan's mixed teams, made up of representatives of different functions (such as product development, purchasing, manufacturing, and sales and marketing) as well as nationalities (French and Japanese), which were in charge of both devising and carrying out the NRP. There is more than meets the eye in Ghosn's assertion, though. Many individuals and organizations have established cross-functional teams to implement ambitious initiatives for the future, but have failed to deliver the expected results. The key is how cross-functional teams are managed to achieve bold aspirations. Here, there are crucial differences between Renault–Nissan's approach and that of other organizations.

Promised	Delivered
Positive annual net income after tax by fiscal year (FY) 2000	(US$6.5) billion in FY 1999 +US$2.7 billion in FY 2000 +US$2.7 billion in FY 2001 +US$4.1 billion in FY 2002
Annual operating margin of 4.5 per cent of sales by FY 2002	+ 10.8 per cent in FY 2002
50 per cent reduction in net debt to US$6.3 billion by FY 2003	Net debt already reduced to US$6.6 billion by September 2001
Reduce purchasing costs by 20 per cent by FY 2003	18 per cent cost reduction already achieved by September 2001
Eliminate 21,000 jobs by FY 2003	19,900 job cuts already achieved by September 2001
22 new car models by FY 2002	All 22 new models launched by FY 2002

TABLE 2 : Some of Renault–Nissan's amazing gentleman's promises

On the one hand, in the case of Renault–Nissan, cross-functional work – involving a hundred executives from both companies – was the norm in the early formation stages of the alliance, within the framework of an open-minded social initiation and experimentation process that lasted about six months. In Chapter 5 we have called this initiation phase tinkunacuy. Corporate tinkunacuy had early on brought three main results for Renault and Nissan. First, it had created an environment conducive to imagining and sharing future dreams about a powerful alliance between the two. Secondly, it had developed mutual trust amongst the hundred executives who engaged in tinkunacuy. Last, it had built a concrete prototype of what a successful alliance between Renault and Nissan could look like. Later on, in July 1999, many of the cross-functional teams that had already been put in place during the social initiation stages of the alliance were now – together with additional new teams – utilized to expand on this early prototype by designing the NRP. The teams themselves did this, following clear rules and without resorting to outsiders such as consultants or industry experts. Explained Ghosn at the 18 October Tokyo Motor Show:

 How did we elaborate the Nissan Revival Plan? On July 5 [1999] we established nine cross-functional teams. Each one was led by two Executive Committee members and headed by a pilot. Team members were selected by the leaders and the pilots [were chosen] from the company's managerial ranks. The composition had to be cross-functional and international. It is not top-down. It is not bottom-up. It is both. Each team had one topic. One goal: Make proposals to develop the business and reduce costs. One deadline: This morning's [October 18, 1999] Board meeting for final decisions. One rule: No sacred cows, no taboos, no constraints. One belief: The solutions to Nissan's problems are inside the company. Only one issue is non-negotiable: The return to profit. [9]

On the other hand, crucially, Nissan's cross-functional teams were not one-off features of the organization, to be disbanded once the promises of the NRP were fulfilled. Rather, they became central elements of the organization, with the overarching task of creating new futures by reinventing the organization from time to time. Thus in 2001, after the NRP's commitments had been delivered and the company revived, Nissan launched another set of gentleman's promises under a company-wide initiative labelled "180". The 1 stood for one million additional car units sold, the 8 denoted eight per cent margin, and the 0 stood for zero debt – all of which Nissan promised to achieve by 2005. As the promises of "180" were being delivered before schedule, however, in June 2004 Ghosn started to publicize "Value Up", yet another company-wide initiative that promised to turn Nissan's and Renault's brands and product portfolio into higher value added items in consumers' minds. The cross-functional teams became a permanent supporting feature in all of Nissan's continuous waves of gentleman's promises. Said Ghosn:

 In my experience, executives in a company rarely reach across boundaries. Working together in cross-functional teams helps managers to think in new ways, challenge existing practices, explaining the necessity for change and projecting difficult messages across the entire company.

Renault–Nissan's peculiar approach to managing its cross-functional teams illustrate that – together with sheer courage, simplicity and clarity – a third key aspect enabling organizations to deliver on seemingly unrealistic gentlemen's promises is the ability to implement an innovation process of sorts. The latter goes well beyond new product development functions. Rather, innovation processes in the Renault–Nissan style are about building an organizational capability to regularly create new futures by reinventing the entire organization around bold gentleman's promises. Such a transformational innovation process builds a group of individuals or an entire organization into a tool for social evolution. To some outsiders, though, this startling capability must look like pure magic.

Inditex, the Spanish holding company that owns Zara, as well as other highly successful fashion retailing brands, offers another powerful illustration of the "magic" of gentlemen's promises in creating radically new and positive futures. Unlike Nissan's dismal 1998 situation, in 1989 Zara was a highly successful, innovative and financially sound Spanish fashion retailer that had no reason to fear for its future economic health. This was mainly the result of Zara's ability to restock its shelves with new cheap-chic fashion items twice a week, every week. This implied a life-cycle for the average Zara item that was a great deal shorter than for the other global fashion brands that, at the time, launched complete collections about four times a year. To completely outclass the speed to market of any other brand in just one small fashion market – Spain – was one thing. But attempting to do it on a global scale was, frankly, unthinkable in 1989. To try in 1989 could have been described as downright dangerous, owing to the catastrophic economic crisis that was then unravelling in Japan – the world's second largest economy at the time – and was dragging the entire global economy in its wake.

Nevertheless, attempting the unthinkable was exactly what Inditex did in 1989. It started an aggressive international escalation for Zara with the opening of its first stores outside Spain. The entire expansion initiative relied on the company's capability to faultlessly deliver on the same gentleman's promise that made the fortunes of the first Zara store back in 1975 – only on a much larger scale: to release new, exciting and inexpensive fashion items twice a week, every week, in every store all over the world. As a result, the original 1975 Zara shop had, by June 2009, become 4,300 stores in more than seventy countries, encompassing a retailing surface larger than many small European nation states such as Monaco or the Vatican. In this immense shopping arena, millions of customers around the globe learned that the company's commitment to delivering "instant fashions" could be trusted, and as a result the entire clothing industry was transformed beyond recognition. After Zara, "fashion" started to mean an exhilarating experience of shopping for fast-changing, stylish and inexpensively priced models that almost everybody could afford to buy, anywhere in the world. Moreover, the company produced vast numbers of new styles in small quantities and would not replace them after they had sold out, so that every customer could buy exclusivity and fresh design at much lower prices than similar-looking models offered by other fashion brands.

If anything, Zara's ability to deliver on its bold "instant fashion" promises was much more impressive than Renault–Nissan's, as Zara's commitment had to be renewed twice a week in front of each of its millions of customers around the world. Bringing them back to the stores depended on that single promise being fulfilled time and again. Behind Zara's seemingly magical capability to do that, one finds the same essential elements at work that allowed Renault–Nissan to deliver on its courageous gentleman's promises between 1999 and 2009. First, together with a small team that included many family members, Amancio Ortega engaged in a tinkunacuy period of imagination and creative socialization that led to dreaming about and building the first prototype of a Zara store in 1975. After a decade of Zara's success in the Spanish market, by the mid 1980s Ortega's team, expanded with new members such as computer expert José Maria Castellano, set a second tinkunacuy in motion that resulted in a revolutionary prototype for fashion retailing, capable of bringing "instant fashions" to life on an international scale. The key to the effectiveness of this prototype was an innovation process underpinned by a unique just-in-time logistical and distribution capability more similar to DHL's or Toyota's than to that of a large clothing retailer. Like the transformational innovation process that Renault–Nissan would implement a decade later, Inditex's innovation engine prototype was designed to produce breathtaking product development, manufacturing and retailing innovations with the potential to radically transform the entire fashion world. Once the new prototype had been successfully tested in Spain, Ortega made the courageous promise to release "instant fashions" for the first time on a global scale. As every one of its bold promises was fulfilled, customers around the world flocked to the Zara stores, resulting in Inditex's dramatically successful international expansion.

Around 2005 the company initiated a third significant tinkunacuy phase, leading to its 2008 unveiling of Europe's largest logistics complex outside Zaragoza. In September 2009 – as the whole world underwent its most severe economic crisis for 80 years – Inditex revealed what its new logistical development was really aiming at when it announced the 2010 opening of Zara's first virtual e-commerce store. Zara's cyberstore would initially be available in most Western European markets and would then be rolled out in every country where the company had physical stores. Thus, between 1975 and 2009, every tinkunacuy period at Inditex had led to a new, reinvented organization that pledged to profoundly transform the global fashion industry – and delivered on its promise. This provided another illustration of how Inditex's transformational innovation process was, in essence, similar to Renault–Nissan's own process, in that it was designed to continuously reinvent the organization in order to constantly shape new and exciting futures around us.

Like Renault–Nissan and Inditex, the US-based Medtronic – one of the world's leading medical technology companies in 2009 – regularly transformed its entire organization in order to deliver on gentleman's promises that radically changed the global medical device industry. As previously mentioned, former Medtronic CEO Bill George, who led the company from 1990 to 2001, maintained that the organization had to be reinvented every five years, and he certainly delivered on that promise. Over the second half of the

1990s, Medtronic pledged to reduce its product release time from 48 months to only 16, a radical promise that entailed reorganizing the entire company around the development of an unprecedented innovation capability. This capability allowed Medtronic to become the company with the youngest product portfolio of any industry in the US, and as a result, the medical community's ability to improve the lives of millions of patients suffering from heart conditions, diabetes and other widespread chronic diseases was fundamentally enhanced. In the midst of this success, in January 2000 George launched another set of courageous promises that committed Medtronic to radically transforming itself into the world's leading medical organization by 2010, providing high-technology lifelong solutions that would dramatically improve the quality of life of vast numbers of patients suffering from chronic diseases, while significantly reducing healthcare costs. This would not only lift the capabilities of hospitals and physicians to previously unsuspected levels, but also had the potential to usher in a new, positive future for the human and economic welfare of entire countries around the world.

Even socially minded organizations such as the San Patrignano community follow a similar pattern, from dreaming about and prototyping a new future, to courageously promising and delivering that new future through the implementation of a transformational innovation process that expands the initial prototype to a much larger scale. The dream of Vincenzo and Antonietta Muccioli was to create a very large family with the outcasts of society as members, all of whom would lovingly embrace and support each other to achieve extraordinary things. By the late 1970s, their prototype was ready to grow. And grow it did. By the late 1980s San Patrignano had become the world's largest and most effective drug rehabilitation community. However, in the words of Vincenzo Muccioli, San Patrignano was a community of Life, built on a two-fold honourable promise. On the one hand, the San Patrignano family promised to lovingly support, educate and help the newcomer build a new future life. On the other hand, the newcomer promised to courageously carry out his or her recovery journey while respecting the rules of the community. As a result of both sides delivering on these simple commitments, San

Patrignano could almost magically achieve the world's highest rehabilitation rates, year after year. However, in addition to honourably observing their commitments, the key to the community's "magical" success was an innovation process that allowed its members to constantly imagine and develop new businesses with world-class standards of excellence. This process expanded upon the Mucciolis' original discovery, back in the mid 1970s, that family support together with community work carried out with the highest standards of excellence were extremely effective tools in overcoming drug addiction and social marginalization.

San Patrignano's moving story highlights a fourth key aspect of the remarkable ability to deliver on gentlemen's promises, even against the odds and in defiance of global economic crises as well as most people's scepticism. As has been mentioned, the community's internal degree of cohesiveness is more like that of a loving family than a "normal" organization – even a socially minded one. Strong cohesiveness is, in fact, a key factor behind the success of the complex and large-scale initiatives that are often required to deliver on a commitment to creating a new future. From Renault–Nissan's NRP and Zara's international expansion, to Medtronic's organizational reinventions or San Patrignano's large family, a strong degree of internal cohesiveness is what often makes the difference between the success or failure of these initiatives. The following chapter looks at the issue of how creators of the future manage to build such a strong internal cohesiveness not only inside their imaginative teams and organizations, but also across cultural, geographic and mental boundaries that most people would describe as daunting, if not insuperable.

7
the seventh key:
common glue

....

SHORTLY AFTER MEETING POPE CLEMENT VII, it
is said that the spirit of Raphael of Urbino entered Francesco
Mazzuoli's body. The main reason for this belief was a series
of remarkable paintings that Francesco subsequently created.
Amongst them, there was a self-portrait painted in such an imaginative way that it stunned not only the Pope's court, but also the
whole of Renaissance Italy. Giorgio Vasari (1511–74), Francesco's
biographer, described how this amazing painting was made:

 [...] in order to explore the finer points of painting, Francesco
one day set himself to do his own portrait, looking at himself in
one of those convex barber's mirrors. And in doing this when he
saw those bizarre effects made by the roundness of the mirror
on the curve of the beams of ceilings, causing them to twist,
and on the doors and other parts of buildings, which recede
in a strange way, he formed the wish to copy all of this just as
he fancied. And so he had a ball of wood made by a turner and
then divided it in half to make it the same shape and size as the

mirror; and with tremendous skill he set himself to counterfeit on it all that he saw in the mirror, and particularly himself, with results so lifelike it could not be imagined or believed. And as all the things near to such a mirror are magnified, and all those away from it diminished in size, he showed a hand that is busy drawing, quite big, as the mirror reflected it, and so beautifully done it seemed absolutely real. And because Francesco had a very fine air about him, and a very gracious face and aspect, more like those of an angel than a man, his likeness on that ball was something divine rather than human.[1]

As a result of his prodigious talents, young Francesco – who was nicknamed "Il Parmigianino" after his home town of Parma – was immediately given important artistic commissions in Rome. However, his success there was to be short-lived. In 1527 the city was sacked by the mutinous troops of Emperor Charles V, causing Francesco to flee Rome and return to Parma, where he was given a hero's welcome and the commission for a very large fresco at the church of Santa Maria della Steccata. It was while experimenting with new pigments for this fresco that Francesco developed an obsession with alchemy that was to prove fatal. Vasari recounts:

> [...] Francesco started to abandon the work for the Steccata, or at least to do it so slowly that it was realized that he went there dragging his feet; and this happened because he had started to study things to do with alchemy and altogether pushed aside those of painting, thinking he must soon make himself rich through solidifying mercury. [...] Finally, still always obsessed by this alchemy of his, like all the others who have once lost their wits over it, and changing from a gentle and fastidious person into an almost savage man quite different from what he was, with a beard and long straggling locks, he was assailed, in this sorry state of melancholy and oddness, by a grave fever and cruel dysentery which in a few days made him pass to another life [...][2]

✳ *common glue as social alchemy*

Il Parmigianino died in 1540 at the age of 37. Vasari's biography on him reads as a cautionary tale against alchemy but does little to explain why this occult discipline wielded such an alluring power over first-rate minds down the centuries. Renaissance philosophers such as Marsilio Ficino, Giovanni Pico della Mirandola and Giordano Bruno were active practitioners of alchemy, which, together with astrology and theurgy (magic), they regarded as the Three Parts of the Wisdom of the Whole Universe. This was an old doctrine that, according to legend, was taught in antiquity by a wise Egyptian called Thoth, whom the ancient Greeks identified as Hermes Trismegistus. The latter name led to the term "Hermeticism", which during the Renaissance stood for the series of doctrines attributed to this ancient sage. Hermes Trismegistus was believed to have created the *Emerald Tablet*, a brief text engraved on stone and summarizing the wisdom of the entire universe. The tablet was the cornerstone of a very popular Renaissance tradition of scholarship called the *prisca sapientia* – the primal wisdom – which claimed that there was a secret, universal wisdom passed down through a line of chosen individuals, usually including Pythagoras and Plato. Sir Isaac Newton, the famous seventeenth-century British mathematician and scientist, who startlingly wrote far more about alchemy than any other subject, translated the *Emerald Tablet* into English. All the evidence suggests that Newton's relationship with alchemy was more than purely theoretical. One of his assistants recorded:

> He [Sir Isaac Newton] very rarely went to bed until two or three of the clock, sometimes not till five or six, lying about four or five hours, especially at spring or the fall of the leaf, at which time he used to employ about six weeks in his laboratory, the fire scarce going out night or day. What his aim might be I was unable to penetrate into.[3]

The British astronomer Sir Arthur Eddington (1882–1944) solved this riddle. In reviewing John William Navin Sullivan's alchemical biography of Newton, he observed that:

> The science in which Newton seems to have been chiefly interested, and on which he spent most of his time, was alchemy. He read widely and made innumerable experiments, entirely without fruit so far as we know.[4]

In the same vein, after reading Newton's alchemical works in

1942, the British economist John Maynard Keynes suggested that "Newton was not the first of the age of reason, he was the last of the magicians."[5] However, the British mathematical genius was not alone in his fascination with alchemy. Most of the great minds of the period – including Robert Boyle, John Locke and Leibniz – shared this fascination. Even in the twentieth century, the Swiss psychologist Carl Jung and the Hungarian philosopher Stephan A. Hoeller saw alchemy as changing the mind and spirit of the alchemist, and in this sense regarded it as a sort of precursor of Western psychology. Jung in particular maintained that he had dreamed about the *Emerald Tablet* in 1912, and that the recurrence of this dream led to his writing *Seven Sermons to the Dead* in 1916.

The *Emerald Tablet* constituted the mainstay of alchemy. From ancient times to modernity, alchemists hung a copy of it on their laboratory wall. Three of alchemy's fundamental principles directly stemmed from the tablet. First, the idea that All is One – in other words, that the universe shares a common origin and unfolds through a single principle of harmony that the *Emerald Tablet*'s texts regard as "The Operation of the Sun". Ancient Egyptians called the latter notion – quite similar to Chinese Daoist or Indian Buddhist principles – *Maat*. Secondly, the idea of the One Mind, or that the universe is a sort of immense hologram that contains, in every small part of it, all of the essential universal principles at work. Third, the notion that all things arose through the Mediation of One, meaning that all things in the universe shared a common essential substance, often regarded by alchemists as the "philosopher's stone". It was by manipulating this substance through an adaptation process referred to in Latin as *solve et coagula* ("dissolve and join back together") and in Greek as *spagyric* ("separation, purification and recombination"), that alchemists of all eras sought to obtain wondrous results, such as the transmutation of base metals into gold or the fabrication of an elixir for eternal youth. It is doubtful whether seventeenth-century alchemists such as Sir Isaac Newton achieved any of these aims, but in the process they played an important role in the birth of modern disciplines such as inorganic chemistry, medicine and metallurgy.

The *Emerald Tablet*'s alchemical principles provide a suitable metaphor to describe how imaginative individuals and organizations go about creating radically new and positive futures for all of us. They are able to do this successfully by performing a sort of social alchemy both inside their teams and organizations and outside them. I call this kind of social alchemical process the *common glue*. It harnesses the diversity of any group by harmoniously building cohesive social relationships amongst their members in ways that lead to radically new ideas, products and services. Inside the imaginative organizations I looked at, the common glue is made up of five elements that interact holistically; in other words each of its constituent parts is related to one another and none works by itself. Only when all five are in place does a group of people or an organization become capable of creating a radically new and positive future. At the same time, the common glue displays a hologramic type of quality in that each of its five constituent elements incorporates fundamental aspects of the remaining four.

Two of the common glue's elements have already been described in the previous chapters. First, a group of *Wiraqocha leaders* passionately sharing a common dream as well as a purposeful mission to realize it, and individually displaying the qualities of wholeness, tolerance, generosity, walk-the-talk and the patience to build a common language. Secondly, the Wiraqocha leaders' ability to make and deliver upon *gentlemen's promises* that commit to transforming small-scale prototypes into new and exciting futures around us. The remaining three elements of common glue – common language, communication rituals and cross-boundary networks – together reveal its internal nature. However, beyond the analytical understanding of its individual constituent elements, it is the way in which common glue is created, nurtured and strengthened as a living totality that explains its amazing ability to delivering radically new and positive futures – even against the odds.

✳ *how to deliver new and positive futures*

However magical it may sound, creating a radical new future for vast numbers of people is a complex challenge. The extraordinary individuals and organizations portrayed in this book dramatically showcase this. In order to create new and positive futures, they all engaged in a plurality of complex and large-scale initiatives that have in common the attainment of astonishing levels of innovation-fuelled growth. This deserves some consideration. Although the positive relationship between leadership cohesiveness and competitive performance has been demonstrated before,[6] successful creators of the future represent an extreme example of this across a wide variety of performance measures. In the cases of fashion retailer Inditex, medical technology player Medtronic or the 1999 Renault–Nissan alliance, their commitment to creating radically new futures resulted in unprecedented levels of new product development, revenue growth, profits and market value. For beverage company Grupo AJE, its 1988 dream to create new high-quality and inexpensive drinks that everybody – even those on the lowest incomes – could afford to buy led to explosive levels of revenue and profit growth that turned it from a small Peruvian start-up into a formidable multinational rival of Coca-Cola in less than two decades. Even social institutions such as San Patrignano in Italy or Delancey Street in the US lived their dreams of rehabilitating the lives of derelicts marginalized by society through creating extraordinary communities where these people could achieve incredible levels of motivational growth at no cost to the state.

Although it is astonishing that these organizations achieved the realization of their dreams simultaneously with record levels of performance, it is even more striking to look at *how* they managed to accomplish both of these things. As already hinted, they did it by successfully orchestrating a myriad complex innovation and growth processes. For organizations like Inditex, Medtronic, Renault–Nissan and Grupo AJE, this variety of processes included the establishment of highly innovative new-product development capabilities inside their companies. Moreover, for organizations such as Medtronic, Renault–Nissan and the leading pharmaceutical giant Novartis, living their dreams of the future involved developing a combined capability for organic growth as well as growth through large-scale mergers, acquisitions and alliances. In addition, for social institutions like San Patrignano and Delancey

Street, realizing their dreams required building the capability to imagine, incubate, finance and grow new start-up business ventures, and turn this capability into the central therapeutic path to rehabilitating the lives of its members – typically drug abusers and convicted criminals. On top of this, for all of these organizations, realizing their radical dreams also meant developing the ability to successfully and fundamentally change their organizations every five to ten years, with all the far-reaching human, organizational and technology-based challenges that this entailed.

Constantly and successfully carrying out multiple complex initiatives such as these represents quite an outstanding ability, especially when assessed against the track record of such undertakings in the global business arena:

> […] some of the business initiatives that best embody the very essence of globalization have evidenced a dismal performance track record. For example, a well-documented body of literature, impressive both in the variety of approaches utilized and in the depth and scope of the underlying empirical analyses, suggests that the failure rate of all mergers, acquisitions and alliances is well over 50 per cent. Strikingly similar findings have been reported in the case of other major undertakings such as large-scale re-engineering, re-structuring and outsourcing, global expatriate programs and change initiatives. In the field of management science, traditionally fraught with contradictory approaches and seemingly opposing views around single phenomena, such empirical evidence has enjoyed a remarkable degree of consensus over most of the 20th century. [7]

How do creators of the future go about managing a variety of complex initiatives that constitute a major challenge to even the most seasoned global players? As indicated before, they do this by developing strong common glue. In other words, a sort of higher social capability that links, coordinates and mobilizes all of the organization's major initiatives towards the attainment of a common dream and a shared purposeful mission. At the heart of this common glue, there exists a group of Wiraqocha leaders in charge of developing and continuously strengthening it. This Wiraqocha leadership group usually represents a highly diverse and multicultural talent pool, with varying numbers ranging from less than 50 people for an organization such as San Patrignano, to hundreds of members for the larger multinational organizations such as Medtronic, Novartis or Renault–Nissan. Typically, apart from developing and strengthening the organization's common glue, the Wiraqocha leaders perform other stewardship roles within the institution, like heads of global functions (such as marketing, product development or finance), or managers of business units in specific geographic areas. When performing these stewardship roles, Wiraqocha leaders follow the agendas of their functional or business units. However, when taking on the role of building common glue, Wiraqocha leaders are responsible for coordinating a variety of organization-wide initiatives, ensuring that a collective idea of the future becomes real at the end of a journey. The art is not in the concept, though. Itself a complex process, developing strong common glue can easily suffer the same negative fate as the global initiatives that have been described above. In order to be successful at it, a group of Wiraqocha leaders need to carefully thread together a few important factors.

✳ *the key to common glue: harmony, holism, holograms*

The first key factor to developing strong common glue is harmony. In other words, its component elements must correspond and work together with the precision and synchronicity of a fit living organism. On the one hand, this means that the emotional core of the individual Wiraqocha leaders must match the organization's purposeful mission. A group of leaders' strong emotional connection with their organization's mission brings harmony to the common glue. Wiraqocha leaders aiming to create new and positive futures deliberately seek after this quality. In 1990, when Bill George started his ten-year tenure as CEO of Medtronic, the company was a successful medical equipment high-tech start-up ripe for acquisition by any of the leading giants of that industry. However, George's dream of turning Medtronic into the world's leading medical technology company implied that the organization had an unrealized value that far exceeded any acquisition premium it could fetch in the capital markets at that time. In order to realize this dream and unleash that unrealized value, George formed a new leadership group for Medtronic that was both culturally diverse and capable of developing unprecedented innovation processes as well as internationalizing the company. When choosing Medtronic's new leaders, though, George looked for one more crucial characteristic. He personally assessed whether the company's mission of restoring people to full health and life genuinely motivated each prospective candidate. If this was not the case, even otherwise highly qualified individuals were told to look for new challenges elsewhere. However, if Medtronic's mission really made the eyes of a highly qualified individual sparkle with genuine excitement and emotion, George made him or her part of the company's new leadership group. The main reason for this was quite simple. Only people who were profoundly connected emotionally with the objective of restoring other people's health could feel motivated to carry out the unprecedented efforts that were required to realize George's dream about Medtronic. In turn, a strong inner motivation was key for Medtronic's leaders to enthuse others into sharing in that mission and realizing the common dream.

Similarly to the Medtronic experience, in 1999, when Nissan's COO Carlos Ghosn described the profile of the two hundred new company leaders he was looking for, he started with two revealing words: "young mavericks". Many headhunters I know were puzzled by this description, as the word maverick contradicted the dependable characteristics that were usually associated with the key leadership roles of multinational organizations. Moreover, these headhunters were doubtful that two hundred corporate mavericks could even be found at all in Japan, a nation that most of them perceived as imbued with strong corporate traditions of reverential behaviour. Nevertheless, as Nissan's turnaround plan was publicly unveiled in October 1999, everybody learned about the company's clear commitments to carry out drastic initiatives such as plant closures, massive layouts, widespread elimination of suppliers and radical new product development initiatives, all of which were, at the time, unheard of in Japan. Nissan's Wiraqocha leaders set out to fundamentally destroy not only an emblematic, historical company, but also a traditional Japanese way of doing things in business, in order to build a powerful new organization that would take its place. This is where the "young mavericks" came in: individuals whose emotional core resonated strongly with the challenge of sidestepping other people's old rules in order to replace them with their own radically new set of rules.

Some of the highest degrees of harmony between an organization's mission and its leaders can be found in social organizations such as San Patrignano. This organization's mission – to train marginalized people and bring them to achieve extraordinary things – completely fits the deep life purpose of each and every one of its members. They are one and the same: identical. When this supreme level of harmony is attained, even the wildest dreams imaginable can become true. This is one of the reasons why San Patrignano's achievements – such as winning world-championship gold medals in Olympic sports, scooping up every available award for Italian premium wines or becoming one of Italy's top designer furniture shops – are hard for outsiders to believe, but represent the routine work of its members.

On the other hand, common glue's harmony also refers to the consistency between an organization's dream about the future, its purposeful mission and its leaders' organization-wide commitments. All of the organizations portrayed in this book show such a remarkable level of consistency between these three aspects that they can be regarded as different facets of the same diamond. First, the dream usually is a bold one and its realization brings forth a radically new and positive future for the organization's customers, be it the creation of a new medical technology leader that opens previously unthought-of possibilities for the lives of millions of suffering individuals (Medtronic); the thorough revitalization of a carmaker on the brink of collapse so that it returns to releasing exciting new products (Nissan); the reinvention of fashion into a democratic experience that almost anyone could afford anywhere in the world (Inditex); or the creation of a very large family where the most marginalized members of society could be included and achieve extraordinary things (San Patrignano or Delancey Street).

Building on their radical dreams, these organizations' purposeful missions – however differently stated – can also be interpreted as realizing the organization's dream. My favourite example to showcase this amazing degree of consistency between an organization's dream and its purposeful mission is San Patrignano's beautifully inspiring mission: to train marginalized people and bring them to achieve extraordinary things. Building upon this consistency, these organizations' promises are geared to simultaneously achieving their purposeful missions and realizing their collective dreams of the future. Thus, San Patrignano's commitment to achieving the world's highest drug rehabilitation rates accomplishes its purposeful mission and realizes its dream. Grupo AJE's commitment to producing high-quality drinks at the lowest possible prices achieves the organization's mission of including lower-income individuals as part of the market in medium-income countries, and realizes its dream of creating one of the world's greatest beverage companies. Similarly, the dream of Greek tycoon Stelios Haji-Ioannou – to build a brand that is popular with the masses – was realized with the creation of the "easy" brand, whose purposeful mission – making out-of-reach products and services accessible to all – was applied to a variety of businesses ranging from low-cost airlines to inexpensive hotels and male toiletries, all of which shared the same all-embracing promise of "providing unmatched value for money to customers". Likewise, Inditex's dream of "democratizing fashion" all over the world was realized by its mission of bringing fashion to the masses and its leaders' startling promise to deliver inexpensive instant fashions twice a week, every week of the year, to anywhere in the world where its thousands of stores could be found. Try to look at Medtronic in the same light. You will certainly find the same remarkable degree of harmony between this organization's 1990 dream, its purposeful mission and its leaders' unprecedented commitment to reduce the company's new product release time from 48 months to just 16.

However, Wiraqocha leaders sharing a missionary dream of the future, together with their associated organization-wide promises, are not by themselves enough to develop strong common glue. As previously mentioned, three additional elements – a common language, cross-boundary networks and communication rituals – also need to be in place for strong common glue to develop. This brings to mind the common glue's holistic characteristic. Under its most common definition, any open system is said to be holistic when the whole is greater than the sum of its parts. This is typically the case of complex living organisms such as human beings. Our manifest lives and mental functions are far more than the sum of our brains, body parts and internal organs, and the same can be said about many other living creatures that populate planet Earth. Life is nature's quintessentially holistic creation. Accordingly, common glue represents a living social phenomenon that is greater than the sum of its five constituent elements, and this "greater than" can be regarded as reciprocal trust, mutual understanding, honourable commitments, connective bridges and cooperative relationships that arise powerfully amongst the Wiraqocha leaders as their journey towards the realization of a common dream of the future unfolds.

The holistic quality of common glue can also be ascertained by the collective mindset and group personality that stems from the individual members of the Wiraqocha leadership team. As already mentioned, all the extraordinary organizations portrayed in this book looked for five qualities in their leaders: wholeness, tolerance, generosity, walk-the-talk and patience in building a common language. This means that, beyond what makes each Wiraqocha leadership group unique, certain common patterns can be expected to emanate from its individual members. Take wholeness, for example, a quality that stands for an individual's natural tendency to transcend dilemmas. Any team made up of individuals possessing this quality tends to collectively develop an imaginative group-mindset, integrating perspectives that look contradictory to most people. This is how organizations like Inditex, Grupo AJE or easyJet conceived the delivery of high value to customers at low cost to the organization. Or how social institutions like San Patrignano imagined delivering world-class products and services designed, manufactured and sold by drug abusers. Wholeness often leads to what in this book has been called a *trade-on mindset* – in other words the mental predisposition to be, do and gain much more with a lot less. When you put together a group of individuals with these mental tendencies and stimulate them to unleash their imagination, a collective trade-on mindset suddenly evolves.

Or take walk-the-talk and generosity. These qualities describe individuals who lead by example, with a natural tendency to give their time generously in order to empathize with and support others, irrespective of hierarchical position. These individual qualities often lead to the development of group traits of courage and determination. In effect, organizations aiming to create new and positive futures often do so by making radical commitments, and this puts the courage and determination of every individual member of a Wiraqocha leadership group to the test. Inevitably, these bold commitments strengthen the resolve and courage of some individuals but frighten others. It is through leading by example and by coaching and encouraging others when they most need it that the best individuals of the group pass on their courage, self-confidence and determination to the whole team.

Finally, consider tolerance and patience in building a common language. Taken together, these inner individual qualities enable a group to develop common language across cultural, professional, age and gender divides. Here, "common language" is not meant just linguistically, but also describes the group process of select-ing words that are key to accomplishing a common mission, and agreeing on a specific meaning for each of these terms. In other words, common language is about a group going through the process of developing a dictionary of key terms whose meanings they all agree to share, just as the leaders of the Renault–Nissan alliance did in 1999. In addition to this process, an organization's common language also includes all the central elements that build mutual understanding inside its Wiraqocha leadership group; in other words a single set of organization-wide performance mea-sures, a shared set of behavioural rules (also called "values" in some organizations) and a common approach to career develop-ment and appraisal for the members of the Wiraqocha leadership group. It requires tolerance, patience and perseverance to incul-cate these elements of common language within the organization.

To sum up, the individual qualities of wholeness, tolerance, generosity, walk-the-talk and patience in building a common language can all be managed to produce a holistic surplus of mutual understanding, a collective trade-on mindset, group courage and self-confident determination within the entire Wiraqocha leadership team.

The fact that, within the organization, each Wiraqocha leader is responsible for stewardship roles other than building strong common glue leads to its hologramic features. A hologram is a three-dimensional photograph made with the aid of a laser. To make a hologram, the object to be photographed is first bathed in the light of a laser beam. Then a second laser beam is bounced off the reflected light of the first and the resulting interference pattern (the area where the two laser beams commingle) is captured on film. When the film is developed, it looks like a meaningless swirl of light and dark lines. But as soon as the developed film is illuminated by another laser beam, a three-dimensional image of the original object appears. The three-dimensionality of such images is not the only remarkable characteristic of holograms. If a hologram of an orchid is cut in half and then illuminated by a laser, each half will still be found to contain the entire image of the orchid. Indeed, even if the halves are divided again, each snippet of film will always be found to contain a smaller but intact version of the original image. Unlike normal photographs, every part of a hologram contains all the information possessed by the whole. Neurologists have discovered hologramic properties in the human brain. Some people who had parts of their brains surgically removed did not lose the body functions governed by the part of the brain they had lost. These functions were later found to have spontaneously moved to other parts of their surgically modified brains.

Like a three-dimensional hologram, every area of the organization where a Wiraqocha leader carries out substantial activities is permeated by common glue. It gives powerful meaning and inspiration to the organization's employees, customers, suppliers and other stakeholders, all of whom become enthused by the common dream as well as its associated purposeful mission and organization-wide commitments. A number of additional elements make this hologramic characteristic a key factor to developing strong common glue. First, the organization-wide commitments that the Wiraqocha leaders carry to every corner of the organization represent guiding lights for employees, suppliers and customers alike, all of whom align their activities and expectations towards the fulfilment of these promises. Thus, the 1999 Nissan Revival Plan (NRP) had clear organization-wide commitments regarding net income, new product development, cost savings and debt reduction. In order to deliver on these promises, nine cross-functional teams were formed, each of which had to deliver on one aspect of these commitments. In turn, every cross-functional team went further down in the organization, establishing multiple commitments with functional areas, business units or suppliers that allowed them to fulfil their own promises, and so on. Thus the NRP unfolded through a process of alignment analogous to those Russian dolls that you open again and again, only to find each time a slightly smaller version of the doll inside the one you have just opened.

Second, the hologramic characteristic of common glue has important implications for the types of cross-boundary networks that evolve both formally and informally inside the organization. Because Wiraqocha leaders not only meet regularly as a group but also perform multiple stewardship roles inside the organization (often involving external constituencies as well), they develop compact networks that connect any pair of individuals in just a few steps and across any kind of organizational boundary. Eventually this creates connective tissue that allows new ideas, information and key resources to move freely within the organization to wherever they are needed to accomplish their mission. This connective tissue becomes akin to a hologramic brain of the organization, in that it allows critical functions, people and resources to seamlessly materialize in different organizational areas where these elements may be required, no matter how far apart. A series of organizational elements ensures that this connective tissue becomes self-generating over time. On the one hand, the customary use of cross-functional teams, task forces, special projects and the like is an effective way to constantly harness the underlying diversity of the organization's internal networks in support of company-wide commitments. On the other hand, knowledge-sharing processes, roles and infrastructure help codify, store, classify and recombine critical information in ways that make it both useful and easily accessible to multiple organizational areas. Moreover, especially within the larger multinational firms, certain global personnel policies can be very effectively used to continuously foster the creation of cohesive networks across geographic, functional and professional boundaries, that is, via expatriate and repatriate schemes, international assignments, development programmes, job rotations and so on.

Moreover, because of its hologramic qualities, every single constituent part of common glue includes essential elements of the remaining four. Take cross-boundary networks, for example. They allow smooth connection with and access to any aspect of common glue: Wiraqocha leaders, organization-wide promises, common language or communication rituals. Or consider Wiraqocha leaders, whose intrinsic qualities offer, to any careful observer, an essential glimpse of the whole organization's dream and raison d'être. This also applies to common glue's organization-wide promises, which immediately evoke an institution's overall commitment to delivering a new and positive future for its customers as well as for its other key stakeholders. Or take common language, whose constituent elements strongly hint at the organization's leadership profile, its whole purpose, its communication approaches and its relationship networks.

However, it is perhaps both the nature and the impact of the communication rituals underpinning strong common glue that give some of the best examples of its hologramic nature. In fact, for organizations developing strong common glue in order to deliver a new future, nearly every action of its key leaders can be elevated to the status of a communication ritual. In 2001, Nissan's COO Carlos Ghosn fittingly characterized this active approach to communication. Asked how much time he spent communicating, he replied:

 Even in brainstorming sessions, even when we elaborate strategy, you communicate all the time.

From the outset, Ghosn, together with his leadership team, instilled a culture of extremely transparent, open, precise and factual communication, both inside Nissan and with outside parties such as the media. This was enacted by the company's leaders' habits of expressing their ambitious commitments as a number and a deadline, and "walking-the-talk" on those commitments. Moreover, daily events and practices became powerful and visible rituals that made the new walk-the-talk approach to communication come alive within the company. For example, in order to communicate his conviction that the solutions to Nissan's problems were inside the company, Ghosn would make surprise visits to Nissan's research facilities and production plants, gathering input from senior managers and line workers alike. The decision to pick English as Nissan's common, official language was backed up with intensive language courses for all the company's employees, regardless of level. In spite of the company's critical state in 1999, Ghosn also started the practice of inviting the media to Nissan's annual shareholder meetings, giving them complete freedom to report what they saw. Moreover, Nissan's choice to communicate the NRP to the outside world at the Tokyo Motor Show in October 1999, at the same time that Nissan employees were learning about it, was a powerful sign of the company's determination to establish transparent, reliable commitments and achieve them in a no-nonsense fashion. In short, over the 1999–2009 decade, Nissan's approach to transparent communications was brought to life through their leaders' daily behaviour, interactions and practices. Ghosn explained:

 Credibility has two legs [...] the first is performance, but [we have nothing to show at the start]; the second leg of credibility is transparency – what I think, what I say, what I do is the same thing. So we have to be extremely transparent.

The above example neatly illustrates the hologramic essence of communication rituals. They are called rituals because they symbolize important meanings that have the potential to emotionally engage participants and stimulate positive responses from them in support of their common mission. On the other hand, these rituals are hologramic in that almost every action of the leader has a communication value, and every communication initiative is linked to a practical result in favour of the organization's commitments. Accordingly, instead of representing the general art of sound message transmission amongst any given set of players, hologramic communication rituals are better regarded as the set of actions conveying actual movement from one part of a social entity to another. Under this broader definition, it is the common actions and daily interactions of an organization's members that in fact communicate. In the case of organizations developing strong common glue to live their dreams, "communications" consist of the set of actions that key individual members carry out together with others in order to reach their shared commitments and accomplish their common mission. From this perspective, the ultimate way to measure the effectiveness of an imaginative organization's communications is whether or not it has delivered punctually and promptly on its commitments.

And that is why you will often learn about the cherished dreams of the imaginative organizations once they have already turned their bold ideas of the future into a new reality.

 **epilogue**

Kashanmi manaraq chayamushaqtin.
(It does exist, though it hasn't yet arrived.)

Qheshwa adage from ancient Peru[1]

IT IS ONE OF THE OLDEST CREATION MYTHS from one of the world's major ancient civilizations, and yet in it we can find subsumed all of the key elements that give imagination its enthralling power to create the future anew. In an ancient time, the powerful Lord Kon (Apu Kon) arrived in the central coastal kingdoms of Pirúa (old Peru). He was a Hamawtha and a Holy Man who spoke with great wisdom. Apu Kon taught about an archaic time when Pacha – our planet Earth – was lifeless, like a rock lost in space. This was the era when there was Ti-Ti (the double Sun) in the Hanan Pacha (the heavens). Then Pacha suddenly awoke, its belly burning with fire and looking like an anxious man – or like a sterile woman. But Ti-Ti noticed Pacha's apprehension with kindness. And He sent her His life-giving sperm – the kamaqen – in the tail of an ako chinchay (a comet). The kamaqen carried fragments of the primordial and eternal cosmic light – that mysterious One Principle which cannot be named nor comprehended (Illa Tecsi). And Apu Kon evoked the memorable time when the ako chinchay plunged into the sea and produced wiraqocha: a fertilizing foam that floated over the surface of the waters. And an endless diversity of cosmic life sprang out in the Pacha from the wiraqocha – the foam of the sea – as the male energy of the kamaqen and the female essence of the water blended themselves harmonically into a unifying whole.

From that time, taught Apu Kon, every year during the *Qhapaq Sitwa* (the month of August), the Father Sun shining in the zenith (*Tayta Inti*) sends His live-giving sperm to Pacha, thus bestowing it with fertilizing powers (*Pachamama*). The Pachamama then blends harmonically with the nurturing powers of the waters – the *Mamacocha* – in order to renovate the cycle of life. Sometimes, warned Apu Kon, cataclysmic events – the *pachakuti* – will erupt like a fearsome warrior and will purify the land, spreading fire, death and destruction everywhere. But the harmonic cycle of life will return with renewed vigour after the pachakuti is gone. And Apu Kon taught that acting in accordance to these great cosmic principles keeps the gentle wind of life in the Pacha regenerating and evolving harmoniously.

Similar to this ancient Peruvian creation myth, our imagination has the generative power to set radical new futures in motion. Entering into someone else's lot with kindness stirs our imagination into fashioning unprecedented images of the future that mesmerize us like radiant beams of cosmic light. These mental images ignite our blazing hearts with boundless passion. And our passion nurtures the imagined future into an alluring dream and a purposeful mission that shape our personal voices. Our single voices soon become a chorus and a collective vision that stimulate others into creative teamwork. As a result, we build a tangible model of the future that grows and propagates wildly, like the life-sustaining foam that floats over the oceans.

Thus mental futures are brought to life. Paradoxically, although it generates an endless variety of new realities that never ceases to surprise us, the process of creating the future is as timeless and immutable as the ancient creation myths of some of the world's oldest civilizations. It always requires motivated individuals with the wisdom to find the seven keys that open the gateway of their own imagination. As a result, these inspired individuals are able to operate the magic of imagining, nurturing and transforming their shared mental futures into reality.

It all starts in the heart. From the moment of empathically taking someone else's perspective, and, as a result, attracting a fragment of light from the unknown future that captivates our minds and sets our hearts on fire. And it also ends in the heart. With the courage of dreaming the unthinkable and the determination to take steps to actually realize it. The heart makes futures that already exist in our minds come forth in the real world.

As we entered a new millennium, it soon became clear that, far from an age of stability, we had embarked on a time of unparalleled opportunities and challenging upheavals. The startling development of science and technological applications across all aspects of human activity – ranging from the medical and communications sectors to the field of clean energy generation – increasingly gave billions of people around the world fabulous powers that sixteenth-century Renaissance magicians like Marsilio Ficino or Giordano Bruno could only dream about. It made technology virtually indistinguishable from natural magic, and turned us all into willing – or reluctant – participants in such technological magic on a daily basis.

At the same time, the capacity of imagination to unleash all that magical power in order to create radical new futures poses very serious moral challenges to us all. Are we endeavouring to create new futures by following the guidance of wise universal principles such as the Golden Rule (Do unto others as you would wish them to do unto you), or will we put our imagination exclusively at the service of our own individual aspirations? In these testing times, every inhabitant of planet Earth holds a piece of the answer to this global dilemma, as even the most unlikely dream of any person anywhere in the world has the potential to spread like wildfire and significantly affect the rest of us.

Imagination has the chance of creating new, radical and beneficial futures as never before in the history of humankind. However, it cannot get there alone. In order to realize wholesome futures, our imagination needs to be guided by our wisdom, supported by our determined courage, and develop in the company of our heartfelt intuition. Because positive imagination does start – and end – in the heart.

 **Notes**

✷ *frequently quoted sources*

Seven sources of original research by Piero Morosini are frequently quoted in this book. They concern the following organizations: the San Patrignano Community, Inditex (the holding company that owns the Zara fashion retailing chain), Renault–Nissan, Medtronic, Novartis and Diesel. Unless explicitly indicated otherwise in the text, all quotes about these organizations and their leaders stem from these seven sources, which have been published in four video cases and three written case studies, as follows:

1   *The San Patrignano Community,* a gripping 19-minute video produced in 2009, from which are taken the third quotation in the Prelude, the single quotation about San Patrignano in Chapter 2, and the first two quotations on the "guardian angels" section in Chapter 4.

2   *Building a Common Glue to Achieve Extraordinary Company Transformation,* International Institute for Management Development – IMD-3-1328-V, 2003; a 12-minute video on Medtronic, featuring an interview with former Medtronic CEO Bill George by Piero Morosini.

3   *Building a Common Glue in a "Merger of Equals",* International Institute for Management Development – IMD-3-1329-V; a 16-minute video on Novartis featuring an interview with Novartis Chairman and CEO Daniel Vasella by Piero Morosini.

4   *The Diesel Way,* Ecole Polytechnique Fédérale de Lausanne

– EPFL-306-144-3; a 22-minute video that recounts the extraordinary rise of the Italian Diesel fashion brand and its founder, Renzo Rosso.

5   *The San Patrignano Community (A), (B) & (C)*, 2001, case study series, International Institute for Management Development – IMD-3-0918, IMD-3-0919 and IMD-3-0920. In this book, all quotations about this community and its members – except those indicated in item 1 above – are from this case study series.

6   *Zara – A cut apart from the competition*, 2009, case study, Ecole Polytechnique Fédérale de Lausanne – EPFL-309-113-1. The 2009 Spanish translation of this case study is coded E309-113-1.

7   *Renault–Nissan: The paradoxical alliance*, 2007, case study, European School of Management and Technology – ESMT-307-0047-8. The quotation by former DaimlerChrysler CEO Juergen Schrempp in Chapter 5 also comes from this case study.

All the case studies and videos above (except for item 1) are available at the European Case Clearing House (www.ecch.com). For additional information about *The San Patrignano Community* video, please contact: sevenkeystoimagination@gmail.com.

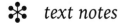 *text notes*

prelude

1   Piero Morosini, *The Common Glue* (Elsevier, Oxford, 2005).

The magic of imagination

1   British historian Frances A. Yates has written a major work on the interpretation of certain Renaissance masterpieces within the framework of Hermetic talismanic symbolism, which remains one of the most insightful of its kind in English language: Frances A. Yates, *Giordano Bruno and the Hermetic Tradition* (Routledge & Kegan Paul, London, 1964). On pages 76–7 and 146, Yates suggests that Botticelli's (1445–1510) *Primavera* can be seen as "a predominantly Venus talisman", whereas the engraving of *Melancholia* by Albrecht Dürer (1471–1528) can be interpreted as

"a predominantly Saturnian talisman". Moreover, observes Yates on page 115 of this volume, "It is in the context of the controversy about Pico [della Mirandola's *Magia naturalis*], in which [Pope] Alexander VI came out so strongly on the side of the Magus [Pico], that one should put the extraordinary 'Egyptianism' in the frescoes painted by Pinturicchio [1454–1513] for Alexander in the Appartamento Borgia in the Vatican. These frescoes were studied by F. Saxl [F. Saxl, 'The Appartamento Borgia', in *Lectures*, Warburg Institute, University of London, I, pp. 174–88; II, Pls. 115–24], who pointed out that within an orthodox programme there are strange allusions."

2   This paragraph, from Pico della Mirandola's *Apologia*, was originally written in Latin. Its English translation has been quoted from Yates, op. cit., p. 89.

3   *Ibid.*, p. 66.

4   Gottfried Wilhelm Leibniz, *Hauptschriften zur Grundlegung der Philosophie* (Meiner, Hamburg, 1966), vol. I: 80.

5   For readers interested in the classical European art of memory, I highly recommend two wonderful books on this subject: Frances A. Yates, *The Art of Memory* (The University of Chicago Press, Chicago, 1974), and Jonathan D. Spence, *The Memory Palace of Matteo Ricci*, (Penguin Books USA Inc., New York, 1985).

6   Mary Carruthers, *The Book of Memory* (Cambridge University Press, Cambridge, 2nd edition, 2008), pp. 19–20.

7   Stephen M. Kosslyn and Samuel T. Moulton, "Mental imagery and implicit memory" in Keith D. Markman, William M. P. Klein and Julie A. Suhr (eds), *Handbook of Imagination and Mental Simulation* (Psychology Press, New York – Hove, 2009), pp. 35–51.

8   Kaspar Schott, *Universal Magic of Nature and Art*, 4 volumes (Würzburg, 1657–9).

9   Lynn Thorndike, *History of Magic and Experimental Science* (Macmillan & Co., London, 1923), vol. 4, p. 598.

10   Frances A. Yates, *Giordano Bruno*, op. cit., p. 449.

11   Marsilio Ficino, *Theologia Platonica de Inmortalitate Animorum – xviii libris comprehensa* (Olms, Hildesheim, New York, 1975). The original edition was published in Paris in 1559.

12   Einstein's insightful quotations on imagination – as well as on many other subjects – can be found at http://thinkexist.com

13   Carl G. Jung, *Man and His Symbols* (Dell Publishing, New York, 1968), p. 82.

14   Stephen M. Kosslyn, *Ghosts in the Mind's Machine* (W. W. Norton & Co., New York, 1983).

15   Alan D. Baddeley, *Essentials of Human Memory* (Psychology Press, Hove, UK, 1999).

16   Giacomo Rizzolatti and Corrado Sinigaglia, *Mirrors in the Brain* (Oxford University Press, Oxford, 2008).

17   Sian L. Beilock and Ian M. Lyons, "Expertise and the mental simulation of action" in Markman et al., op. cit., pp. 21–34.

18   A. M. Glenberg, T. Gutierrez, J. Levin, J. Japuntich and M. P. Kaschak, "Activity and imagined activity can enhance young children's reading comprehension", *Journal of Educational Psychology*, 96, 2004, pp. 424–36.

19   N. Epley and D. Dunning, "The mixed blessings of self-knowledge in behavioral prediction: Enhanced discrimination but exacerbated bias", *Personality and Social Psychology Bulletin*, 32, 2006, pp. 641–55.

20   Ruth M. J. Byrne, *The Rational Imagination* (MIT Press, Cambridge, Massachusetts, 2007). Nearly all of the examples on "counterfactual imagination" in this chapter are based on Byrne's excellent book and research results. Readers interested in this particular subject or willing to learn about these research experiments in more detail are highly recommended to read Byrne's book.

21   Piper Fogg, "How to be happy", *Chronicle of Higher Education*, vol. 51:2, 3 September 2004, p. A 10. This article can be found at http://chronicle.com

22   R. C. Curtis (ed.), *The Relational Self: Theoretical Convergences in Psychoanalysis and Social Psychology* (Guilford Press, New York, 1992), p. 123.

23   Elizabeth W. Dunn, Noah D. Forrin and Claire E. Ashton James, "On the excessive rationality of the emotional imagination: A two-

systems account of affective forecasts and experiences" in Markman et al., op. cit., pp. 331–46.

24   William M. P. Klein and Laura E. Zajac, "Imagining a rosy future: The psychology of optimism" in Markman et al., op. cit., pp. 313–29.

25   William L. Gardner, Elizabeth J. Rozell and Fred O. Walumbwa, "Positive and negative affect and explanatory style as predictors of work attitudes" in Mark J. Martinko (ed.), *Attributional Theory in the Organizational Sciences* (Information Age Publishing Inc., 2004), p. 73.

26   The complete definition of "imagination" from which these quotations stem can be found online at the Encyclopedia of Psychology (http://www.enotes.com/gale-psychology-encyclopedia/imagination).

27   In October 2009, these statements could be found in an article entitled "imagination" at the online encyclopedia (http://en.wikipedia.org).

28   Arnold H. Modell, *Imagination and the Meaningful Brain* (MIT Press, Cambridge, Massachusetts, 2003).

Unleashing the wizard within

1   This quotation is from a speech in Spanish by Ángel Añaños, accessible on YouTube at http://www.youtube.com under the title "Testimonio Ángel Añaños (Presidente del Directorio – AJE)". The English translation is by the present author.

2   "Ángel Añaños' dio la bienvenida a más de 1200 alumnos que iniciaron ciclo académico en la Universidad ESAN", *El Comercio*, Lima, Peru, 30 March 2009. The original quotation is in Spanish; the English translation is by the present author. The article can also be found in the "Sala de Prensa" section of http://www.esan.edu.pe

3   Lynda M. Applegate, *Medtronic Vision 2010* (Harvard Business School Case -9-807-051, Harvard Business Publishing, rev. 30 April 2007), pp. 10–11.

4   Peter Drucker's quotation comes from a 1998 interview entitled "An afternoon with the Master" (http://mfinley.com/experts/drucker/PeterDrucker_Precis.htm)

1 The first key: trade-on mindset

1   "Mario Cucinella: Il mio piano casa", *Wired* (Italian edition),
       May 2009, p. 57. The original quotation is in Italian; the English
       translation is by the present author.

2   Barry J. Nalebuff and Adam M. Brandenburger, *Co-opetition*
       (Currency, Doubleday, 1996).

3   "Emiliano Cecchini: Off-grid, quell miracolo all'idrogeno", *Wired*
       (Italian edition), May 2009, p. 62. The original quotation is in
       Italian; the English translation is by the present author.

4   Carol S. Dweck, *Mindset: The New Psychology of Success* (Random
       House Inc., New York, 2006).

5   Bronislaw Malinowsky and Robert Redfield, *Magic, Science and
       Religion and Other Essays 1948* (Kessinger Publishing, US, 1948).

6   Additional information about this 19-minute video by Piero
       Morosini and Patrizia Italiano, entitled *The San Patrignano
       Community*, is available by contacting: sevenkeystoimagination@
       gmail.com

7   "The Big Easy enters choppy waters", interview with Stelios Haji-
       Ioannou by Jane Martinson, *Guardian*, Friday 5 May 2006.

8   *Ibid.*

9   *Ibid.*

10   "Stelios Haji-Ioannou: The serial entrepreneur", *Prague Tribune*,
       1 December 2004.

11   This quotation is from a 1 March 2008 article entitled "Northern
       Rock, private equity and Sir Stelios", which can be found at the
       Cass Business School website (http://www.cass.city.ac.uk).

12   Michael E. Porter, *Competitive Strategy* (Free Press, New York,
       1980).

13   Michael E. Porter, "What is strategy?", *Harvard Business Review*,
       November–December 1996, p. 69.

14   *Ibid.*, p. 68.

15   *Ibid.*, p. 68.

16 W. Chan Kim and Renée Mauborgne, *Blue Ocean Strategy: How to Create Uncontested Market Space and Make Competition Irrelevant* (Harvard Business School Press, 2005).

17 "In search of France's black gold", *Independent*, Saturday, 31 December 2005.

2 The second key: customer obsession

1 C. Daniel Batson, "Two forms of perspective taking: Imagining how another feels and imagining how you would feel" in Markman et al., op. cit., pp. 267–79.

2 *Ibid.*, p. 268.

3 E. Stotland, "Exploratory investigations of empathy" in L. Berkowitz (ed.), *Advances in experimental social psychology* (Academic Press, New York, 1969), vol. 4, pp. 271–313.

4 Batson, op. cit.

5 Michael W. Myers and Sara D. Hodges, "Making it up and making do: Simulation, imagination and empathic accuracy" in Markman et al., op. cit, pp. 281–94.

6 *Ibid.*, p. 287.

7 *Ibid.*, p. 288. The study by Kilpatrick et al. is: S. D. Kilpatrick, V. L. Bissonnette and C. E. Rusbult, "Empathic accuracy and accommodative behavior among newly married couples", *Personal Relationships*, 9, 2002, pp. 369–93. The study by Gottman and Levenson is: J. M. Gottman and R. W. Levenson, "Marital processes predictive of later dissolution: Behavior, physiology and health", *Journal of Personality and Social Psychology*, 63, 1992, 221–33.

8 Found at the on-line etymology dictionary (http://www. etymonline.com).

9 Nicholas Epley and Eugene M. Caruso, "Perspective taking: Misstepping into others' shoes" in Markman et al., op. cit., p. 295.

10 Myers and Hodges, op. cit.

11 "Stella Adler, 91, an actress and teacher of the method", *New York Times*, Tuesday, 22 December 1992. This article can be found at http://www.nytimes.com

12   This quotation – originally from the online edition of Italy's *Corriere Della Sera* – is from *The Diesel Way*, a 22-minute video by Piero Morosini that recounts the extraordinary rise of the Italian Diesel fashion brand and its founder, Renzo Rosso. The video is available at http://www.ecch.com

3   The third key: purposeful mission

1   Roger Ebert, "Fitzcarraldo (1982)", 28 August 2005. This article can be found online at http://rogerebert.suntimes.com

2   Werner Herzog, *Conquest of the Useless: Reflections from the Making of Fitzcarraldo* (Harper Collins, New York, 2009), p. 1.

3   *El Istmo de Fitzcarrald – Informes de los Señores La Combe, Von Hassel y Pesce: Publicación de la Junta de Vías Fluviales* (Imprenta La Industria, Desamparados No. 15, Lima, 1904), p. 238.

4   Cecilia Monllor, *Zarápolis* (Editorial Planeta, Barcelona, 2001), pp. 51–2. Original text in Spanish; English language translation by the present author.

5   Rhonda Byrne, *The Secret* (Atria Books, New York, 2006), p. 23.

6   Bill George, Peter Sims, Andrew N. McLean and Diana Mayer, "Discovering your authentic leadership", *Harvard Business Review*, February 2007, pp. 6–7.

4   The fourth key: Wiraqocha leaders

1   During my Peruvian treks in the footsteps of Hamawtha Wiraqocha, I gathered information not only about His legends but also about the unlikely antiquity that a number of pundits and local Andean communities have claimed for them. In early 2007, I posted what I found on my blog, under the title: "The Path of Wiraqocha – VII – Tiwanaku, 23 January 2007" (www.commonglue. com). Some readers may find the information in my blog useful, interesting and perhaps even inspirational.

2   Piero Morosini, *The Delancey Street Foundation: "The Harvard of the Underclass"*, (ESMT-2006-case-12, European School of Management and Technology, 2007). All quotations about the Delancey Street Foundation in this chapter come from p. 2 of the case study, except for the last quotation, which is from pages 1 and 6.

3   Haziel, *Notre ange gardien existe* (Editions Bussière, Paris, 1994).

5   The fifth key: tinkunacuy

1   José María Arguedas, *Canciones y cuentos del pueblo quechua* (Francisco Moncloa Editores, Lima, 1967), p. 26. English language translation by the present author.

2   The original and complete text in (ancient) Spanish, from which these remarkable excerpts have been translated into English by the present author, can be found in José de Acosta, *De procuranda indorum salute*, Libro VI, cap. XX, pp. 585–7 (Salamanca, Spain, 1588).

3   Barry J. Nalebuff and Adam M. Brandenburger, *Co-opetition* (HarperCollins paperback edition, 1997), p. 16.

4   *Ibid.*, p. 18.

5   *Ibid.*, p. 21.

6   *Ibid.*, p. 18.

7   *Ibid.*, p. 27.

8   "Kerkorian sues Daimler", *CNN Money*, 28 November 2000. This article can be found at http://money.cnn.com

9   Monllor, op. cit, p. 53. Original text in Spanish; English language translation by the present author.

10   These quotations are from the 1999 ABC *Nightline* report on IDEO, entitled: "Nightline: Deep Dive: 7/13/99". The video is available at http://abcnewsstore.go.com

6   The sixth key: gentlemen's promises

1   Anthony Everitt, *Cicero* (Random House Inc., 2003), p. 298.

2   *Ibid.*, p. 311.

3   *Ibid.*, p. 312.

4   *Ibid.*, p. 317.

5   Henry Mintzberg, "The fall and rise of strategic planning", *Harvard Business Review*, January–February 1994, p. 109.

6   *Ibid.*, p. 110.

7   Excerpts from Carlos Ghosn's speech at the Tokyo Motor Show on
      18 October 1999. The complete transcript of this speech, under the
      title "Ghosn: We don't have a choice (transcript)", is available at
      http://www.accessmylibrary.com

8   This quotation is from a 2004 corporate video by Nissan entitled
      "Nissan is back". For additional information about this video,
      contact Nissan's headquarters at Nissan, 1-1 Takashima 1-chome,
      Nishi-ku, Yokohama-shi, Kanagawa 220-8686, Japan.

9   Ghosn, op. cit.

7   The seventh key: common glue

1   Giorgio Vasari, *Lives of the Artists*, vol. II (Penguin Books, London,
      1987), pp. 187–8.

2   *Ibid.*, pp. 195 & 196.

3   This quotation, originally from A. Cockren's *Alchemy Rediscovered
      and Restored*, can be found online in an article by D. W. Hauck
      entitled "Newton the Alchemist" (http://www.alchemylab.com).
      The alchemical biography of Isaac Newton by John William Navin
      Sullivan undoubtedly remains the classic work on the subject.
      D. W. Hauck is also the author of *The Emerald Tablet: Alchemy for
      Personal Transformation* (Penguin Books, 1999).

4   See note 3.

5   This quotation is from a 21 October 2004 online article by James
      Gleick entitled "What you don't know about Isaac Newton" (see
      http://www.slate.com/id/2108438/). James Gleick is the author
      of the US National Book Award winner *Chaos: Making a New Science*
      (Penguin Books, 1988); and of the Pulitzer Prize finalist biography
      Isaac Newton (First Vintage Books, 2004).

6   Piero Morosini, *The Common Glue* (Elsevier, Oxford, 2005).

7   Piero Morosini, "Competing on social capabilities" in Subir
      Chowdhury (ed.), *Next Generation Business Handbook* (John Wiley &
      Sons, New Jersey, 2004), p. 248.

Epilogue

1 This Qheshwa proverb is taken from Federico García and Pilar Roca, *Pachakuteq* (Fondo Editorial del Pedagógico San Marcos, Lima, 2004), p. 33. This source also provided important material for the ancient Peruvian myth of creation that is recounted in this chapter.

Index